Paying for Pleasure

Paying for Pleasure
Men Who Buy Sex

Teela Sanders

WILLAN
PUBLISHING

Published by

Willan Publishing
Culmcott House
Mill Street, Uffculme
Cullompton, Devon
EX15 3AT, UK
Tel: +44(0)1884 840337
Fax: +44(0)1884 840251
e-mail: info@willanpublishing.co.uk
Website: www.willanpublishing.co.uk

Published simultaneously in the USA and Canada by

Willan Publishing
c/o ISBS, 920 NE 58th Ave, Suite 300,
Portland, Oregon 97213-3786, USA
Tel: +001(0)503 287 3093
Fax: +001(0)503 280 8832
e-mail: info@isbs.com
Website: www.isbs.com

First published 2008

ISBN 978-1-84392-321-3 paperback
      978-1-84392-322-0 hardback

British Library Cataloguing-in-Publication Data

A catalogue record for this book is available from the British Library

Project management by Deer Park Productions, Tavistock, Devon
Typeset by TW Typesetting, Plymouth, Devon
Printed and bound by TJ International Ltd, Padstow, Cornwall

Contents

Preface

From conducting research in the sex markets in the UK since 1999, I have been privileged to meet hundreds of people who are involved in the sex industries as sex workers, receptionists, sauna owners, advertisers, landlords, dominatrices, outreach workers, photographers, website managers, dungeon makers, fetish artists, lap dancers, telephone sex workers, partners of sex workers, swingers, club owners, security workers, drivers, activists, advocates, union members and those who study and write about sex work. Men who buy sex, the clients of sex workers, were always at the periphery of my research and visible in the ethnographic setting. Having delved deeply into the lives of female sex workers (Sanders 2005a), it felt logical for the next step to concentrate on the client's perspectives. There was a seamless transition from researching sex workers and the organization of the industry, to researching men who buy sex. Intellectually there were many questions, not a significant body of current evidence and as many myths to dispel about male customers as there are about female sex workers. Questions about the complexity of human sexuality were raised when considering the relationship between the sex worker and the male client. As my understanding developed it became evident that there has been a fundamental flaw in sex work research because viewing the sex industry only from the position of the female sex worker (normally street based) denies the reciprocal relationship of any 'supply and demand' chain to be exposed in its entirety. This book, and the research that supports it, had an organic birth, a life of its own with no time to wait for funding or be trampled down by the prudery of the academy or inflated concerns about ethics.

My agenda

Applying Goffman's (1983) sociology of the 'interaction order' requires that observations are made of the microscopic interactions that happen between individuals in their everyday ordinary interactions. Following on from this tradition, the details of men's interpersonal and intimate lives form the basis of this work. My intentions for the outcomes of this project are fourfold:

1. To examine the presumed 'deviant' status of men who buy sex through their conventional sexual stories and the construction of the sexual self in order to question whether sex work is only and always a symbol of male domination;
2. To illustrate how client conduct is not necessarily oppressive, damaging or disrespectful, but that sexual and social scripts performed by male clients are normative and can be used to make sex work a responsible industry;
3. To critically analyse the complex social, personal and emotional mechanisms that fuse in late modernity to produce a thriving sex industry, where particularly middle-class clients seek pleasure, refuge and intimacy;
4. To provide a critical voice against the criminalization of commercial sexual behaviour between consenting adults and to persist with the campaign to provide sex workers with safe working conditions through civil, human and labour rights.

Chapter outline

The opening chapter examines why the focus has shifted to men who buy sex in recent years to fully understand the politics of prostitution and sex work and the organisation of sex markets. Outlining the methodological difficulties of researching men who buy sex, this chapter offers some insight into the politics of this research in the wider context of sexual and social politics. The second chapter sets out the parameters of the research: the research questions; the access and recruitment process; the men I interviewed; reflections on the nature and dynamics of the researcher–respondent relationship including trust, emotional labour and the therapeutic element of the interview process. Chapter 3 presents some overall findings about the behavioural conduct of clients. I discuss the 'push' and 'pull' factors that motivate the purchase of sex from men's perspectives and their opinions on exploitation and 'danger' across the sex markets. Using a five-category typology of involvement in the sex industry, I apply the 'life-course' approach to understand at what stages of their lives men turn to the sex industry. Morality and rules that govern their involvement in the sex industry are described alongside mechanisms used by individuals and the sex work community to benchmark standards and etiquette.

Chapter 4 explores the role of the Internet in men's experiences and processes of buying sex. Arguing that new technologies have provided a space for a 'sex work community' to develop which moves between on and offline interactions, the role of the Internet in male social networks is explored. The role of message boards as an arena for male bonding, for learning about sex market etiquette and as a place to find emotional support are examples of how specific websites for male clients go beyond the textual surface of 'field report' accounts of sexual encounters. Chapter 5 examines the role of intimacy in the commercial sexual relationship, the process and reasons for becoming a 'regular' client to the same sex worker and the emotional and psychological impact of buying sex. A range of reactions such as emptiness, vulnerability, emotional consumption and 'falling in love' are explored, challenging the false dichotomy between commercial and non-commercial relationships. Chapter 6 examines the stigma attached to men who buy sex and the ways in which male clients subvert or manage the stigma. This chapter explores how men who are involved in the sex industry as purchasers confront the stigma attached to buying sex, how they make sense of the stereotypes, the need to keep their activities hidden and the consequences of secrecy in their lives. Drawing on 'discourses of respectability' (Skeggs 1997), I argue that male sexuality, particularly that associated with the working classes, has been recycled in recent policy to reinforce what is considered to be 'acceptable' and 'unacceptable' sexual behaviour.

Chapter 7, 'Criminalizing the customer', examines the recent government strategy to 'tackle demand' and heavily enforce the kerb-crawling laws. I trace the repositioning of the client as a criminal over the past two decades and critique the ideologies behind the current prostitution policy in relation to 'demand'. The support for kerb-crawler rehabilitation programmes are critically analysed in relation to displacement, legal theory, the resource intensity of the programmes and the ineffectiveness of the long-term outcomes. The cultural implications of criminalizing clients and the impact of demonizing clients on the continued vulnerability of sex workers are discussed. Chapter 8 continues to examine the discourses attached to the 'punter' by applying key criteria of the theory of moral panic to the case of the male client. Here I establish that through concern, hostility and disproportionality men who buy sex, particularly from the street, are constructed as sexually dangerous. The consequences of this construction on the status and vulnerability of female sex workers are outlined.

The final chapter discusses why there has been a growing increase in the use of sexual services in late modernity. Cultural conformity to masculine practices and the dominance of the consumerism and the entertainment industry provide the 'pull' factors that perpetuate the desire to buy sex. In other areas of social and personal life, the desire for emotional and physical intimacy, the stresses of everyday life and unsatisfying marriage provides the 'push' factors to seek out commercial sex. These observations are discussed in the broader context of sexuality and changing sexual and social attitudes, behaviours and values.

Note of thanks

Initial gratitude must go to the men who responded to the call for research, volunteered their time and were so open with their intimate lives. Without them this book would not have been written. Thanks go to Helen Self, Michael Goodyear, Christopher Keefe and Caitlin McKiernan for sharing their time, energy, wisdom, information and critical insight to help me clarify my ideas, writing and views. A special thank you goes to 'Hugh Jampton', for his integrity and support and for reading the whole manuscript, and also to Keith Soothill for his ever-present injection of the bigger picture. I am indebted to my colleagues in the School of Sociology and Social Policy at the University of Leeds for facilitating my study leave. Thanks once again to Brian Willan and his team for supporting this specialist subject. On a personal note, I thank Rosie Campbell and Nerys Edmonds for their constant care, Thelma Knight for hoodwinking me into expanding my horizons, and Sharon Elley for taking this part of the journey with me and being a true soulmate. My parents, as always, have been a solid rock.

Chapter 1

The genesis of the study

Convention suggests that engaging in the purchase of sexual services is somewhere on the spectrum of 'deviance'. Notions of men visiting massage parlours or the 'red light district' to pay women to perform various sexual services conjures up images of lurid sexual contact in dark and repellent surroundings. Those judges, politicians and celebrities who are caught in compromising positions with 'hired' women appear to have flouted civilities, disgraced themselves and shamed their families. Attitudes that negatively frame the purchase of sexual services are bound by mythology about commercial sex, failing to entertain that perhaps commercial sex goes beyond physical release but provides intimacy and pleasure. Myths are supported by strong expectations that commercial sex can only produce hollow and cold sex acts that are momentarily pleasurable, that quickly subside to be replaced by guilt, regret and loneliness. Commercial sexual interactions appear to be sharply at odds with the 'special' and 'pure' forms of intimacy that modernity upholds as the ultimate goal in personal relationships (see Giddens 1992; Jamieson 1998). We, in the West, are socialized into believing that this 'pure' form of intimacy is 'right' and 'proper', that the only legitimate route to mutually satisfying, healthy relationships is to be found in the 'comfort zone' of orthodox sexual relationships. Sexual relationships are only considered 'proper' when they are within a committed, long-lasting, monogamous dyad. But are we not dealing with a spectrum of commercial intimate relationships? The 'trade-offs' that are evident in extreme cases such as the celebrity marriage between the late Anna Nicole Smith and billionaire oil tycoon J. Howard Marshall, 63 years her senior, are surely predicated partly on an economic exchange? Are there not economic, material and social capital trade-offs in all relationships?

Despite economic exchange as the basis of many forms of relationships, whether explicitly stated or tacitly agreed, anti-prostitution discourses that stigmatize sex workers, and to a lesser extent male clients, are strong in the UK and Northern Europe. The condemnation of many forms of commercial sex (while hypocritically accepting forms such as 'gentlemen's clubs') is not simply sexual conservativeness reacting against a contemporary society awash with the provocative sexualization of almost every cultural manifestation and product. Contradictory beliefs about buying sex have framed our understanding of commercial sex for a long time, and form the point of departure for a book about men who buy sex from women in a commercial context.

There are some initial sociological observations to be raised in this first chapter which explain why a book on men who enter into commercial sexual transactions with women is important and how the findings contribute to a wider understanding of sexuality, relationship formation and sexual culture in contemporary society. These observations connect to broader themes of the book: the diversity of social and sexual stories in late modernity; the transformations in technology, commerce and sex; changes in sexual attitudes and the temporality of mores; the forms and spaces of 'community'; the spectrum of intimacy, emotional consumption and the false dichotomies between commercial and non-commercial sexual interaction; and sexual citizenship, 'discourses of respectability' and the common place of commercial sex in society. These broader social and cultural themes are an important backdrop to understand the complexities of the sex industries and human sexuality.

As I write, direct (purchasing sex acts) and indirect (erotic dancing, telephone sex for example) sexual services in many different markets and forms flourish around the globe (Harcourt and Donovan 2005). The UK escort and parlour markets have been estimated at grossing £534 million yearly earnings, an equivalent expenditure to that spent on visiting the cinema (Moffatt and Peters 2004). One reason for the continued customer base and the growth of commercial sex as part of the entertainment industry is that the sparkling neon lights of the visible erotic landscape present many more possibilities, promote multiple facets of sexual desire and expand the explicitly erotic to an unprecedented level. 'The media has become sexualized' (Plummer 1995: 4) leading to the commodification of sex permeating our everyday lives through digital TV channels, high street shops, magazine racks and supermarket aisles. We are surrounded by a sexual culture lead by dominant advertising agencies. Sex subtly becomes part of all aspects of consumerism, leisure (Attwood 2006), work spaces and governance (Phoenix and Oerton 2005). Hawkes (1996: 17) neatly summarizes: 'In the sexual landscape, desire for sex is ever-present, of no more moral consequence than the desire for food. Like food, this product is prepared and presented in an ever-expanding variety.' One of the interviewees in this study aptly remarked: 'We live in a society which is bombarded by sexuality. You can't buy anything without it being advertised – like Pot Noodles are advertised by sex – you know.' In a society dominated by 'sex as culture', where suggestions of eroticism and insinuations of racialized sexual exoticism sell the obvious perfumes and less obvious commodities such as mobile phones, washing powder and insurance cover, it is somewhat expectable that the desire for sexual interactions, albeit in a commercial exchange, is more visible than ever before.

There are other considerable changes in the sexual and social landscape, or what Plummer (1995: 4) more aptly describes as the 'erotopian landscape', that contribute to the expansion and diversification of the sex industry. Mores about sexual acts have changed – what was considered 'correct' or 'proper' sexual acts at the beginning of the 1900s have altered in the last century (see Gagnon and Simon 1973). Haste (1992) explains how the rules governing sexual desire have been redrawn since the First World War, largely due to the separation of sex from procreation, enabling new possibilities for eroticism to emerge for both sexes. Oral sex is now much more acceptable both as pre-coital foreplay and as a substitute for penetrative sex (Chambers 2007; Shostak 1981) yet continues to be the most popular sex act purchased.[1] Indeed, former president of the United States, Bill Clinton, exalted the act of oral sex to everyday acceptability when he claimed that fellatio was not even full sexual relations in his famous denial statement: 'I did not have sexual relations with that woman.' With the acceptance of fellatio and other less orthodox sex acts in 'ordinary' heterosexual relationships, it is perhaps surprising that commercial sexual services are still popular for providing a range of sexual services alongside emotional and physical intimacy.

Despite a more liberal repertoire of 'ordinary' sexual conduct, the commercial sex industries that provide direct sexual services go way beyond 'the missionary position' and oral sex. Domination, fetishisms, role play, romance, touching, kissing, erotic talk, socializing, bondage, massage, sex emporiums, dancing, stripping, tantra, swinging, webcam virtual sex (see Bernstein 2001): the list of desires and matching services that are available at a price is endless and increasingly inventive. The sex markets appear to be both diversifying and specializing as the female sex worker–male client traditional markets become infused with characteristics of modern capitalism (Brents and Hausbeck 2007). Although not the concern of this book, the sex markets are catering for a range of sexualities and sexual orientation. There are various groups of men who sell sex to men: male sex workers for gay, bisexual and straight men (Browne and Minchiello 1995; Gaffney and Beverley 2001; West and Villiers 1992); transgender sex workers (Slamah 1999; Weinberg *et al.* 1999) and other men who have sex with men for the exchange of a range of commodities. Men sell sexual services to women as 'cads', male strippers (Dressel and Petersen 1982) and in various guises as 'gigolos' (such as dance teachers) in sex tourism sites such as Cuba and the Caribbean (Cabezas 2004; Sanchez Taylor 2001). The personal adverts in mainstream magazines for lesbian and bisexual women identify that female sex workers do sell sex to women and couples (see *Diva* for instance). As couples are finding more entertainment venues where mutual sadomasochistic practices can be facilitated and purchased, fetishes once considered subversive are making their way onto the mainstream (see Hoff 2006). Markets are ever-changing to the extent that research and policy has not kept up with the changes and the fluidity of the ways in which sex is sold and sexuality is packaged (Gaffney 2007).

Beyond the cultural recognition of the fluidity of sexuality, there are clear tensions between the state's willingness to embrace human rights and the freedom to express sexuality and the need to control certain types of sexual 'pleasures'. Men, and to a lesser extent women, buying sexual services are somewhat outside the construction of intimate citizenship and 'respectability' that is an underlining feature of New Labour rhetoric on how the model citizen should conduct their life. On the one hand, recent changes to allow civil partnerships between gay couples demonstrate significant shifts in institutional thinking about diversity, sexuality and family life. Yet, under the Sexual Offences Act 2003, it is now a public offence of indecent exposure if caught having sex outside in a public place. Further desire to constrain the sex lives of individuals is evident in the *Consultation: On the Possession of Extreme Pornographic Material* introduced by the Home Office in 2005. Sexuality and sexual behaviour continues to be a point of tension where definitions of 'pleasure' and how they should be policed are at the heart of institutional and organization change.

The 'pleasures' associated with commercial sex are contested in moral debate, pragmatic policing and the law. For example, the political desire to prevent certain types of prostitution (namely street based) which are framed as 'harms' are at the forefront of recent policy that aims to 'disrupt the sex markets' (Home Office 2006). At the same time, there is less political will to interfere in the private sexual lives of consenting adults by outlawing the sale or purchase of commercial sex, while some forms (such as lap dancing) have seen unprecedented expansions into every night-time entertainment district in UK towns and cities (Jones *et al.* 2003). Hence, because of the complexity of the law (some would say contradictions), managing activities like commercial sex occurs on a spectrum between law enforcement (with many variants) to that of self-regulation. Kagan (1984: 45, cited in Miers 2004: 337) assesses that markets are more likely to be regulated rather than policed with a view to enforcement if the benefits to society outweigh the costs: 'In the case of regulated business [however] their offences, even if irresponsible or socially harmful in and of themselves, are more likely to be viewed as negligent, non-malicious side effects of socially useful activities.' This leads us to suggest that the policing of pleasure and its associated industries may fluctuate according to perceptions of commercial sex as socially useful or inevitable, therefore warranting less formal styles of control.

The lack of regulation over the UK brothel industry and the indoor sex markets in general is a case that testifies to the 'self-regulation' argument as the moral and practical will to ban such sex work venues is absent (Sanders and Campbell 2007b). One interpretation suggests that the absence of law enforcement and law reform relating to brothels, while directly rendering women vulnerable to violence and exploitation, is also an implicit acceptance that some forms of sex work provide a positive social function and should continue to exist.[2] Yet in formal policy (see Chapter 7), the government constructs commercial sex not as a 'pleasure' to be regulated but as a social harm. Unlike countries such as New Zealand and Australia, the UK government has chosen a management style that opts for strict law enforcement for certain markets (street) and virtual non-regulation of others as the 'harm' argument is arbitrarily applied to suit political and moral agendas.

The tensions surrounding commercial sex and how it is managed can be traced back to the general template for intimate citizenship. It is difficult for any government to operationalize the reality of sexual relations for many people. Despite the radical and religious right promoting a conservative sex ethic, the monogamous, long-term hetero-sexual relationship is no longer the defining feature of modern Western sexual relationships (Roseneil 2007).[3] Sex lives are not homogenous and the experience of sex with a stranger is not a rare event for some, and no doubt a point of recollection for many readers. Accounts of one night stands and other temporary relations suggest that liaisons with strangers can be immensely erotic and satisfying – sexual and emotional pleasure between adults is not predicated on knowing someone 'inside out' or for a set amount of time, or commonalities such as age, ethnicity, language or sexual orientation. Sexual and emotional intimacy leading to fulfil-ment is not the sacred property of only conventional relationships that have civic and/or religious approval. In much of the West it seems that when commerce is introduced to sex other issues immediately take precedence: issues of tradition and morality override the strength of attraction, difference, need and intimacy. Which political party included in their manifesto definitive plans to sanction when and where consent-ing adults should find satisfying sex?

While I paint a scenario that lends itself to the varied nature of contemporary sexual conduct predicated on a concoction of sexual and relational difference, a point of clarification made throughout the book is that buying sexual services is not always about strangers engaging in sexual acts. Chapter 5 describes strong trends that establish how men become regular clients to the same sex worker(s), forming conventional relationships beyond the sexual but within the commercial context. Taking the lead from Bernstein (2001), I describe how intimacy is not exempt from the commercial sexual experience, but for some an essential part of the criteria and satisfaction of commercial liaisons. Western formal politics promotes conventional sexual intimacy and citizenship of a certain kind, pushing commercial sexual services to the margins of acceptability to the extent that it is generally a taboo topic or unacceptable unless under specific cultural conditions such as stag parties, birthday celebrations or a 'boys' night out'.

The politics of researching 'punters'

In recent years, when I have presented at conferences or raised issues with policy-makers about men who buy sexual services, I have often been met with a mix of reactions ranging from genuine perplexed questions, quiet disdain, or spineless scoffing at the value of such a subject. While Plummer (1995: 4) eloquently describes how 'telling your sexual story' in contemporary Western culture is performed in endless ways and through endless mediums (from pop songs to 'reveal all' talk shows), the story of the man who purchases sexual services has not been a topic exploited by the media in the way that stories of infidelity or abuse have been exposed. Men do not come forward because of their preference for secrecy and also because the stigma attached to buying sex is intensifying. In the academic corridors of research, where we expect a commitment to discovering knowledge and pushing the boundaries of what has already been established (especially among scholars of human sexuality), negative attitudes of suspicion and distaste towards men who buy sex still prevails. I am not alone in experiencing rejection based on the subject matter. Don Kulick (2005: 225), upon presenting a critical analysis of the Swedish legal changes that criminalize the buying of sex, describes how audiences displayed 'unsettledness', resulting in persistent requests that he stated 'his agenda' in order to justify the research.

Men who buy sex are seen by some extremists to be the perpetrators of oppressive acts, or indeed in some people's minds those responsible for a culture that accepts violence against women. In the radical view of commercial sex, the basic premise is that sex work is an act of violence against women whether there is consent between adults or not. Men are considered to seek out paid-for sex entirely because of power and their dominant social and economic position. Sometimes this view rejects the legitimacy of the study of male clients because of men's perceived immorality, dangerousness or criminality. Even writers who are not as extreme in their thinking still (usually silently) have issues with men being pushed onto the agenda in research. In their opinion, any research funding, journal airspace, conference papers or media outputs that speak about men who buy sex is diverting the focus away from the exploitation, harm and dangers associated with selling sex. Researching male clients is assumed to go hand in hand with a positive blanket agreement that the sex industry should be legitimized: researchers who do engage in studying clients are considered to be anti-feminist and in favour of loose sexual mores (Kulick 2005). Where a switch in research focus has been considered acceptable, it is usually when there is a call for more knowledge about men who buy sex for the purposes of further criminalization. Sometimes men who buy sex are considered a legitimate target for research only if the agenda is to eradicate prostitution. It is this background of academic conservatism, moral entrepreneurialism and radicalism that this research attempts to balance. Men who buy sex are as legitimate a topic as women who sell sex in the quest to find a system that enables safe commercial sexual interactions between consenting adults. Apart from that, men who buy sex tell us much about human sexuality and the human condition in general.

The traditional absence of the male client

Despite a plethora of knowledge about the sex industry, in particular the street sex markets, the historical concentration of research has been overwhelmingly on women who sell sex. This has its origins in the state control of prostitution: the legal aspect of prostitution has traditionally concentrated on women who sell sex and not the men who buy (see Self 2003). Until very recently, commentary has focused on women's sexuality and not men's because of an explicit acceptability that men who buy sex are doing what is 'natural'. A Royal Commission report in 1871 stated:

> We may at once dispose of [any recommendation] founded on the principle of putting both parties to the sin of fornication on the same footing by the obvious but not less conclusive reply that there is no comparison to be made between prostitutes, and men who consort with them. With the one sex the offence is committed as a matter of gain; with the other it is an irregular indulgence of a natural impulse. (Cited in Goodall 1995: 47)

Scrutiny of male clients has traditionally been protected by the power of religious doctrine, medical discourses and the law as their involvement in seeking out sex has been considered a legitimate, if crude, biological necessity. Women's sexuality, as seen in the quote above, has been targeted because of its doubly deviant nature: working as a 'prostitute' goes against many laws and the ideology of 'proper' femininity and 'acceptable' womanly conduct. Public health discourse, medical practices and state regulations continued to view women in the sex industry as 'carriers of disease' in the nineteenth Century, amid concerns for the spread of syphilis (Walkowitz 1980). These outdated correlations between sex workers and the spread of sexually transmitted infections continue in current policy as sex workers are considered a 'high-risk' group whereas evidence suggests rates of infections are in decline and condom use is high (Boynton and Cusick 2006; Cusick and Berney 2005; Goodyear and Cusick 2007).

Not studying men who buy sex is detrimental to wider sociological understandings of human sexuality, gender, personal relationships and, of course, commercial sex industries. McLeod (1982) states that the invisibility of the male client means that there are limited views on prostitution and that the debate is informed only by one side. Men's experiences of daily life are not understood in relation to how buying sex manifests in their constructions or understanding of their self and sexual identity. Campbell (1998: 157) explains: 'It has been easier to pay attention to the women who sell sex and label them as a category of "irrespectable" deviant women than pay attention to clients and examine reasons men pay for and create a market in commercial sex.' Unlike the proliferation of testimonies from sex workers, there are only a few examples of clients 'speaking out' (Egan *et al.* 2006; Korn 1998; Loebner 1998).[4] In this sense, men who buy sex have been for some time marginalized by researchers and commentators on the sex industry. While Lowman and Atchison (2006), in their review of the large body of research on clients in Canada, note a swing in the research pendulum, the reasons for the relative invisibility of the male client, up until now, are a combination of sexual politics, structural silencing, the limitations of feminism and the over-focus on female sex workers by law, police and health discourses.

Why include men in research on the sex industries?

Given that the subject of 'men and masculinities' has somewhat flourished into a discipline of its own since the 1980s (see the work by Hearn and Morgan (1990) and Connell (1995)) and embodies a wide range of research activities (see, for instance, the Research Unit on Men and Masculinities at Bradford University), specialist journals, handbooks and this specific research community have been slow to feature men who buy sex as a subject for academic inquiry. Male sex workers and men who buy sex from men have been at the periphery of research (Gaffney and Beverley 2001; West and Villiers 1992) and policy (Gaffney 2007). Men who buy sex from women have also been marginalized in terms of knowledge production. Alongside more contemporary writers (Campbell 1998; Kinnell 2006b; Monto 2000; Weitzer 2000), Winick and Kinsie, in their book *The Lively Commerce* (1971), call for further research on men who buy sex but advise that the social ecology of men alters with the social and sexual culture. This essentially means that the knowledge we do have needs updating as the sex industries and behaviours shift in response to broader social and sexual changes.

Beyond understanding for the purpose of sociological knowledge, there are real, practical policy reasons why more exploratory and critical material needs to be produced about this group of men. Ward *et al.* (2005: 470) state that 'greater understanding of the changing nature of commercial sex, and the engagement of men who pay for sex in both descriptive research and the design of interventions is an essential next step'. Despite documented need for a targeted sexual health intervention programme (Groom and Nandwini 2006), currently, there are no sexual health outreach projects directed at men who buy sex.[5] Sexual health education and prevention in the sex industry is entirely focused on the woman, echoing similar safety and crime prevention messages (Stanko 1996). Health messages and practices promote that women need to be responsible for keeping themselves physically safe, while men will be exempt from any direct education or awareness programmes whether it is safe sex, condom use or that violence against women is unacceptable (Sanders 2006b). Health promotion policies are not likely to succeed if only one party is engaged or targeted. If the spotlight continues to be averted from men who buy sex, there will be little basis or impetus for ensuring that men take responsibility for sexual and social relationships that are both commercial and non-commercial. Research knowledge on men who buy sex must feed into social and health policy in order to reduce health concerns and gender inequalities.

The policy and legal changes within and beyond the UK justify a need for new, sociologically grounded research that centres on men who buy sex. As Phoenix and Oerton (2005) describe, the 'problem of sex' has been reduced to the 'problem of men'. In policy, the law and government, decisions have been made on the basis of the construction of a specific form of male sexuality that is considered threatening and dangerous and therefore warranted to be at the forefront of sex regulation. This 'problem of men' discourse is powerful and draws from the discourses of political correctness. The strength of the argument is evident in a refocusing of the perpetrator as men are targeted as buyers of sex in legal changes led by Sweden and adopted in various forms by

Norway, Finland and Scotland recently (see Chapters 7 and 8). Broader European political change in the management of the sex industry also calls for more integrated approaches to understanding the complexities of men who buy sex, sex workers and those who manage sex businesses (Groneberg *et al.* 2006; Kilvington *et al.* 2001). In the UK, the government's tolerance is decreasing towards sex work, preferring to focus on other wider global changes relating to immigration, migrancy, 'trafficking' and organized crime. These global issues appear to have overridden the quest to understand the social meanings, relevancy and functions of the sex markets in the domestic and local context. The panic about the 'global' impact on the domestic order has resulted in the criminal justice system earmarked as the legitimate place where sexuality should be regulated. Human rights issues and the generalization that coercion and masculine domination underpin the whole of the commercial sex industry lead to commentary and policy starting from the premise that men who buy sex are inherently doing wrong. 'Demand' for sexual services has been understood as intrinsically oppressive for women and only an expression of male dominance. Such a premise immediately discounts a realistic perception of the diversity of the sex industry and appropriate ways to regulate for safety.

The research and policy agendas of human rights and exploitation on the one hand and voluntary organized sex work on the other are not mutually exclusive: there is room for research, policy and practice to concentrate on both the harmful side of prostitution and the movement to formalize sex work as genuine labour. Where all men who buy sex are considered dangerous and all sex workers as dishevelled victims or rational, calculating criminals, a discourse is produced (some would call this propaganda) that is barely short of manhating. This work bucks against this trend, sheds light on the humanity of men who buy sex, and by locating their stories in the sociological imagination, provides a platform for those who have rarely been consulted or represented. While the radical feminist perspective has been counteracted by real voices from female sex workers (for instance, see Delacoste and Alexander 1988; Kempadoo and Doezema 1999) and 'identity politics' through the sex workers' rights movement (Gall 2006), men who buy sex have no platform for their voice. This group is a powerful group in their everyday status position yet has no political power or voice regarding their sexual identity and practices.

Despite the call for a new research agenda where there is a refocus in studies on sex work that reflect the complex reality of sexual relations and commerce (Agustin 2005, and see the Special Edition of *Sexualities*, 2007), there are still very clear gaps in what we know about men who buy sex. The literature has concentrated on the psychological and psychiatric enquiry which pathologizes behaviour: epidemiologists count prevalence and suggest trends, while disciplines across health, law and psychology, which are empirically driven, focus on individual behaviour rather than the social context of the sexual purchase. The sociological perspective that attempts to understand the context in which men buy sex, how sexual services feature as part of their everyday lives and how they view the purchase have been in the minority (see Egan 2006; Frank 2002). Taking the 'sociology of stories' (Plummer 1995) as its departure point, this study looks at the experiences of men who are within their legal right in the UK to buy adult consensual sexual services. This reality has been sidelined by the strong political agenda of 'eradication' and judgements about the rights and wrongs of sexual morality. How does buying commercial sex fit into men's lives, hopes, fears, failures, self-esteem, relationships, life plans, budgets, emotions and, of course, their pleasures? How are their sexual selves constructed through commercial sex? Moving towards answering these questions about the culture of sex work is essential in order to fully understand sexuality in late modernity.

A brief word here about the title of the book, *Paying for Pleasure*. Using a title that refers to the purchase of sexual services as 'pleasure' has several risks attached to it, but my intentions are as follows. Stemming from a wider critique of modern politics that has taken the pleasure out of sexuality, the title reminds the reader, in particular the sociologist, that pleasure and sex are still desired, achievable and acceptable aspects of human interaction. In Bauman's (2005: 39) summation: 'Today, sexuality no longer epitomizes the potential for pleasure and happiness. It is no longer mystified, positively, as ecstasy and transgression, but negatively instead, as the source of oppression, inequality, violence, abuse and deadly infection.' Referring to sexual services as pleasure recognizes the possibilities that not all sex work is damaging, coerced or against the sex worker's will. Many sex workers are providers of emotional labour and sexual satisfaction that produce pleasure as well as a range of other intimate physical, sexual, emotional and psychological services. The title also recognizes that the relationship between the sex worker and client has the capacity to go beyond the sexual act and can represent similar sexual, emotional and psychological relationships found in non-commercial contexts. Challenging the trajectory of one aspect of feminist commentary that has traditionally framed men's sexualities as essentially problematic (either because of aggression or sexuality), this book attempts to understand men's experiences of personal intimate relationships outside an essentialist discourse. Men, particularly heterosexual men, are often not explored as subjects in their own right, as sexual beings with legitimate desires, attractions and pleasures. Contextualizing these stories in the context of the global sex trade, structural inequalities between men and women and the need to understand commerce, sex and intimacy provides a springboard for moving this debate beyond that of the 'kerb-crawler' as a modern folk devil.

Notes

1 Monto (2001) found that 81 per cent (n=995) of men arrested for attempting to hire a street worker were more likely to request fellatio than any other sexual practice.
2 The Home Office (2006) *Coordinated Prostitution Strategy* included a proposal to change the law so that two or three women could work together from the same premises within the law. However, there appears to be a backtrack on this proposal as no action has been taken and the law still stands in contradiction to safety advice (see Sanders 2007a).
3 For example, as Ashbee (2007) and Busza (2006) document, sexual politics that preaches abstinence, and opposes abortion and sex work shapes US government policy, and homophobia prevents sexual orientation overtly featuring in sex and relationship education programmes in schools in the UK (Thatcher 2001).
4 There are many more examples of sex workers testimonies. See Annadale (2005), Daniels (2006), Delacoste and Alexander (1988), Efthimiou-Mordant (2002), Jaget (1980), Kempadoo and Doezema (1999), Levine and Madden (1988).
5 A project was set up in Bradford where outreach workers visited saunas where men bought sex to initiate sexual health education but it was short-lived and unfunded.

Chapter 2

Researching men who buy sex

The research literature has noted consistently that there are general methodological barriers when designing and executing research with men who buy sexual services (for instance, McKeganey 1994: 290). This is largely due to the taboo and sensitive nature of the subject, the secretive nature of the sex industry and a general desire for anonymity among the customers who come and go in the shadows of brothels and discreet apartments. I was aware of issues of anonymity, secrecy and the hidden nature of the patrons of the sex industry from my observations in brothels and massage parlours. In the previous ethnographic study (Sanders 2005a), the managers of brothels often did not want me to be overtly known as a researcher to the clients, so I had a peculiar double status: the staff knew I was a researcher but the clients, who would come and go throughout the day, would assume I was a friend or another worker. This presented interesting encounters and my covert status also acted as a benchmark with which the sex workers could test my pledge of confidentiality (Sanders 2005d). The nature of the sex industry, and my 'tales from the field', suggested that creative access strategies were necessary to reach clients of sex workers. This chapter describes the methods through which I made contact with men who buy sex, the complex access and recruitment process and some personal method-ological reflections on the researcher–respondent relationship.

Locating the population

The problem of where to find this group of men is further complicated because of the unclear legalities surrounding prostitution: many men I have spoken to are not clear what is and what is not illegal as many aspects of prostitution and running a brothel have been recently legislated against, or are in the news as a topic for potential legal change and criminalization. Clients' concerns about their legal status have been compounded by the criminalization agenda that has turned the focus equally on men who buy sex (see Chapter 7), particularly those that visit the street market, putting further barriers between the researcher and the population. For instance, research by Coy *et al.* (2007: 5) had difficulties recruiting men who paid for street sex, despite using the police as gatekeepers and placing several advertisements in newspapers, resulting in a study mainly on men who visited off-street locations. Despite these hurdles, much of the research with men who buy sex is of a qualitative nature. To account for the under-reporting of involvement in commercial sex in large-scale surveys (Brewer 2000), qualitative samples are usually purposively selected, achieved through a myriad of strategies that rely on official agencies that are in contact with men (usually health professionals and the police), informal contacts, existing networks in the sex industry, sex workers and recruitment through the media.

To recruit male clients for research a range of data collection techniques and access routes have been adapted, with varying degrees of success:

- approaching clients directly on the street (Freund, *et al.* 1991);
- at police stations and through arrest operations (Brooks-Gordon 2006; Sharpe 2000);
- sex workers conducting questionnaires with clients (Faugier and Cranfield 1995);
- rehabilitation programmes/prison/court diversion (Monto 2000; Monto and Hotaling 2001);
- court file studies/documentation (Atchison *et al.* 1998);
- street and indoor sex work venues (Freund, *et al.* 1989; Gomes do Espirito Santo and Etheredge 2002; Pickering *et al.* 1992);
- advertisements in the media that generate telephone interviews (Barnard *et al.* 1993; Prasad 1999);
- Internet (chatrooms, message boards) (Earle and Sharpe 2007; Peng 2007);
- sexual health clinics and case notes (Gibbens and Silberman 1960; Groom and Nandwini 2006);
- participant and/or covert observation (Stein 1974; Thomsen *et al.* 2004);
- sex workers' accounts/diaries of their clients (Kinnell 1990).

These recruitment techniques are often heavily dependent on third-party introductions and gatekeepers, making the access process lengthy, time-consuming and out of the researcher's control. The ethical integrity of some of the methods must also be brought into question. For instance, approaching men who are on the street (usually looking to make a negotiation with a sex worker) can have implications for the street sex workers who are trying to attract customers, as well as present issues for the researcher's own safety given the precarious nature of the street environment. The case of mistaken identity can also land the researcher in confrontational scenarios: a male researcher could be seen as a 'punter' by sex workers or the police while a female researcher could be mistaken for an offender or competition from other workers. Other recruitment methods where researchers pose as clients is similar to entrapment and against social science standards of informed consent. Holzman and Pines (1982: 98) note that researching 'johns' through accounts of sex workers has epistemological weaknesses because women inhabit a different reality to men, preventing men's stories coming to the fore.

Asking sex workers to introduce their own clients to researchers also has limitations. This can become a burden on sex workers when their object is to make money and retain 'good customers' as regulars. Using indoor sex work venues may appear an ideal recruitment ground. However, the occupational culture and everyday activities of a brothel or massage parlour are based on tight schedules and set routines (see O'Connell Davidson 1998; Whittaker and Hart 1996): a researcher's presence could be disruptive and even discourage customers who do not expect researchers to be present when they are in the process of engaging in an intimate and private activity.

Relying on accessing men through various points in the criminal justice system means that only those who visit the street and have been subject to a policing crackdown will be targeted. This is largely because men who visit indoor premises are rarely arrested as they are usually totally within their legal rights and parlour raids are infrequent. Researching men who visit the street market is becoming particularly difficult because traditional 'red light districts' are being dispersed geographically, spatially (they are taking different forms) and temporally (they are happening at different times). Observations based on feedback from outreach projects suggest that in locations where policing has been consistently intense for some time, the street market in its traditional form is less visible – making the population of men who visit street sex workers difficult to access for research purposes.

The methodological history of researching men who buy sex reflects, and is at the same time influenced by, the legal and political climate at the time of the research. As the means through which clients contact sex workers alters and adapts to the modes of consumption and new technologies, researchers have to adapt traditional methods of recruitment in order to access this hidden population (Sanders 2005e). Whatever methodological tools are adopted or new innovative methods emerge, most samples of men who buy sex are self-selecting respondents who volunteer to participate.[1] In this sense, it is very difficult to achieve representative samples as the known quantity and characteristics of the whole population remain an unknown entity.

The empirical study

The sociological questions that stimulated this project stem from two traditions. First, as Plummer (1995) outlines, the narration of life has become an everyday feature of late modernity. Therefore the 'sociology of stories' has become a key aspect of qualitative research as we piece together the narratives of individuals, groups and cultures. Learning again from Plummer (1995: 13) that sexual stories are at the heart of the individual's sense of self, such stories also reveal complex social relationships of our time. The stories of men who buy sex are as important as the 'suffering, surviving and surpassing' stories that are so frequently retold and revealed. Similar to these stories of trauma and strength, the sexual stories of men who buy sex are not only about sexual relationships but are equally social stories of how their sexuality merges with other parts of their lives, needs, desires and roles. In short, the lives and perspectives of men who buy sex tell sociologists something about sexual and relationship formation in contemporary modernity. In this sense, the broad research question was to explore 'socially produced stories in the social contexts of people's [male clients'] everyday lives' (ibid.).

The research questions

The overarching questions driving the research were to explore how men negotiate, make sense of and experience buying sexual services in their everyday lives. This question was posed at different levels to enable information to be elicited about men's experiences of buying sex, their sexual scripts as clients and their conduct within the sex industry. Key themes were established to build up data in the following areas.

- *Nature of the sex industry.* Descriptions of what the sex markets looked like from the client's point of view were explored in relation to the organization of the different markets: routines, prices, changes over time, the rise of the Internet and the characteristics of websites/ message boards. Experiences of risk-taking and risk management, health, scams and 'dangers' were probed. Within these questions, motivations for buying sex were explored (why they started, length of time involved, experience of being a regular customer to the same sex worker and the overall pattern of their engagement).

- *Stigma and secrecy.* In describing how men went about researching, planning and organizing visits to sex workers, usually in secret from several different audiences, the nature of how the sex industry featured in men's lives was explored. Closely related, the struggles men had with different types of stigma and the reasons they discounted or absorbed these stereotypes were significant questions. Techniques of 'passing off' and strategies to maintain and protect their 'respectability' were a central focus. Opinions on the socially disapproved 'deviant' status of buying sex were discussed alongside the negative implications of secrecy and their impact on conventional relationships.
- *Emotions, identity and networks.* Men were asked about their emotional interactions with sex workers, their role as a 'regular' client, love, emotional loneliness, intimacy, friendship, social networks and the nature of the virtual communities. These themes built up the bigger picture of masculine identity and performance in their role as a client.
- *Sexual scripts and social conduct.* Inquiry was made into the minutiae of the conduct of men in all aspects of their encounters with the sex industry and sex workers. How they locate establishments or individual women, the role of the Internet in enabling access to the sex industry and processes of 'learning' to be a client were explored. How they prepared themselves for the visit, the 'presentation of self' (Goffman 1959) in the establishment, their interactions with sex workers and how men adopted the client role was key to unravelling the clients' part in the stage of the sex work venue.
- *Law and policy.* Men were asked about the regulatory system, the place of the sex industry in society and the long-term prognosis of the nature and shape of the sex industry. Also the merits and potential outcomes of the Home Office (2004) consultation on prostitution, *Paying the Price*, that was taking place at the time featured in the policy questions.

Recruitment: the procedure

As this project gained life and momentum from a previous ethnographic study (Sanders 2005a), it was predictable that gatekeepers and access routes would take similar forms and depended on existing contacts. To kick-start this project I used my established research contacts who were still involved in the sex industry in various capacities. In many senses, gaining access to men who buy sex was relatively easier compared to the trials of gaining access to sex workers (see Sanders 2006b). It has been documented that among this group there is a 'desire to confess' their sexual habits (Grentz 2005: 2098). Elsewhere I have described the eggshell path I trod as I originally attempted to break into the sex work community as a novice and complete outsider with no connections and no experience of this industry (Sanders 2005a). Developing a bona fide research status was not something that could have been done on my own with male clients, just like I needed introducers the first time round with female sex workers (Sanders 2005e).

The first boost to this project with men who buy sex came through the media. I gave an interview on the ethnographic findings from the book *Sex Work: A Risky Business* for BBC Radio 4 with Laurie Taylor on his *Thinking Allowed* programme in June 2004.[2] Laurie's concluding question asked: 'What are you going to do next?' I briefly mentioned the idea of speaking with men who were involved in the sex industry as 'buyers' and he promptly put out a call for people to get in contact. Within 24 hours I had over 200 e-mails to sift through from men volunteering themselves for the project. This was a totally different experience from when I had spent hours and weeks building up trust with gatekeepers and sex workers in their places of work. The men seemed so eager to talk, I had to think of a strategy to manage the numbers and filter out genuine participants from those who were time-wasting – a process that sex workers go through every working day.

The second main point of access was through the Internet. I was already aware of the Internet sites where interested parties congregate to advise, discuss and argue about various issues as well as sex work 'stuff'. In the summer of 2005, it was on these websites that I initially posted messages advertising the study and asked for volunteers to participate. I had gained the trust of three Internet hosts and they endorsed the aims of the research and my integrity as a researcher, offering me privileged access:

> I've just heard the programme on Radio 4 about the sex industry. I thought it was a well balanced view of escorting. Your request to survey the men who do it, feel free to post on the XXX board, and any relevant links I will be happy to add. I could open up a thread for you and you could conduct a survey via the message board.

Aware of the inhibited and secretive nature of the client, and motivated by propelling the research forward, respondents also advised me on how to go about encouraging others to participate. One interviewee helpfully e-mailed:

> The approach that I would suggest that you take would be to register [with a particular website], then make a post introducing yourself and explaining what you are interested in doing and why, then see who replies – if there are any people who you are particularly interested in interviewing as a result of what they have

posted, then you could send them a personal message via the site. Alternatively I could make a post with your contact details on if you are interested in pursuing this line of enquiry.

One respondent had such faith in the research process, and was particularly keen that different types of men were in the sample, that he contributed this message to a popular website headed 'Not exactly a field report' to encourage other men to participate:

> There was some mention a couple of months ago re: this researcher from Leeds Uni, who has a book published about working girls and is currently doing research about the punters' view of things. She had good 'references' from XXX (name of a sex worker) amongst others. She's just visited me for an hour and recorded an interview for her research. I just thought I'd let you guys know that she's a nice, friendly, street-wise, down-to-earth lass and easy to talk to. As a sometime social sciences researcher myself I can confirm that she knows her stuff and can be trusted to do a good job. She's doubtless interviewed one or two other guys from the board as well – I know she's conducted some interviews by phone and interviewed some in her Leeds office. She's looking for others to take part, partly to ensure a balance of different types of punter (age, ethnic group etc.) and partly so she can hear from guys who use different sectors of the market (street, parlour, indies etc.). So, if you want to have your say, I'd encourage you to contact her. For me it was interesting to be able to talk through my thoughts about punting to a neutral observer – not often you get the chance.

It was important that I was considered among the gatekeepers as someone who did not have a narrow 'agenda', especially an overtly radical view of male sexuality as a direct threat to women. Potential respondents were often aware of my previous research with sex workers and were reassured by my awareness of the complexity of sex work as an organization and the interactive emotional, physical and psychological relationships that male clients have with female sex workers. This reputation for 'balance' was helpfully endorsed by others I had made strong links with through the previous ethnography. Three sex workers with whom I still had contact posted messages to verify that I was a bona fide researcher and not a journalist. The snowball sampling technique gathered momentum. Sex workers referred me to clients, clients referred me to other men they knew visited sex workers and website hosts promoted the study.

From June 2004–January 2006, I received 457 e-mails from men who expressed an interest in the research project and wanted more information. All inquirers were sent e-mail replies with an information sheet attached and a consent form. The first included details of the project, who I was, what the research objectives were and what 'participation' would mean. The consent form stated the boundaries of confidentiality, what would happen with the recorded interview tapes, the contract I had agreed with the transcription service in terms of confidentiality and how the information would be used in the writing up and dissemination process. I asked all those who were interested in taking part to write an initial biography about themselves, sketching out a brief factual history of their involvement with sex workers. The invitation to submit a biography was essentially a filtering system that enabled me to scan and select individuals that I considered suitable for the aims of the project (see criteria below) and identify those men who were serious about participating with the available time to invest in the process. As Plummer (1995: 10) recalls, there needs to be some degree of flexibility over choosing whose sexual story to pursue as taking sexual life histories from those who are different can be problematic on a pragmatic, personal and political basis.

I received 134 biographies (129 by e-mail and five by post). Other types of information were also volunteered: eight men sent spreadsheets which recorded their involvement with sex workers and their financial expenditure (often over several years). A few men had websites of their own where they recorded blogs of their activities. Others were prolific contributors to websites and would copy me into discussions and threads from message boards. After the biographies were received I read each carefully and screened them for validity in as much as I considered them to be useful to the study and 'genuine' clients. Only a few biographies did not seem genuine as they read as inflated fantasies or grandiose accounts of sexual antics. A few were 'cries for help' because they had fallen in love with sex workers and wanted me to mediate, or because their wife or girlfriend had found out and they wrote laments of regret and remorse. In all, there were nine respondents I did not consider suitable for an interview. Of the 125 who were offered interviews, 64 agreed in principle, and of these I made appointments with 56. Four people did not keep the appointment and gave no explanation for withdrawing. One man left the country before an interview could be arranged and another man cancelled as he had stopped visiting sex workers.

In total, 52 interviews were carried out. I terminated two interviews: on one occasion the participant was visibly upset and I felt it unethical to continue; another telephone interview was terminated because the man became verbally hostile (see below). Of the 50 interviews that took place, 37 were face to face and 13 were over the telephone either because of geographical distance (three of these were overseas) or because men preferred to remain entirely anonymous and not meet in person. The majority of the face-to-face interviews (31/37) were conducted in my office at the university. The other six were conducted in other safe places: one in the man's house (he was recommended by a trusted contact), two in bars, one in a participant's place of work and two in sex workers' apartments.

Recruitment: me, men and motivations

Key features of the research relationship influenced the type of men that were contacted and the composition of the sample, the experiential 'feeling' of doing research with men who buy sex, the data that was eventually collected and the final outputs. The personalized, subjective nature of qualitative research and dynamics between my identity, individual respondents and the wider sex industry influenced the production of knowledge.

Framing the official context

The research was presented to potential participants and the wider sex work community as a serious, 'official' piece of enquiry that was set within disciplinary procedures, followed ethical guidelines (for instance a consent form was part of the process and there was no 'off the record' contact which is natural and normal in ethnographic study) and required the participant to actively engage with the research process. Questions were e-mailed to respondents before they were interviewed with the expectation that they would do some 'homework' in preparation for our meeting. It was clear from the questions I sent that the participant would have to think and consider their own position. I was not asking them to relay their sexual exploits as if they were chatting recreationally or with fellow hobbyists online.

After seeing the length and depth of the questions, some participants were a little surprised that there were so many topics of inquiry or were a little anxious over the subjects such as 'emotions' which they confessed not to consider in their everyday lives. Yet this procedure enabled the interactions and relationships I had with the male respondents to be framed within a research context that was, as much as possible, devoid of the sexualized context and behaviour that underlined the subject matter. The official research procedure which I invited the participants into set out the 'territory' and boundaries for the research relationship. The physical context of where the interviews took place, usually in my office, bolstered this formal context and provided a professional atmosphere which somewhat protected me from any potential ambiguities.

The two interviews that were conducted in bars did have a different 'feel'. The absence of the official context of the university meant that the liaison between a male and female stranger meeting to discuss sexual behaviour in an arena that is a significant part of the seductive night-time economy had a different context and potential meaning. It was clear that when interviews were conducted in my office, my status as an employee of a public institution and as a formal researcher reduced opportunities for my role to be sexualized or for any ambiguities about my intentions to emerge. I can say this because I did not experience some of the overt sexual comments or attempts to objectify my role that some researchers of male clients have disclosed when they advertised for clients in less official or substantiated environments. For instance, when Peng (2007: 317), researching as an undergraduate student, asked for interviewees for a study on men's motivations to buy sex through an Internet bulletin board, she was met with sexual remarks, personal and inappropriate questions and solicitation such as 'Let's go to a motel and I will tell you every detail'. Other researchers (notably Grentz 2005: 2094 and O'Connell Davidson 1994) report sexualized interview experiences and explicit sexual requests by potential participants. Surprisingly, all I had to avoid were some lunch invites and a trip to Rome to conduct the interview face to face rather than on the telephone. Men who were willing to visit the university were equally stating their belief in this topic as a serious academic subject that deserved inquiry. Some respondents had been to the university before, others commented on their own higher education experience that came flooding back when they stepped onto the campus, a few had never visited a university before and were intrigued by how it all worked. The research setting of the university for the 31 respondents who visited had an impact at some level which framed the researcher–respondent dynamics.

While I confess that I have somewhat intellectualized the physical and psychological context and meaning within which the research was framed and organized, I clearly had vested interests in researching from the comforts of the establishment. Setting up the interviews so that participants visited my place of work gave me security and control on several levels. Obviously, time was gained by men travelling to the university and there were clear advantages of meeting strangers in the safety of a public workplace as well as fulfilling my obligation to abide by risk assessment safety protocols. It was feasible to slot in interviews during the humdrum of term-time teaching duties and at the same time I had the luxury of private space and research facilities for interviewing. Generally, conducting the interviews on 'my territory' meant that the complexities of negotiating the cultural context of the sex industry were largely avoided. No doubt recruiting and interviewing in a parlour, a strip bar or another such sex work venue would have changed the dynamics and made the process more complex as the sexualized context of the commercial sex setting would have positioned the research and the researcher. Where I did venture into the sex markets, it was in massage parlours or sex workers' apartments with which I was already familiar and had trusted gatekeepers nearby. In this regard the muscle memory of doing previous research came into play and few new negotiations had to take place.

Trust and power dynamics

This entry in my fieldwork diary reveals some key themes of the fieldwork experience:

> I agreed to visit XXX in his home because he was referred to me by a trusted contact. The meeting went well and he seemed to have considered my questions and was thoroughly prepared for the interview. He had also done some of his own social science research in the past and appreciated why qualitative inquiry was meaningful. As he told me about how he prepared for escorts to visit him at home I realized that the interview had been planned in pretty much the same way. He had cleaned his house from top to bottom and we had gone through the same process in terms of the information he imparted to me as he would give to an escort – pseudonym, telephone number, address, directions to his house. He chose not to tell me his real name just as he chose to conceal his real name from sex workers initially. After the interview, he commented on the usefulness of the session, how he thought the research of import- ance, and how he would post a 'field report' about our meeting on the message board to encourage other volunteers. The next day he stuck to his word and posted a complimentary message about the research experience, my skills and personality. This generated more interest, several e-mail exchanges with potential participants and finally, three interviews. It became apparent that the Punternet message board was becoming a place where I and my project were being marketed. So far, the responses have been positive, but I am braced for trouble. The message boards can be unforgiving at times and while the vibe is going in my favour at the moment, this could easily change. (Extract from fieldwork diary, August 2005)

It was a recurring theme that men would go about arranging our meetings (both practically and emotionally) in the same way that they had done many times with sex workers (this is also reported by Grentz 2005: 2104). Men would rely on familiar skills, cover stories and trusted procedures for setting up a meeting with a researcher as they did when making clandestine arrangements with sex workers. This was because, like the meetings for sexual services, engaging in research about being a male client was also secret, undisclosed and private.

Being involved in research about the sex industry implicated individuals directly as clients which meant that the same protocols they adopted to keep their involvement in the sex industry secret were employed in our relationship. For instance, when I visited a chief executive in his plush office I was given strict instructions about who I was (a cover story) to tell the secretary who screens all his visitors. Another participant, who offered to take part in a telephone interview even though he lived overseas, scheduled our call for the time he usually took his morning run before work (the time difference was to my advantage!). E-mail replies, such as the following, were standard when I was negotiating a time and place: 'Very happy to talk to you but it would need to be prearranged so that "the coast is clear".' The respondents were experts in arranging meetings without other people knowing (usually intimate partners) and therefore defaulted to these familiar skills and processes when faced with the unfamiliar scenario of speaking with a researcher about a secretive and intimate activity.

For two reasons I also suspect (I have no proof of this) that some men were aroused, excited or enjoyed the attention of arranging an interview with me and being given the opportunity to discuss, at length, their sexual behaviours and relationships with sex workers. First, some men engage in the sex industry because they are compelled by the process of thinking about, planning, organizing, negotiating and executing the visit to the brothel, escort or street market, more so than the actual sexual interactions. The scenario of arranging to meet a female researcher (also a stranger) to discuss their sexual behaviours and experiences of the sex industry may not be that far removed from the same emotional processes that are the product of visiting a sex worker. One interviewee, Kelvin, directly refers to these similarities when describing his attraction to commercial sex: 'I think it's just the fact that you know, two strangers meet and agree, however, they agree to this extremely intimate act, it's somehow endlessly fascinating. And I have to say there's a certain irony in this interview, is there not?' Such similarities between the interview negotiation and commercial sex negotiation influenced the power relations of the process, demanding emotional labour from the researcher. Yet these similarities were ultimately beneficial to finding out knowledge and learning how men understood their own experiences (Hoffman 2007).

Some readers, especially those who may think that the trend in reflexivity in the 'sixth moment' in qualitative research may have been taken too far, could make the charge that this analysis of the motivations of men who buy sex to be interviewed is contrived, exaggerated or simply reading too much into the dynamics. To rebuff these criticisms, I refer to Plummer's (1995) insistence that the making of sexual stories is an equally important sociological process that can be as revealing about sexuality as the content of the stories. What urged men to speak to me about their sexual selves and why they appropriated me as a 'listener' and gateway to publicize their private story is as intriguing to the symbolic interactionist as making sense of the sexual behaviour. Secondly, for several respondents, the motivations for engaging in research about the sex industry were along similar motivations for purchasing intimacy and comfort through sexual services. Feedback after the interview on the 'usefulness' of the interview process was revealed as cathartic, similar to that of relaxing with a sex worker to discuss personal trials and tribulations. The emotional labour that I engaged with as a researcher was faintly comparable to the emotional labour that sex workers provide as part of the sexual service (I will return to this theme below).

Age, status and social class were determining factors that produced different power dynamics in the researcher–respondent relationship. As the age of many of the respondents was one or even two generations above mine (respondents would comment about their own daughters being at a similar life-stage/age to me), this age dynamic produced different effects. My relative youth left some men with the image that I was 'fresh faced', 'naive' and in some way 'protected' from real life (all words used by interviewees), which translated into my enquiries being non-threatening in nature, curious and without hostility. Trust was often afforded because I appeared as an 'ordinary' middle-class young woman whose questioning was harmless. This did not stop some of the older clients 'turning on the charm' by inviting me to lunch. I believe that these were not solicitations but usually (in their eyes) sociable progressions from our exchanges in the research relationship. Similar affections, invites and boundary crossing were produced in the research relationships I had with female sex workers whereby their invitations into their homes, to meet their families, partners and children were testament to the strength of the research bond. In my relationship with sex workers, the power dynamics were different as some of the women occupied marginalized positions in society, marred by abusive experiences and welfare dependency. Although critiques from feminist standpoints would argue that the dynamics between a young middle-class female researcher and an older, middle-class male are riddled with complex undercurrents that are inherently sexualized or at least based on gender differences, I did not find this necessarily the case as other dynamics became defining.

The power dynamics were often there, but this was usually based on life-stage, status in the community, and cultural and economic capital rather than gender difference. In the case of men who were in professions and had similar educational backgrounds, the relationships felt equal. With some of the manual workers who came to my office to be interviewed there were different power dynamics that framed the relationship. A younger woman, in a different social class, who had an 'elevated' status in society (working in a university apparently gives you that!), meant that with the male working-class respondents the power lay with me, and I had to work hard to make interviewees feel comfortable in unfamiliar and intimidating surroundings. In a few cases where the men were very wealthy (five respondents held prestigious jobs that gave them significant status) and lived very different lifestyles to that of the public sector worker (in fact, with one respondent, we joked that he had spent more on sexual services in a few years than my salary!), the power relations were different. In these scenarios, there were feelings of disempowerment as these wealthy older men had financial and social power that afforded them freedom to control all aspects of their lives. Differences in economic capital and access to resources meant that implicit aspects of their lifestyles and values meant our 'starting points' in the interview were at polar positions.

During the e-mail exchanges some interviewees expressed reservations at my ability to understand the sex industry, given that I had not worked in it. A potential respondent wrote: 'One of the difficulties might be discussing the subject with someone who hasn't actually done the job herself as it were. That's not meant to be as negative as it might sound, and I certainly have no objection to meeting sometime to discuss.' Caution was common during this early stage of the access process: 'I am interested in at least a preliminary chat to establish scope and context, and establish how relevant my experiences and views are.' Often through a couple of e-mail exchanges, any caution was ironed out and full interviews took place in these two cases.

For the younger men who contacted me and with whom I met for interviews, there were more uncomfortable experiences. If we were of similar ages, I had the feeling that some of the men found me intimidating and that the power balance lay with me as the 'coaxer' of the sexual story. The younger men were often more conscious of their assumed 'deviance' when there is a strong convention of freely available sexual relationships in contemporary culture. When younger men revealed their sexual secrets, there seemed to be more expectation that I would make judgements, or that they were breaking some golden rules of youth in their admissions of buying sex. For three of the younger interviewees, the research process seemed 'confessional' in nature: men were treating the experience of being quizzed on their sexual habits and engagement in the sex industry as a way of evaluating their behaviour, lifestyles and relationships. In these cases, gender dynamics were important. A male researcher discussing these secret sexual antics, their need for affection, comfort and sexual pleasure, and the state of their conventional relationships would undoubtedly construct a different researcher-relationship and therefore an alternative 'story'.

During the interviews I did not feel that the respondents sexualized or objectified me in the ways I was expecting. The ground rules and clear statement of the appropriate topics for discussion that I sent before the meeting established what I was interested in hearing about and what was 'off the agenda'. Essentially, I spelt out that I was not interested in descriptions of sexual encounters men had paid for (I was fully aware of these through studying 'field reports' (Soothill and Sanders 2005a)), but that other experiences and feelings were more pertinent to the research questions. Although emotional labour was an intricate part of the research relationship (see below), the social relationship between myself and the respondents was based on my identity as a researcher rather than as a woman or advisor. Despite acknowledging that the process of telling their sexual, personal, intimate stories identified me as a unique 'listener', my lack of personal investment or disclosure in the research relationship protected my 'self' from experiencing the intimacy, friendship and personal closeness that can be produced through the qualitative interview (see Cotterill 1992; Duncombe and Jessop 2002). For other researchers who collect data in the context of the sex industry, where the environment is constructed on seduction and sexual promise, their research experience, and ultimately the 'stories' they collect, may be clouded by solicitation and sexualization.

Turning a secret story into a public testimony

Plummer (1995: 13) asks why people tell their confidential, deeply personal sexual stories to researchers or anyone else. My fieldwork diary captures the reasons why some men willingly volunteered for the project:

> Matthew, a primary school headteacher, was my first interviewee who agreed to travel to Leeds to be interviewed. I liked Matthew – he was a gentle looking man with the look of a school teacher – summer slacks and cotton shirt – I could imagine him being quite a hippie. Our conversations began with talking about education – both our lines of work. This was a safe familiar topic that broke awkward silences before we were in the privacy of my office. Someway into the interview, Matthew clarified that he had prepared for our meeting in the same way he would when arranging a meeting with an escort. No one was aware we were meeting and he had

orchestrated the event so that he didn't have to lie to his wife. Incidentally, that week he had arranged to meet three sex workers while his wife was away. Matthew was open about why he had so readily taken up the offer of being a research participant – he saw it as free counselling. He went on to reveal that he had paid a sex worker who was training to be a counsellor £50 for an hour of her time so he could talk about his activities with someone who understood the business. He saw our interview as another chance to explore some of the areas of his life that he did not think about often, certainly did not have the opportunity to talk about to others and in his mind, clarify some decisions about his continued involvement in buying sex. He admitted that some of the questions were challenging and had raised guilt about his secrecy which had 'hit a raw nerve'. He wanted to be interviewed again – but after going through all the questions he accepted that this would not be helpful for the research. (Extract from fieldwork diary, August 2005)

Many men found engaging with research about the sex industry, although equally daunting and nerve-racking, a cathartic process. Although the interviews were not designed to be 'therapeutic', it was clear (and expected) that the interviews would appeal to men who wanted to talk about their purchasing sex and their private intimate lives and selves. There was indeed a 'spectrum of catharsis': some men, like Matthew, were explicitly motivated by wanting to discuss their emotions and experiences, whereas others (see quotes below) did not consciously enter into the process for emotional reasons but on reflection had gained insight as an outcome.

Some men contacted me after the interview to express how useful the interview process had been. The interviews often sparked off questions and trains of thought that were not promoted in their everyday worlds of secrecy: 'Just e-mailing you to say that I enjoyed meeting you today and being interviewed. It was a good experience and I am glad to have helped with your research' (Adam, 32, long-term partner, sales). For others, the opportunity to speak freely was enlightening: 'Thanks for the chat the other day – it really made me think (not always an easy thing in this age of unreason!). If you need any further info then don't hesitate to get in touch, and I look forward to seeing the fruits of your research' (Boris, 56, married, retired accountant).

For others, it was the first time they had spoken to someone outside the sex industry about buying sex. Several men described the experience in terms of an 'emotional awakening'. In three cases the interview led men to conclude that they would benefit from professional therapeutic help to discuss some of their thoughts, feelings and experiences about sex, emotions, love, relationships/marriage, so had decided to contact psychologists or specialist counsellors. Two men, who were already in the process of leaving the sex industry behind, found the interview a useful milestone that resulted in them deciding finally to stop buying sex.

Smashing stereotypes and contributing to knowledge

There were other more philosophical and altruistic reasons that motivated men to answer requests for interviews. First, men were disconcerted and offended by the negative press that was attached to the sex industry, sex workers and men who buy sex. Terry (68, married, lawyer) had political reasons for becoming a participant:

> One of the reasons why I wanted to do this was that I believe that it is right that some sort of correcting influence on the stereotype should exist and the fact that you are working in this field and trying to bring a bit of balance into the picture made me feel I really wanted to contribute.

Respondents were motivated by the overall research objectives of wanting to challenge negative stereotypes about who the 'punters' are. One respondent posted a message on a board to encourage others to participate stating: 'This is a good opportunity to do something to persuade the world that we are not sleazy scumbags in dirty macs!' Some of the interviewees had an interest in the wider parameters of ensuring that a study of this kind featured men 'like them' and that they were able to contribute to smashing down stereotypes: 'As your work appears to be to the common good if you are able to guarantee anonymity and safe contact procedures I may be willing to assist as a "current" regular user of massage parlours.'

The final motivating factor for a smaller group of respondents was their interest in policy and specifically legal reform regarding the law on prostitution. At the time of the recruitment process, the Home Office (2004) were conducting the *Paying the Price* consultation on the management of prostitution in the UK. Those who contributed to and read message boards would have picked this up as well as some media attention given to the review. Three of the interviewees had studied the consultation document and had contributed to the process by submitting their own responses and ideas about how best to regulate and manage the sex industry. When asked why he had contributed to the project, Edward, a 38-year-old engineer with a long-term partner, stated: 'I suppose altruism really. You know, it would be nice to think that control – you know, improvements would come along and academic research may be a part of that kind of process.' Some of the interviewees were actively aware of the politics of prostitution and the state of the policy arena and saw this research as another route to making small steps to change.

Emotional labour and the therapeutic interview

Conducting research with men who buy sex was emotionally charged in several ways. Some of the questions were challenging to the participants and therefore provoked defensive, confrontational responses. This usually happened around my questions about unsafe sex, exploitation of women and the power relationships between sex workers and clients. A minority of respondents' misogynist attitudes challenged my own views, my probing skills and my politeness! One particular interviewee, who was not counted in the final data collection because I terminated the interview, held extreme views on race, nationalism, migration and women. His claim that 'all women were whores at heart' as a preamble to a rant about his hatred for women was not conducive to the research objectives – which I explained before terminating the call.

A proportion of the interviewees (20/50) revealed that at some point in their involvement with sex workers they had not used condoms for either penetrative or oral sex. Challenging were the stories offered of paying more money for sex without condoms, believing that sex workers wanted sex without condoms because they had a 'special' relationship beyond the commercial contract, as well as distorted views that they were somehow exempt from contracting sexually transmitted infections or passing them on to other intimate partners. These controversial and simply incorrect attitudes and practices were usually met with my rebuffs about sex workers' preferences and safety risks, the risks of passing on infections and the importance of condom use for sex workers. At times, like sex workers often do (Sanders 2006b), I felt like a health educator explaining the importance of condom use to male clients. In these instances, the interview became a site where masculine practices could be reproduced (Schwalbe and Wolkomir 2001).

True to the dilemmas of interviewing men (Lee 1997), another interviewee left me with angry and defensive emotions. The telephone conversation we had was fairly brisk, short answers and abrupt in tone and manner. He riled me on three points: first, he was blasé about requesting oral sex from street sex workers without a condom, claiming there were 'no risks'. Second, he directly blamed his involvement in the sex industry on his wife's pre-menstrual tension, her lack of interest in sex and her unwillingness to perform fellatio. Third, he ended the conversation with details that he had visited Thailand on a few occasions where he had bought sex from young women who were probably underage. He accepted this as the norm claiming that this was what legitimately happened in other cultures.

Reflective revelations (for instance by Hart 1998; Maher 2000; Melrose 2002; O'Neill 1996; Sharpe 2000; Shaver 2005) have begun to reveal the emotional labour, tensions and difficulties of researching aspects of the sex industry. The negative responses to researching men who buy sex, usually in the gritty reality of the sex markets, has been reported by few (see an account by O'Connell Davidson and Layder 1994: 216–17). Emotional labour was part of my research experience not only because, on a few occasions, I had to deal with sexist attitudes and ignorant practices but because I had to work hard to absorb and appropriately react to difficult emotions that respondents revealed. For instance, the laments of love, unhappiness, confusion and loneliness were significant parts of some interviews. Equally other stories of fun, pleasure, connectivity, and good sexual and social relationships balanced these outpourings. Listening to, responding to and entering into conversation about emotions with interviewees, although somewhat anticipated, affected the research–respondent relationship to the extent that the therapeutic element of the qualitative interview became the data collection. As Hoffman (2007) describes, it is through emotional labour that the researcher comes to understand the data, the participants and the stories at a deeper level.

In reflecting on the process of the interviews with men who buy sex, the reflexivity and understanding provided by Birch and Miller (2000) has been most helpful in making sense of the social relationship constructed with my participants. Referring specifically to the qualitative researcher who explores the 'intimate sphere', Birch and Miller ask: 'Can the invitation to narrate past and present experiences, together with future hopes, avoid offering potential therapeutic opportunities?' Clearly in the case of my research, the qualitative interview/er mimicked the therapeutic encounter by 'creating a space in which individuals can reflect on, re-order and give new meaning to past, difficult experiences' (*ibid.*: 190). Of course, not all of the men I interviewed had difficulties or tensions to reflect on, but a significant proportion did and openly admitted their motivation for participating was therapeutic. The depth of the questions and the nature of the topic also dictated that the interview would create a distinct social relationship between the researcher and the respondent, a space where respondents were asked to tell a story, a personal, intimate and sexual story, in a certain way and for a certain audience. Any interaction that involves telling sexual stories requires the researcher to be reflexive about the performance of how and why sexual stories are told, what gets left out and how the researcher is part of the process (Plummer 1995: 13).

As a researcher my position mirrored that of the 'therapeutic mediator' (Birch and Miller 2000: 194) as I was privy to, and the initiator of, personal sexual narratives retold and disclosed (often for the first time). As a 'coaxer' of sexual stories (Plummer 1995: 23), it was not simply my task to invite men to tell their story but I was responsible for the production and dissemination of their sexual stories. In doing the data analysis and writing this book the data has been transformed from 'our' one-to-one research relationship where the man took the role of the storyteller and I adopted that of the listener to the narrative that is recorded, disseminated and applied. This process adds a therapeutic element to the research and also places the researcher in a dilemma. Some of the interviews were 'confessional' in the Foucauldian sense of admitting behaviour that is often frowned upon. When these stories were retold in the formal context of the research interview, they were implicitly subjected to a process of judging and monitoring from the benchmarks of social attitudes and norms of sexual behaviour. Birch and Miller (2000: 194) explain how this process of monitoring is the point where the personal intimate story becomes a public story for the researcher to disseminate to audiences beyond the qualitative interview dyad. The formal storytelling process that qualitative research becomes (see Plummer 1995: 5) propels the personal, intimate story into the public arena. This chapter has alluded to why male clients of sex workers are compelled to take part in this formal storytelling that allows them to lay bare their sexual souls for the scrutiny of those who are curious about, damning of or sympathetic to their reasoning.

The data sources

What is used as data in this book is reminiscent of the anthropological fieldwork data collection methods of researchers who live among communities and groups to make sense of their lives (see Shaffir and Stebbins 1991). There is an attempt to triangulate information from different sources as a strategy that enables the researcher to confirm patterns of behaviour and interactions. The data sources these findings are drawn from largely fall into four categories: interviews with men who buy sex, observations from Internet websites, sex workers, and grassroots knowledge from sex work outreach projects. The bulk of the verbatim quotes are taken from the formal in-depth, semi-structured interviews as this chapter has described. Other verbatim quotes are taken from e-mail correspondence, message boards, chat rooms, and written letters that men have contributed to the project. Three key Internet websites were observed intermittently over a period of 18 months and whenever I was guided to interesting discussions. Factual details are reported from biographical accounts that respondents recorded and spreadsheet records of their purchasing habits and tables of expenditure.

On several occasions in the book, data has been included from men who were not interviewed but offered 'their story' through e-mail correspondence. Some men constructed lengthy e-mails which were in effect narratives of their lives that revealed their relationships, sexual habits and engagement with the sex industry. In whatever form the data was presented, all of the sexual and social stories have been constructed from an amalgamation of many different influences including: society's view of the sex industry, the stigma surrounding being a client, the views of other 'punters' and those of the 'punting' community, written sexual stories from others, website information, magazines and guides that are in the form of self-help manuals, legal statutes, media accounts and exposés, opinions from close intimates, sex workers' tales, brothel folklore, therapeutic 'experts', religious doctrine, and medical texts. In addition, material and verbatim quotes from the previous ethnography that included 50 interviews with women involved in the sex industry are incorporated when relevant to illustrate a wider point about the sex industry (Sanders 2005a).

Another set of data has been explicitly and implicitly triangulated with the original sources of data. My active involvement in two different types of grassroot organizations that support women involved in the sex industry has provided a privileged, almost daily update of the changing nature of the sex industries. As an associate member of the UK Network of Sex Work Projects and an active member of their Safety, Violence and Policing Group, I have drawn on the observations, concerns and patterns of behaviour and policing and the ongoing policy climate that are reported by outreach projects across the country.[3] In addition, I am currently the Chair of the Board of Trustees with the outreach charity Genesis in Leeds.[4] This enables me to have close contact with the dynamics of a local sex market and stakeholders who are involved in managing prostitution. For me, the awareness of a broader picture beyond my own research agenda enables a more holistic view of the state of the sex industry in contemporary Britain, the failure of policy and the conditions of late modern capitalism that have a direct bearing on the sex industry.

The participants

A chart in the Appendix provides details of the 50 men who are in the sample. The characteristics of the men who were interviewed were as given in Table 2.1.

Table 2.1 Socio-demographics of sample

Socio-demographic feature	Distribution in sample (n = 50)
Age	Range: 22–70 years Mean: 45 years
Ethnicity	White British: 42 Asian British: 4 White Irish: 1 Italian: 1 Australian: 1 British-born Canadian: 1
Marital status	Married: 18 Long-term partner: 8 Widowed: 4 Single: 12 Divorced/separated: 9
Fathers	39/50
Education	Degree or higher: 34 Vocational qualification: 9 No formal qualifications: 7
Employment	Retired: 9 Full-time employed: 36 Part-time employed: 2 Student: 3
Monthly expenditure	Range: £45–£500 Mean: £170
Length of time buying sex	Range: 1–33 years Mean: 9 years

Age and marital status

Unlike other studies that have utilized the Internet and bulletin boards to attract younger clients (Peng 2007), the average age of the participants in my study was 45 years. There were four men interviewed who were in their 20s with the youngest at 22 years. At the other end of the spectrum, the oldest interviewee was 70 years old. The most frequent age bracket was men in their mid 40s to mid 50s. Some consideration in relation to why the self-selecting sample was generally older men relates to a general trend of older men appearing in prevalence surveys (see Chapter 3). Older men tended to be widowed, divorced or separated. Having no spouse could mean that men are more inclined to volunteer themselves to take part in research of this kind because there was no one else to consider when negotiating the process. Men in this age bracket may have more disposable income than younger men, and therefore may be the largest group in the population of men who buy sex. Of the sample 29/50 lived alone. As expected and concurrent with other demographic studies, half of the sample (26/50) were in committed long-term relationships: 18 were married and eight had long-term partners (although four of these did not live with their partners). This status corresponded with the majority of participants having children (39/50).

Ethnicity

All of the respondents had had British residency for a considerable number of years. The majority of the sample was White British (42/50). An Australian, Irish and Italian, all of whom lived permanently in the UK, were in the sample. Despite efforts to recruit Asian men, only four interviewees came forward. There were no Caribbean or African interviewees in the sample, most probably because of the socio-demographics of the Internet message boards where the research opportunities were advertised (see Chapter 4).

Education and employment

Like many studies on clients (Holzman and Pines 1982), this study is predominantly a study of middle-class white men who buy sex in the UK massage parlour and escort sex markets. The class status of interviewees was determined by a combination of their current employ-ment and their educational background. Of the interviewees 34/50 had been to university and had at least one degree: six had postgraduate qualifications. Nearly half of this group (16/34) had jobs in what Lash (1990) calls the 'new middle-classes': white collar jobs in the service sectors of media, information technology and computers, and sales. The other 18 worked in traditional middle class jobs such as law, teaching, academia, the armed forces, senior management, finance and engineer-ing, and one man was a pilot. A further nine had professional vocational training (relating to occupations such as accountancy and law). A minority of the sample (7/50) would be described as working class. These respondents occupied manual jobs such as driving, manufacturing and factory work.

Buying sexual services

Only two men I interviewed currently bought sex from the street market. This corresponds with the small numbers of working-class men in the sample. The relatively high amount of money spent each month on sexual services (see below) and the popularity of the Internet as a method of arranging meetings with sex workers are also characteristics of a middle-class sample with disposable income. Although eight other respondents said that they had bought sex from the street (either in the UK or abroad), this was often several years ago and they would not return to the street market (this is discussed in Chapter 3). Table 2.2 indicates that 48 of the sample considered themselves to be customers of the indoor sex markets only: a combination of visiting massage parlours and escorts in their own apartments. Nine men only saw escorts, six of whom only saw escorts in their own home.

The type of involvement in the sex industry differed among the interviewees. Of the whole sample, 28 participants described themselves as 'regulars' who visit the same sex worker (sometimes more than one sex worker). Sixteen other participants described themselves as 'repeat' customers who visited different sex work venues in different locations and with different sex workers. Six other clients described their habits more as 'one-off' purchases, often sporadic and without a pattern.

Information was gathered on the amount that respondents spent in the sex industry each month. The average expenditure was £170 and the range was £45–£500. The range denotes the price spent over a month: £45 represents the amount spent by a respondent who went to the street on two or three occasions in a month.[5] The same amount could represent only one visit to a massage parlour for another respondent. Some of the respondents did not purchase sex every month (due to finance or planned reduction for instance) so provided an average expenditure over the year. Men who visited indoor markets on a weekly basis usually paid £80–£100 per visit. Men who spent more money would not necessarily be visiting sex workers more frequently: £250 could buy two hours with an escort at the top end of the market – so £500 a month could represent only two visits.

Table 2.2 Respondents' preference for sex market

Type of market	Number of respondents
Street only	2
Street in the past	8
Both massage parlour and escort	32
Massage parlour only	7
Escort only:	
At own home	9
Working flat/hotel	3

Table 2.3 Number of years purchasing sexual services

Number of years buying direct sexual services	Number of respondents (n = 50)
1 year	5
2–5 years	20
6–10 years	6
11–20 years	10
21–30 years	6
31 years or more	1

The length of time that men had been buying sex varied significantly (see Table 2.3). At the time of the interview, five men had only recently started to explore direct sexual services[6] whereas others had been regular visitors to different markets for 30 years. The majority of men had been visiting sex workers for up to five years while 17/50 were long-term patrons who had been involved for more than ten years. Seven men described how buying sexual services had been a permanent part of their lives for a very significant proportion of their adulthood. Although these lengthy years of involvement were interspersed with some disengagement, this group of 'permanent' purchasers considered buying sex a part of their life. Due to seven 'permanent' purchasers involved for many years this means that the average number of years for buying sex was nine years, which could be misleading for the majority of the sample.

Notes

1 The exception here is those large-scale surveys that take place in the criminal justice system where a captive audience provides a more representative sample. See Monto (1999).
2 Teela Sanders speaking with Laurie Taylor in a BBC Radio 4 interview 'Managing the Sex Industry' can be listened to on: http://www.bbc.co.uk/radio4/factual/thinkingallowed_20040630.shtml.
3 http://www.uknswp.org.uk
4 http://www.genesisleeds.org.uk
5 The price of sexual acts on the street varies geographically but generally it is £10 for fellatio (a common request) and £20 for sexual intercourse. Other touching or manual masturbation costs less. The Punternet website, which hosts 'field reports' from clients' experiences with sex workers (mainly escorts and some sauna workers) boasts an impressive 40,582 accounts (as of 13 January 2007). The average cost per visit is £123 which illustrates the different price range for each market.
6 The term direct sexual services is used because this data does not refer to pornography or experiences with strippers or in lap dancing clubs.

Chapter 3

Client conduct: motivations, markets and morality

This chapter develops and reinforces the point that men who buy sex are not a homogenous group. The heterogeneity of male clients does not only mean that they represent men from all walks of life but that men's motivations and reasons for engaging in the sex industry represent a myriad of lifestyles and backgrounds. There are various patterns of involvement as a 'punter'. Rarely is buying sex permanent or consistent over the life-course. The length of time involved and the trajectories of client behaviour cannot be reduced to singular categories or characteristics, reducing the meaningfulness of the label 'men who buy sex' in policy. This chapter discusses how clients culturally understand their own motivations to engage in commercial sex, their views of the markets, how they make decisions about the markets and how they create their own rules and etiquette. Before the cultural and contextual nature of buying sex is discussed, a brief review of some empirical data is worthwhile to place this sociological investigation in the context of what is already known.

Evidence from surveys

Recently, the prevalence of men who buy sex has been studied by sexologists and epidemiologists in both small-scale local studies and national sex surveys. In the UK, Ward *et al.* (2005: 468) compared results from a survey of men aged between 16 and 44 in 1990 (n = 6,000) and with a survey in 2000 (n = 4,672). This comparative study showed that there had been a significant increase in the prevalence of buying sex over the decade with 8.8 per cent of men in 2000 admitting to buying sex in their lifetime, compared to 5.6 per cent in 1990. The authors conclude 'this population based study shows that a significant proportion of men in Britain pay women for sex and that this proportion is increasing' (*ibid.*). In Scotland, Groom and Nandwani (2006) reviewed 2,665 retrospective case notes of male attendees of a sexual health clinic and found 10 per cent had reported paying for sex. These more recent statistics challenge the comparative evidence from European and American sex surveys that show a decline in the prevalence of men buying sex (see review in Brooks-Gordon 2006: 82–3). Wellings *et al.* (1994: 138) in The National Survey of Sexual Attitudes and Lifestyles conducted in the UK, found that single men were least likely to buy sex while the most likely group were widowed, divorced or separated men. Paying for sex also increased with socio-economic status and age.

Large-scale surveys in the US that test for correlations show that there are no differences in men who buy sex across ethnicity, educational background, socio-economic group, religious affiliation, household income, political spectrum and marital status (Sullivan and Simon 1998). Sullivan and Simon (1998: 150) found that where men identified high numbers of sexual partners in their life, they were more likely to engage in commercial sex, suggesting that 'hypermasculinity' may be connected to why some men visit sex workers. Although from survey results there is conflicting evidence about whether there is an increase or decline in buying sex in postwar times, factors of older age (see Pitts *et al.* 2004; Santos-Oriz *et al.* 1998), working away from home (Johnson and Mercer 2001) and a range of marital status seem constant variables across studies of men who buy sex. Given the ageing population, the increase in divorce and cohabitation, and mobile work patterns, these socio-demographic changes point to a likely increase in the desire to buy sexual services.

Motivations

Knowledge about the reasons why men buy sex is where research in this field has been successful. Echoing similar findings from Kinsey *et al.* (1948), McKeganey and Barnard (1996) interviewed 143 male clients in Scotland and concluded that there were five key motivations: the capacity to purchase specific sexual acts; access to a wide variety of women; the ability to contact women with certain characteristics; limited, temporary relationships; and the thrill of the activity (also see Kinnell 2006b; Monto 2000). Adding further to this literature, Atchison *et al.* (1998) reviewed the literature and proposed six reasons why men buy sex: physical unattractiveness, social unattractiveness/psychological maladjustment, psychopathology (poor sexual development), manifestation of cultural gendered role expectations, avoidance of gender role responsibilities and buying sex as an exercise of power for disempowered men. Many of these motivations existed among the men I interviewed, suggesting there is a spectrum of universal reasons that motivates men to enter into commercial sexual relationships. I want to add to this literature by suggesting that motivations for buying commercial sex fall into 'push' factors – elements of men's lives that are lacking, and 'pull' factors – aspects of the sex industry that are attractive and are promoted as 'entertainment'.

Push factors

The key push factors appear to be:

- emotional needs;
- stages of the life-course;
- unsatisfactory sexual relationships;
- unease with conventional dating etiquette.

Campbell (1998: 164) explored in her interviews with men the impact of loneliness and the inability to form a sexual relationship as important factors for visiting sex workers (also see Jordan 1997). One of the central motivations for men seeking sex is their emotional and physical dissatisfaction in current relationships: Andy (31, married, sales manager), who frequently worked away from home, stated that 'boredom and loneliness sort of were the push factors' for seeking out escorts. As Bryant (1982: 294) and Xantidis and McCabe (2000) identify, reasons for seeking commercial sex often go beyond sexual gratification:

> It's more for intimacy ... I am a hermit if you like, I am a lonely guy. I don't have many real time friends or I don't see them that often. There you are for five years, most of the time sleeping in your own bed alone ... it's very nice to have a cuddle. (Steve, 47, divorced, IT)

> I think it's probably more about being single and the traits of my personality. I mean I'm naturally shy, was as a child. I continued into my teenage years and I guess I have the typical things like poor self-image, that sort of thing. And it seemed the only alternative. (Ron, 51, divorced, teacher)

Findings I describe elsewhere (Sanders 2007c) note how men living with impairments are a specific group of clients that visit sex workers because of the disabling effects of the modern social world that prevent engagement in everyday social and leisure events where relationships are sparked. In this study, given the older demographics of the sample, there was further evidence that older men seek sexual services not simply to satisfy sexual motives. Some look to commercial sex because of their status as widowers, or after experiencing a lack of intimacy in a long-term marriage, while others were motivated by a final chance to experiment with different sexual relationships. Santos-Oriz *et al.* (1998) established that older men over the age of 60 were visiting sex workers regularly for a range of sexual services: both the desire for sexual pleasure and the absence of a partner were explained as motivations. Ten men in my sample with different marital status, who were all aged over 55, explained their intrigue in sexual experimentation and their hedonistic approach to finding sexual partners:

> I would consider it as probably, as a phase that I'm going through actually. I'm sixty and I suppose if I were the kind of person who liked to travel I would blow five grand on a round the world cruise or something. But I'd rather travel in inner space than geographical space. So this is a way of exploring a new part of myself in new ways. (Tom, 60, widower, social care)

> I think the older you get the more you realize you can do things that you never – you wouldn't have done when you were younger. For a variety of reasons, money being one; confidence; enjoyment; pleasure. (Jeff, 57, married, senior management)

Reasons for visiting sex workers can change over a lifetime. There appeared to be no fixed patterns but instead involvement fluctuated as men's lives changed and personal relationships took on new forms. Where older men made decisions about how to improve their quality of life, 'push' factors (age, lack of relationship, sex or intimacy) worked together with the 'pull' factors of the sex industry: the fact that temporary sexual relationships with beautiful women can be purchased in safe environments that can be sympathetic to the needs of older men. As discussed in Chapter 5, commercial sexual interactions for many men are based around social relationships (desirable commodities such as companionship, socializing, 'common' interests, rituals of courtship, romance, pseudo-conventionality and the purchase of intimacy) which act as 'pull' factors for experimenting with new sexual lifestyles and relationship formations.

The life-course trajectory is an important lens through which to further understand the different motivations or 'push factors' for some men. Age and its relationship to the sexual marketplace did not only throw up issues for older men. Four men under the age of 30 described how meeting other single women had become problematic:

The trouble is that when you get to my age and you haven't got a girlfriend, it's very difficult to meet new women, especially working in the kind of industry I am. It's a very male dominated industry so it's now very difficult to actually meet ... I mean there's a few people at work who've met their girlfriends and spouses at work but it's getting increasingly rare. (Minty, 27, single, IT)

Early biological arguments suggested that men who are married or have existing sexual outlets will not look for additional sex and can control sexual impulses, but those who do not will use commercial sex as an outlet for their sexual 'needs' (see Davis 1937). If biological argument prevailed then men who are actively sexual would not be among the clientele of sex workers. Contrary to this, men explained specific domestic situations which meant that their sex life in their relationship was unsatisfactory or had deteriorated. Patrick, a 39-year-old social care worker with a long-term partner, explained recent changes which had led him to see an escort once a month:

One of the motives was my partner, who always had a higher sex drive than myself, had a difficult pregnancy with our child who was born two and a half years ago. She was left with a number of not chronic but irritating clinical issues which means she finds it physically difficult to be a sexual person again. It's not quite as simple as, 'therefore I need meaningless sex' because in previous relationships I have actually been celibate with my partner for two years, and I don't have that urgent sex drive.

A common story is presented by Tony, a 55-year-old pilot who had been married for 24 years and had not had an affair or visited sex workers for most of his married life until two years ago. He explains how the lack of sex and emotional fulfilment in his marriage had promoted the need to look for intimacy elsewhere:

TS: What do you think prevented you from exploring the sex industry before?
Tony: Just loyalty I think to my wife really. And I probably hadn't stopped and analysed that I wasn't really you know, completely happy or satisfied. And, as I say my wife had been my only real sexual experience in life before this anyway and I was sort of conscious that perhaps I'd – well, to a degree led a sheltered existence and it had been on my mind for some time perhaps that I just wanted a little more experience in life. I haven't had sex at home for a good two years I suppose, and I think the intimacy has somewhat gone from the relationship for the moment at least.

The rudimentary biological argument also burdens marriage and other conventional relationships with the expectation of sexual and emotional fulfilment. The myth that marriage is the vehicle of personal fulfilment is one social factor that fuels the sex industry rather than dissipates its function in contemporary society. The sex industry may be popular not because of the absence of marriage or long-term relationships but in spite of institutionally sanctioned relationships.

Understanding why men buy sex needs to look beyond the psychological and psychiatric perspectives that tend to individualize the desire to buy sex, but instead, the 'push' and 'pull' factors that fuel the sex industry are largely sociological in nature. Hawkes (1996: 14) describes how 'sex as entertainment' is promoted through cultural forms (such as reality television) but that the sex is a certain type: 'without commitment, transitory, anonymous and promiscuous'. A desire for this type of sex was described by some men who sought convenient sexual relations without the added burden of the 'courting' rituals that are an expected part of heterosexual interactions. Nine men related their preference for the simplicity of commercial sex in comparison to their depressing experiences of the hazy night-time economy rituals of finding a female partner even for a temporary, singular sexual experience. Men described the classic pub/club, alcohol-induced socializing scene, which was considered the normative route to casual sex or meeting a woman for a potential relationship, as grossly distasteful, vulgar and, for some, intimidating. Stuart, a 38-year-old single, media specialist, explains how he understood his options:

> My motivation was I'm pretty bad in relationships but I still want to have sex [laughing] so you're left with basically, to be crude your right hand sometimes loses its appeal! So you know it is nice to actually have a sexual relationship with people even if it's just on a temporary basis. As I say to be horribly blunt about it, in my experience going to a prostitute is cheaper than a night out and you are guaranteed. So I think for me that's why I do it because especially now that I have got more of a talking relationship with some of the girls, you know, I get the benefits. I get to talk with them. I get to have sex with them. They get the money. You know I like to think that they are reasonably kind and I'm not completely hideous.

Stuart's account could lead some to interpret his pragmatic approach as an example of how men who visit sex workers commodify the woman's body as a sexual object, focusing on her sexuality as her primary function. However, Stuart explains that the relationship, at least for him, goes beyond that of simply the availability of sexual organs, and entails non-sexual characteristics and intimate elements he describes as a 'talking relationship'.

Alcohol-induced, competitive and pressurized scenarios in nightclubs were recounted where men had felt obliged to take a woman home after rituals of 'chatting up', flirting and buying drinks. Noah, a single 30-year-old manufacturing worker, explains the downfalls of some conventional sexual liaisons which burden men with the expectation of fulfilling Western courting and dating etiquette:

> I just can't be doing with the hassle of having a one night stand and then giving somebody my phone number I don't want to see again and then not getting stalked, but having continuous blumin' text messages being sent. I don't want that.

For the majority of the single men in the study, these familiar stories of trying to find a female partner (even for the night) had been replaced with the straightforward and, in their opinions, more 'honest' business transactions with sex workers:

> With being like young as well and busy, rather than going out, going through the whole rigmarole. Like, I don't like going and finding the girls, like going out and then to the meal and blah, blah, and all that. So then you just go to a parlour and its simple, no hassle. (Trey, 24, single, student)

Motivations that are driven by social as well as sexual needs challenge the pathologizing of earlier theorists. Drawing on Freud, Glover (1969) argued that men who buy sex suffer from a psycho-pathological condition, where they regress to an infant stage of sexual development and have subconscious separations between love and erotic desire. Gibbens and Silberman (1960) suggested links between psychological problems and buying sex. The psychoanalytical theory of Stoller (1976) took the pathologization of men who buy sex one step further by suggesting that it was a perversion stemming from internal anxieties relating to one's painful sexual history resulting in the erotic manifestation of hatred and revenge. No doubt some of the explanations of fantasy, excitement and danger have deep-rooted internal origins, and buying sex can be a dysfunctional attempt to resolve unrelated life problems. Equally, the violence directed at sex workers by some men who pose as clients suggests psychological imbalance that could be based on hatred for women and female sexuality (see Kinnell 2006b). Yet overwhelmingly the evidence from my study (and others such as Campbell 1998; Holzman and Pines 1982) suggests that there are strong sociological and cultural as well as psychological and emotional reasons that act as 'push factors' that lead men to visit sex workers which are not explained by the Freudian-based psychoanalytical theories.

Sociological reasons underpin the purchase of sex: the dissatisfaction with conventional relationships, whether trying to find them or the weariness of their longevity; the personal desires for emotional and sexual fulfilment born out of a lack of satisfaction; the pressures of not 'doing masculinity' but instead finding a temporary relationship that provides time and space out of the taxing constructions of heterosexual masculinity. Yet these factors of the contemporary social and economic landscape do not exist in isolation but combine with the sultry seductiveness of the sex industry in its contemporary form.

Pull factors

Men are attracted to the nature of the sex industry, what it offers and the glitzy or gritty images and promises that emanate from adverts, websites, stereotypes, pictures and the allurement of fantasy created specifically for those who want to trade cash for pleasure. Brents and Hausbeck (2007) use the case study of the legalized brothel industry in Nevada to illustrate how the sex industry is beginning to use the marketing strategies and business forms of wider economic structures in late capitalism to sell an 'individualized, interactive "touristic" experi-ence'. Strategies that aim to mainstream the sex industry, such as upscaling, market specialization and expanding markets and services, are evident in designer brothels and gentlemen's clubs that normalize the industry and the experience in many towns and cities in the West. These upscaling trends are identifiable in the lap dancing bars in the UK (Jones et al. 2003: 215), the 'macro-brothels' in Spain (Tremlett 2006) and luxury corporate brothels (such as Artemis) advertised as 'adult multi-entertainment venues' opened specifically for the World Cup Football Tournament 2006, located within 20 minutes' walking distance of the main Olympic stadium in Berlin, Germany.

Aside from the overt attractions to buying sex that sit alongside the everyday 'sexualization of the night time economy' (Illouz 1997), engaging in commercial sex is dressed up as normalized leisure pursuits in tourism, sport and entertainment. Yet, still the images and discourses that surround the sex industry are of a non-normative, 'deviant', naughty activity, which in turn can act as a strong attraction for some men. As Holzman and Pines (1982) note, the illicit nature of commercial sex and the taboo of entering an underworld secret market can be a core motivation. Twelve interviewees in my study concurred:

> Maybe it's an addiction to the thrill of it, the excitement of actually going to the establishment, rather than what goes on once you're

there. It's like when my football team, when we win, where I get just the buzz. Like I say, I go as a season ticket holder to my football club and going to a parlour is the same thrill you get on match days. (Craig, 31, single, sales)

I've always liked pushing things as far as they would go and walking that fine line, particularly between something that's kind of legal and illegal and moral and immoral and – I mean that kind of shadowy world; literally shadowy world ... I've seen too many James Bond films. (Kelvin, 36, single, charity worker)

Described exquisitely by sociologists who have worked in exotic dance (Egan 2003; Egan *et al.* 2006; Frank 1998; 2002), consuming sexual services, whether direct or indirect, is constructed through fantasy. The sex industry is predicated on meeting the desired fantasy of the paying client. Sex workers (particularly exotic dancers) work hard to exploit their femininity, sexuality, bodily capital and emotional labour to provide the customer with his ultimate fantasy, albeit for a few hours (see Egan 2005, 2006; Sanders 2005b; Wood 2000). The very presence of the 'opportunity' to buy something that is unobtainable in their 'real' life is perhaps the seduction for many: 'You have the opportunity to have sex with someone who looks on the web site an attractive girl ... You know, almost a girl of your fantasy really' (Tony, 55, married, pilot). The desire to suspend reality, experience something outside their mundane routine and take some 'time out' are strong pull factors that the sex industry entrepreneurs exploit.

Trajectories of being a client

One significant finding of this study is that the majority of men were clear that they would not be a client forever or that their purchasing sex habits was not consistent or a permanent feature of their lives. The psychological desires and needs that find expression in the sex industry are often transient. Graham, a 52-year-old, who had separated from his wife four years previously, had been visiting parlours for three years. Graham had been dating a woman regularly for the past year and had found his interest in commercial sex had reduced:

Because part of my motivation for doing it was the excitement and the danger. It's exactly the danger, you know, the risk. And I'm just not interested anymore. So much of my life has changed, you know, and in my forties I was – I lived a much more edgy kind of existence than I do now.

Developing conventional relationships was the most likely reason for a waning enthusiasm for buying sex. Often sexual services were seen to be incompatible with a conventional relationship:

> I've met somebody through one of these websites, so this [buying sex] is hopefully going to come to an end. She's great and you know, I won't be going short, let's put it like that! So there'll be no need to do it really. So this is kind of probably the end of the line as far as the experiments go. (Kelvin, 36, single, charity worker)

There were also very practical economic reasons for some men to reduce their visits to parlours. Fazel, a 22-year-old single student, states bluntly: 'I'm like cutting down now . . . I'm trying to save some money. Because I want to buy a car.' For those who admitted there were issues of compulsive visiting, a process of reducing their involvement was motivated by other life changes: 'At some point, my wife and I would like to have kids and when we do that, well obviously the money is not going to be there, so I have got to get myself to a point where I think I can stop before we do that' (Andy, 31, married, sales). Holzman and Pines' (1992) phenomenological study of 30 men who buy sex found that being a client is a process: a series of interrelated decisions and acts that leads to the interaction. This process is not straightforward or necessarily pattern forming and is usually not permanent. Despite this trend of fluctuating involvement in buying sex, 15 of the 50 respondents could not see an end to buying sex at the time of the interview: 'I always say you never say never, but at the moment I can't see a time when I wouldn't do it. Because I enjoy it, and it's very easy to do it now. Very enjoyable and it's very accessible' (Darren, 38, long-term partner, customer services). The varied involvement in buying sexual services suggests that the process through which men become and stop being clients is under-theorized. How buying sex features in the trajectory of the life-course is important for understanding why and when sexual services are purchased.

Typology of involvement

Although there have been several typologies that categorize clients who buy commercial sex from women (Brewis and Linstead 2000a; O'Connell Davidson 1995; Sawyer *et al.* 2001; Stein 1974) and those who buy sex from men (Browne and Minichiello 1995), there has been little attention paid to the patterns of and length of involvement among men who visit female sex workers. Men I interviewed engaged in the sex industry in different ways and at different times of their lives, and displayed a range of separate characteristics that defined

Table 3.1 Typology of men's involvement in buying sex

Pattern of involvement	Life-course stage	Characteristics
Explorers	Any stage or age	Start at any stage; sexual experimentation/curiosity/fantasy; single or in relationship; short-term involvement; becomes dissatisfactory; filters out.
Yo-yoers	30s +	Pattern-forming behaviour; reduces when conventional relationships start; involvement subsides when in relationship; starts when relationship becomes dissatisfactory; repeated pattern; attracted by 'danger', excitement and the process rather than sex or interaction.
Compulsives	Any stage or age	In or out of a conventional relationship; compulsion is the planning/arranging/Internet rather than sexual experience; unpleasant and uncontrollable consequences; usually ends with satisfying conventional relationship or change in relationship and/or therapeutic help.
Bookends	Beginning (20s) and end (mid 50s–60s +) of life-course	Initial sexual experiences and experimentation; incompatible with relationship; long period of absence during marriage; returns to buying sex in later life; widower/final chance for sex life; companionship not just sex; often regular clients to one sex worker/romantic courting rituals.
Permanent purchasers	Throughout the life-course	Sporadic over lifetime; abroad; travelling with work; away from home; long-term partner; not usually regular clients; driven by sexual needs.

their commercial sex involvement. Table 3.1 identifies five categories of client through a 'typology of involvement' that refers to different patterns of behaviour that fluctuates over the life-course.

These five categories of types of involvement challenge the general lumping together of 'men who buy sex' as a homogenous group in policy. This study has recognized that the pattern of men's involvement in buying sex is complex and that there needs to be a more nuanced understanding when 'men who buy sex' are targeted by punitive criminal policies or other health and social interventions. Involvement can be fleeting or permanent; it can occur at a particular stage of the life-course; there are those who engage in compulsive commercial sex and others who integrate sex workers with other relationships in their lives. These nuances are important qualitative detail that determines the nature of the sex industry.

Markets, exploitation and morality

The study uncovered attitudes that clients had towards the markets they chose to engage in, their justifications for avoiding certain markets and the overall understanding of the shape and characteristics of the sex industry. There were strong discourses about the dangers of the streets, the legitimacy of some aspects of the indoor markets and the complexi-ties of how women could be exploited by third parties and the system within which the markets operate. Opinions about the markets and exploitation were interlinked with the client's own morality of deciding when, where and who it was legitimate to buy sex from and when it was 'wrong' or 'immoral'. These findings directly challenge those that argue 'paying for sex, per se, raises no moral issues' (Earle and Sharpe 2007: 38) for male clients.

Dirty and dangerous streets

Only two men said they visited the street market to buy sex at the time of the interview while the other 48 interviewees visited parlours or escorts, suggesting that men who buy sex from indoor markets are not the same group of men as those that visit the street. Those who stated they would never contemplate the street as a legitimate place to buy sex connected this market with concerns about a range of risks. Street prostitution represented 'danger' for many of the men in the study. Tom (60, widower, social care) summarized the chief concerns: 'The main reason why I wouldn't go to the street is because of drugs and under age sex and disease.' Dangers were described in terms of their own health and the risk of experiencing violence or robbery:

> There is more risk of criminal offence. More risk of getting ripped off, more risk of violence, more risk of disease. Just feel – would feel very, very uncomfortable – I just wouldn't be happy. (Sol, 58, widowed, self-employed)

> It's all far too risky and it's dangerous in a physical sense, it's also dangerous in the hygiene sense and you know, it's just ridiculous. I

mean I'd rather spend money than take those sorts of risks. (George, 58, married, IT)

Attempting to understand clients' perspectives of the commercial sex interaction, Plumridge *et al.* (1996) draws on Mary Douglas's theory of contamination and risk and have applied the concept of 'cordon sanitaire' to refer to a discourse where 'men structure a hierarchy of infection' based on certain types of women, spaces and places. I suggest that part of the contemporary 'cordon sanitaire' of 'who' is dangerous relates to perceptions of drug use as well as disease and risk. Among my sample there were strong associations, often similar to those represented in the media, of the street markets and the women who work in them, evolving around drug use, addiction, and drug markets. Darren (36, long-term partner, customer services) had moral objections against street prostitution:

You know it's totally morally wrong. You know there's a lot of programmes about it. There was a programme on TV last night about it. And it just shows a bad side to it [the sex industry]. You know its all drug related. It's a grim life and it's bad.

Images of street prostitution brought with them expectations of violence, dangerous men controlling the activity and a wholly unpleasant environment:

The girls who work on the street a lot of them, I can't speak for all of them but I am positive that a lot of them are there to feed drug habits or coerced by pimps or don't really want to be there. I think there is a lot of violence and unsavoury characters that are involved in street prostitution. (Jeremy, 24, single, student)

Reiterating findings from Leonard (1990: 46), clients adjusted their behaviour in terms of 'selecting a "clean" sex partner' in attempts to avoid health implications. The 'risky' nature of the street market was often used to compare the 'safety' and 'legitimacy' that men found in the indoor markets, whether this be in the suburban parlour or the more upmarket escort scene. 'Risk' and 'safety' were equally applied to types of sex workers who operated in different markets:

A street girl I think, well I certainly feel more pity towards somebody on the streets . . . they're sort of trapped there almost . . . a few years ago some of my friends lived very close to the red light district, so I was aware of the prostitutes there and unfortunately a lot of them were hard drug users and that's not something I am really into because again that's a form of coercion because they are actually trying to do this to feed their addictions. I don't really want to be involved in that obviously for their sake and also for my health as well. You know I think it's a very difficult moral issue that because they really aren't doing that by choice. (Darren, 36, long-term partner, customer services)

The narratives of men who morally objected to the street market displayed 'discourses of respectability' (Skeggs 1997) that differentiated their behaviour as acceptable compared to that of other men who exploited women who were vulgar and 'unacceptable' (see Chapter 6).

Eight men described how they had previously visited the street market in the UK and had stopped because of a negative experience. Reasons for not returning to the street market included four men disclosing they were victims of robbery and one other man who had been physically beaten by someone he called a 'look-out pimp':[1]

I have not used street markets for some time now. I stopped simply because I was feeling more frightened and was robbed by one woman. I think the massage parlour markets are easier to access as there are adverts in nearly every local paper. It's easier to see if they are well run and afford some form of protection from being caught. (Boris, 56, married, retired accountant)

In fact one of the times I was ripped off was by a woman who I'd picked up in the street. And we had sex. She stole my wallet. She had amazing guts, this woman. We were parked in a lonely kind of industrial estate somewhere. And she nicked my wallet! I just let her go, you know, I just thought that was very brave really. I mean because she just coolly denied it. And she just walked away. So I left it till the next morning and then reported it to the police who stopped the cards and everything. And when I looked at the card statement it was all baby clothes. Sad. (Graham, 52, separated, public sector worker)

One of the 'permanent purchasers' in the sample had been a visitor to various sex markets, at home and abroad, for 25 years. He had started off visiting the street markets on occasions and progressed to parlours after being arrested for kerb-crawling:

I had a mishap fifteen years ago . . . I did get arrested and I haven't been to the street since. I never used it much. It sort of came about purely by coincidence that I used to drive home from the sports centre on a weekly basis through what was then the red light district and I just stopped one night out of curiosity because there was a girl stood on the corner but unbeknownst to me there was also a marked [police] car further up the street and it spotted me. (Norman, 50, married, engineering)

The charge of kerb-crawling was enough to stop this client from returning to the street market but did not reduce his involvement in buying sex. True to the theory of displacement (see Chapter 7), Norman shifted his purchasing habits to the invisible and less criminalized markets of the parlour. Another interviewee who had experimented with the sex industry for a year initially had sexual encounters on the street but then reconsidered what he was doing as he faced up to the reality of the social position of many street drug-using sex workers:

I mean really it's too risky and it's too quick and too uncomfortable. And to be honest I feel it's exploitation. The people on the street are there because they're desperate and they've nothing else to do and there's no other choice for them. I mean . . . I don't feel happy about doing that because I'm aware that some of the people I saw on the street I think were fairly obviously drug addicts. Quite a lot of them I suspect may have been quite young; sort of sixteen, seventeen. It's hard to tell in the dark when they're very made up . . . I mean I wasn't proud about going out on the streets at all. It was interesting and it was fascinating but wrong. (Kelvin, 36, single, charity worker)

Several men who had never engaged with the street market described the idea as distasteful because they saw the environment, the sexual acts and the position of the women as contrary and incompatible with their needs for intimacy, companionship and sexual fulfilment:

The danger doesn't concern me, it's just that I think that is not how I would behave. I cannot imagine picking up a woman in the street and going to a doorway or a car or something. I mean that is just absolutely making physical lust, presumably, just get your rocks off and, you know, I'm not interested. (Liam, 70, widower, retired academic)

Fucking in the back seat of my car does not turn me on in any way, shape or form. You know, I mean it's sordid and degrading and crappy. (Tom, 60, widower, social care)

One encounter was enough to certify to Patrick that buying sex from someone advertising on the street was not a good experience for either the sex worker or the client. His concerns for the vulnerability of women meant that in the future he only visited women who he judged to be more in control of their work and working environment:

> I didn't particularly enjoy it because what happened was I actually drove back to the girl's flat. I didn't enjoy it because she's obviously wary of punters. And I sensed she was very nervous. She felt vulnerable, I could tell. So that sort of spoilt it really for me, you know, because at least – I mean at least in brothels they know they're safe because if there's any problem they can call on someone and that makes it more relaxed. So that was the one time sort of from the street really, so I wouldn't do that again. (Patrick, 39, long-term partner, social care)

Several themes came out of the men's narratives about the morality of sex markets and their choice of market. These were constructed from a concern with the exploitation on the street and objection to this as a viable or acceptable place to buy or sell sex. This market was considered 'unacceptable' to their way of conducting themselves and the treatment of others. Respectability was a strong characteristic through which men accounted for and justified their own behaviours. Morals and ethics were a constant framework for understanding their own behaviour and were always present in their decision-making.

Assessing exploitation

The discourses surrounding the illegitimacy of the street were bound up with men's views on exploitation, freedom to choose to work in the sex industry and the characteristics of the different markets. Street sex workers were considered to be generally coerced by boyfriends or 'pimps', either physically or through their drug addictions, and therefore the notion of consensual engagement in the sex industry was dubious. This sample of men made assessments of which sex markets were overtly 'exploitative' and these judgements supported their own principles of not wanting to be linked to or seen to perpetuate harms against women: 'I certainly wouldn't want to get involved in anything involving exploitation. I mean I have some principles' (George, 58, married, IT).

Most men demonstrated an awareness of the types of exploitation that are associated with the sex industry in relation to the classic notions of 'the pimp' or 'being trafficked' or under age. Often their views on which women worked against their will informed which markets they approached. Age, immigration status and control over the working environment were upheld as measuring units against which exploitation was assessed:

If the girl is about thirty or so and she's working from home, she's not being coerced. You don't know why she's embarked on that as a career but she's not being you know, pimped or held against her will. But at times obviously – you know, because I wouldn't really – I wouldn't want to be involved with somebody who would be in that situation where they're being held against their will. (Anthony, 31, long-term partner, customer services)

Certainly before a lot of Eastern European countries became part of the EU I was slightly uncomfortable with the way that some of the places that I had been visiting were going. In terms of lots of Eastern European girls, they were all illegal immigrants. It was obvious that they had pimps who weren't very nice to them and that worried me and I stopped visiting those sorts of establishments and went to more expensive ones where it was a lot more obvious that the women were there completely by choice . . . my views have changed because you start thinking a lot more about the cheaper end of the market and some of the coercion that obviously goes on in there and that becomes a bit more distressing. You know because I don't want people to be doing things against their will because that's not what I – you know I, like, I am a bit of a soppy liberal in that respect but you know I don't want people to be uncomfortable in what they're doing. (Dean, 34, single, sales)

Most respondents held familiar media-led discourses about sex workers who were 'foreign' and in particular from Eastern European countries as involuntarily working in the sex industry and victims of human trafficking crimes. Noah (30, single, manufacturing) expressed concern at the extent of trafficking of women into the sex trade:

I'm a little concerned with a lot of the Eastern European girls, because I think there's a huge trafficking problem going on. If you look on a lot of the forums I think there's a huge kind of influx really of, you know, European girls coming in and being exploited by blokes from that area.

The complexities of the relationship between migrancy and voluntary involvement in the sex industry were not evident but equally organized crime as a feature of the sex industry was only mentioned by three respondents:

The organized crime aspect does concern me. I suppose that it's more the worry of things like the illegal immigrants and women under duress. I think it's that aspect of duress that sort of concerns me as much as anything. And it's always a fine line isn't it, as to what counts as duress. (Matthew, 39, married, teacher)

These views on exploitation concur with the findings from a multi-site pilot study across six countries by Anderson and O'Connell Davidson (2003). One of the conclusions from this project was that 'clients are not a unitary group in terms of their willingness and propensity to consume the sexual services of trafficked or otherwise unfree prostitutes' (O'Connell Davidson 2003: 58). Men showed repulsion at the idea of buying sex from women who were vulnerable or coerced.

Among the men I interviewed, perspectives on exploitation were not simply based on whether women worked on the street or indoors. Several interviewees were more nuanced in their understanding of the potential unfair treatment of sex workers in parlours and often rated women who worked independently through websites. These signs of 'independence' were judged to be a more trustworthy sign of the absence of overt exploitation from a third party: 'Owners are the worst. Some are quite greedy by all accounts. But it's a business relationship really in most of the cases. But some of them [sauna owners], I think they are taking quite a sizeable chunk of what they're [sex workers] earning' (David, 45, separated, social care).

A 'hierarchy of markets' was constructed in relation to exploitation, based on space and place, which included a sliding scale of levels of working conditions and treatment:

If somebody's working in a – whatever you call it, a parlour – then I think you've got really no way of knowing what they're doing. And if they're on the street then obviously things get very dodgy. But if they're independent then clearly they're operating in an independent way, you can tell. I mean if you arrive somewhere where it's a one-roomed flat or whatever, and there's clearly nobody else about exerting any influence – when you get to know somebody you can tell these things. (Adam, 32, long-term partner, media)

The awareness of types of exploitation described in these verbatim accounts does not extend to a critical account of the arguments against prostitution. Respondents clearly explained how they assessed potential exploitative situations and engaged in commercial sex based on a set of ethics that protected themselves from any involvement in their perceptions of the chain of exploitation. Yet respondents never identified their own behaviour as potentially exploitative because of the very nature of their displays of money as a sign of economic and social power. There was a failure to connect wider social and gender inequalities to their individual privileged male position. However, not putting themselves in the frame as 'exploiter' did not mean that clients were blasé about the tremendous strains of the sex industry or the potential damage that sex work could cause.

Rules, etiquette and benchmarking

The research questions attempted to draw out how male clients perceived their role as a client and how they understood the sexual exchange. Although sexual health and condom use were not a driving research question, differences in respondents' perspectives and experiences form an important lens that exposes men's views of sex workers. Challenging the view that clients do not think about the ways in which they engage in the sex industry, how they treat sex workers and expectations of their own behaviour, this section explores the rules and etiquette that inform client engagement when purchasing sex.

Condom use, safe sex and sexual conduct

Knowledge of the behaviour patterns in relation to condom use among men who buy sex and their attitudes and perceptions of health-related risk has been researched over the past two decades in response to HIV/AIDS (see review by Vanwesenbeeck 2001). Epidemiological concerns about the spread of the disease were raised during the 1990s and patrons of sex workers were considered a high-risk group. Buyers of sex were considered to be risks to themselves, their partners and part of a wider public health risk caused by commercial sex. Despite initial concerns about non-condom use, some research suggests that condom use among some clients is consistent. Vanwesenbeeck *et al.* (1993) interviewed 91 men about the costs and benefits of using a condom and found high condom use was reported with sex workers but this was reduced in their personal relationships (also found by Chetwynd and Plumridge 1994; McKeganey 1994; Morgan Thomas 1990). Plumridge *et al.* (1997) explored male clients' perspectives of control in the commercial sex encounter and found that they were passive in the negotiation and performance of sexual services and that the sex worker was in control of the sexual interaction. Relinquishing control stemmed from an apparent respect for the sex worker to have control over her own body but at the same time this discourse abdicated the men from any responsibility for safe sex: sex workers supplied the condoms and were blamed for condom failure. Confirming concerns set out in the 1990s that male clients engaged in 'high levels of risk taking' (Faugier and Cranfield 1995; Morse *et al.* 1992), 20 respondents in my study said they had had unprotected penetrative sex with a sex worker at some point in their history (see Thomsen *et al.* 2004 for '50 reasons for unsafe sex'). Andy (31, long-term partner, sales) explains his remorse and stupidity at not using a condom in one of his first encounters with a street sex worker and adopts the same blaming discourse described by Plumridge *et al.* (1997):

It was a total disaster in that she sort of went into her bag and said, 'Oh I don't have any condoms but that's probably all right. We don't need to use a condom.' Which was probably on her part good judgement because obviously she faced no danger from me but obviously once I'd sort of sobered up and realized what I had done I was really kind of anxious about that and ended up getting quite badly depressed in the period before having an HIV test.

Although none of the respondents 'confessed' to not using condoms for full sex in their current involvement with sex workers, twelve men said that they still purchased oral sex without a condom. Ill-informed attitudes were expressed about the risks of unprotected oral sex where the decision had been made that pleasure overrides safety: 'I mean all sex is covered, except for oral. Which, if you weigh up the pros and cons, I don't think it's a massive risk anyway. It's one that I'm prepared to take' (Darren, 36, long-term partner, customer services). Directly demonstrating how a discourse of a 'hierarchy of infection' exists among clients, one interviewee, made judgements about 'risk' and 'safety' based on the woman's 'cleanliness':

I've never done it without a condom. When I perform cunnilingus there's no barrier but that's normally with regular girls that I have been to a couple of times or I'm fairly sure of and I've spoken to them before and thought, 'Well, yes, I think she's telling me the truth. She is clean. She goes for regular check-ups'. (Paul, 56, married, retired bank manager)

Respondents spoke about the prolific online advertisement of the availability of oral and penetrative sex without condoms:

There is, I think, quite a lot of unprotected sex. I think a lot more than you might imagine. And if you went onto that adult site you could look up Bareback or whatever the term is for it. I've seen girls who offer it, they won't offer it until they've seen somebody, till they know who they're dealing with basically. (Matthew, 39, married, teacher)

Oral, and perhaps to a lesser extent penetrative, commercial sex takes place without a condom because often men subscribed to a belief in their own 'invulnerability' to risk (Plumridge *et al.* 1996). Yet, what this research has uncovered is that an equally strong discourse supports the practice of safe commercial sex among customers. Clients expressed concerns for their own health and some stated that it was their responsibility as much as the sex worker's to take precautions: 'I've never done anything uncovered. I always take the necessary precautions and I've had tests. I have one every year at least' (Morris, 55, married, academic). Further examples were offered of the 'punter community's' view on condom use and the methods that reinforced 'good practice' to protect all clients, not just individuals. The Internet was a key vehicle for impressing the view that condoms are a necessary part of commercial sex for everyone's safety:

> I mean anybody who mentions 'bareback' on the Punternet gets flamed pretty well straight away. So there is a consensus there that it's not the done thing. One reason it's not the done thing is that you know, some people come up and say 'oh, it's my personal choice' and all that. But well, for Christ's sake, you know, you're spreading it to a community. There's a whole group of people here. No man is an island and all that. There is a kind of self regulation there in terms of what's the accepted morality. (Tom, 60, widower, social care)

Just as there was evidence to suggest unsafe commercial sex is commonplace, there was strong evidence to suggest that this could not be generalized and that a safety discourse existed among clients. A client's view on sexual health often motivated their choice of market. Some of these perspectives were fuelled by beliefs that some sex workers were inevitably 'clean' based on their working routines, environments and backgrounds while others were as 'dirty' and 'unsavoury' as the environments they worked in. Clients are then involved in stigmatising some sex workers and perpetuating negative ideas about street prostitution.

Self regulation and client misconduct

Evidence among the respondents suggests that patrons of sex workers engage in processes of benchmarking, or setting and maintaining standards about the 'client role', the 'proper' way to interact with sex workers and the overall collective responsibility of male patrons. Soothill (2004a: 21) notes that misogynist attitudes displayed by some male patrons about sex workers, particularly street sex workers, were persistently challenged on message boards by other clients. Soothill (2004b: 50) also refers to message board discussions on the age of sex workers and strong criticisms of the promotion of a 16-year-old working in a parlour.

In this instance, this age was rebuffed with outrage and concern by male contributors, who took it upon themselves to check out the legalities and inform the parlour that this was unacceptable and illegal. One respondent in my study referred to a similar incident: 'Somebody had started advertising on the web as being 16 and that was mentioned on the message board and there was a lot of discussion about that not being right, so that again was setting standards' (Daniel, 41, single, teacher). The Internet chat rooms act as a 'quality control mechanism' that Soothill (2004b) describes as a means of 'order maintenance' in the subculture of male clients.

In his response to the Home Office (2004) *Paying the Price* document, one of the interviewees stated clearly how criminalizing men who buy sex was a sure way to reduce the 'community' that reinforced good practice:

> Anything which contributes to freer communication and a sense of community tends to result in users and providers finding their own benchmarks. Peer pressure from within the community is a more powerful tool than moralizing from without. Thus any moves towards criminalizing mainstream punting activities will fragment the community and create more dark corners for vile things to flourish.

On three occasions, clients recounted how they had approached the authorities after having concerns over particular women or establishments:

> A few of us believed that a new girl was being pimped ... We are pretty sure that she was trafficked from XXX. You can't prove these things very easily and I spent the best part of a month using every contact I could to contact the appropriate person in the police or immigration or whoever to get it sorted and they just didn't want to know. (Steve, 47, divorced, IT)

Half of the clients stated that the age of the sex worker was a deciding feature when planning and researching their visits: 'My main concern is "Is the girl old enough or not", you know. You don't want to be breaking the law do you' (Murphy, 28, single, sales). Not only motivated by the legalities of prostitution and sex with minors, generational issues were at the forefront of many clients' minds: 'Of course you see pretty girls in the parlours but suddenly you look at this woman as if she's your daughter and it all changes. I've no interest in younger girls because of the association with my daughters, because I've one of 28 and one of 23' (Sol, 58, widower, self-employed). Other men described how they vetoed certain markets because they held a reputation for younger women, preferring parlours or escorts where older women could be found: 'I don't tend to go to parlours because most of the girls are much, much younger and I don't like it, to be honest. All I can think, "Oh god, you're old enough to be my daughter!" That's why I like XXX who is older, closer to my age' (Paul, 56, married, retired bank manager).

Referring to clients who buy domination or straight services, O'Connell Davidson (1998: 150) argues that 'the sexual pleasure they find in their encounter with prostitutes is predicated on the notion of prostitutes as socially dead, sexual "Others" . . . refusing to acknowledge her as anything more than her sex.' There are men, of course, with such attitudes, whether they buy sex or conduct private relationships with all women with hatred, disdain and objectification. Discourses from men in my sample suggest there are equally dominant attitudes that are respectful of sex workers as women and as workers rather than simplifying their identities as 'Others':

> You know they're just ordinary people. I mean they're no different to anybody else. You know, they've got the same problems, same concerns. I think they're offering quite a valuable service really. (Sol, 58, widowed, self-employed)

> I admire them because it can't be an easy job sometimes. I understand why a lot of them do it. It's a lot of them supporting children or to get themselves a better way of life. So I don't look down, I certainly don't look down on them and I treat them with respect. Why should they be stigmatized? (Ross, 54, single, engineering)

Peng (2007: 334) interviewed Taiwanese clients and also found that men had respectful commercial relationships, leading her to conclude that the relationships are not necessarily defined by an essentialist link between buying sex and male domination: 'Instead of totalizing sex buyers as problematic, therefore, I suggest that we distinguish among acceptable and unacceptable clients and practices.' Peng's view appears to be one that recognizes that patrons of sex workers are not homogenous and therefore neither are their practices and views of sex workers and women in general. Although there is ample evidence on websites, sex worker testimonies and Internet data of debasing requests, dire attitudes of misogyny (Peng 2007: 333), the spectrum of client attitudes, behaviours, practices and interactions goes beyond the simple construction that they are sex exploiters.

To conclude, this chapter has made the argument that there are strong sociological reasons that create 'push' and 'pull' factors that lead men to look to commercial sex for pleasure, intimacy and emotional needs as well as sex. This research adds to the cultural understanding of how men engage with the sex industry and individual sex workers, illustrating that some male clients have a moral conscience about their behaviour, actively impose subjective rules about how and from whom they buy sexual services and are not necessarily passive when they come across harms and distress. Not only does individual morality about 'right' and 'wrong' guide their choice of sex worker and market, but a collective pressure exists through the Internet and client etiquette in parlours which reinforces key standards of 'good' behaviour that achieves some success in standardizing client conduct. There is strong evidence to suggest that some clients, those in privileged social positions, were abreast of the broader issues of exploitation, poor working conditions, degradation and force that have been exposed as being connected to some parts of the sex industry in recent years. Not only were respondents aware of the different types of exploitation, the complexities of the sex markets and forms that exploitation could take; some showed nuanced understanding of the moral issues relating to the processes of selling and buying sex. This evidence speaks directly against an analysis of male clients as inhabiting 'a moral world in which such debates have simply been bracketed out' (Earle and Sharpe 2007: 38). Morality is often high on the agenda in the personal and public narratives of men who buy commercial sex.

Note

1 Finnegan (1979: 116) uses this term to describe interactions among clients and sex workers in the Victorian age in York, including the pickpocketing and stealing conducted by street walkers. (This reporting shows historical continuity.)

Chapter 4

Buying sex online: virtual regulation

Despite 'sex' being reportedly the most frequently searched topic in the information superhighway (Cooper *et al.* 2000: 522) and long-standing concerns that the Internet contains mainly unsuitable, offensive sexual material that is uncensored (Hamilton 1999), 'computer erotica' (Durkin and Bryant 1995) has not attracted the critical analysis that would have been expected (Waskul 2004). Investigations have begun to assess the broad impact of cyberspace on sexuality (Cooper *et al.* 2000), the digital economy's relationship with pornography and censorship (Attwood 2006; Cronin and Davenport 2001) and psychological issues relating to online sexual compulsivity (Carnes 2001; Griffiths 2000). Still, there has been a striking absence of research on the specifics of the interpenetration of sexual commerce and the Internet. In this chapter, I argue and provide evidence of how commercial sexual practices have been re-shaped away from the 'linear, irreversible, measurable, predictable time' to produce 'timeless time' (Castells 1996: 429). The virtual has become a marketplace for sex industries, particularly entrepreneurial sex work, and a meeting place for men who buy sex to express and form their sexual and personal identities. The aims of this chapter are to explore the changes that new technologies and computer-mediated communication have had on the way that sex work is available and operates. The focus is on how men use the Internet to learn about and negotiate the sex industry, and how the Internet features in their negotiation of and access to experiences of intimacy, identity and networks. In short, evidence in this chapter will argue that there exists a thriving 'sex work community' which goes beyond the facilitation of commercial sex and the concerns of 'cybersexploitation' (O'Connel 2003; Hughes 2004).

Technology meets the sex markets

The social repercussions of the availability of the Internet to the 'information rich' are still unfolding and will continue to attract the attention of social observers for some time. The Internet as an everyday feature of millions of people's lives across the globe has wider implications for social relationships: 'Computer-mediated communication and cyberculture are dramatically changing the nature of social relationships' (Ebo 1998: 1). It is not an exaggeration to state that the implications of computer-mediated communication on the sex industry have been nothing short of revolutionary. The changing nature of the sex markets due to technological advancement has reshaped, expanded and re-packaged the availability of all types of sexual services over the past decade. The expansion of Internet-based advertisements for direct sexual services from escorts and sex work venues is unquantifiable. Although critics will argue there is no hard evidence, any perusal of the Internet for sexual service websites illustrates the growth in businesses and both male and female sex workers advertising sexual services.[1] The growth both of women setting up as entrepreneurial sex workers and the methods through which men come to know and negotiate sexual services is almost certainly attributable to the prevalence of computer-mediated communication that has occurred in late modernity (see Earle and Sharp 2007; Soothill and Sanders 2005). Case studies such as freelance sex workers in Thailand adopting the Internet to make higher earnings and pay less fees suggest new technologies are a tool that sex workers are using across the developed and developing world (Veena 2007). Which came first in the rise of the sex industry – sex workers, business entrepreneurs or clients – is rather like the 'chicken and egg' conundrum. What is undisputable is that new information technology has created new conditions for sexual commerce and consumerism in the digital age.

The Internet became a promoter of the sex industry when the first online escort agency based in Seattle, USA, was advertised in 1994 (Hughes 2001: 2). In the UK, the first website, Punternet, which facilitates adult consensual sexual services, appeared in 1999 'to facilitate the exchange of information on prostitution in the UK'. Designed initially as a site for men looking for sexual services, the website sets out its primary functions: 'Here you will find information on where to find services, what to expect, legalities etc. . . . and read reviews of encounters with working girls.' Another regionally based website states that its aims are 'to play parlours off against one another. It increases the stakes and competition between rival parlours such that the best survive and prosper and the worst places vanish.' These types of websites receive, at times, several hundred contributions each day and an unknown amount of observers, known as 'lurkers', who simply read and use the information without contributing. Soothill (2004a) recorded that one website for the Northwest of England hosted 900 topics in 2003 and received 3,900 replies. Since the Punternet website pioneered these forums in the UK, several others have sprouted with a geographical specificity.

Publicly available without membership fees, Punternet was originally aimed at facilitating information for male clients who were looking for like-minded peers to discuss their 'punting' habits and disclose their own experiences through what are known as 'field reports' (described below). However, there was always an acknowledgement that the site was accessible for female sex workers and organizers of sex work venues: 'This website aims to promote better understanding between customers and ladies in hope that everyone may benefit, with less stressful, more enjoyable and mutually respectful visits.' Over time, Punternet became a website visited and contributed to by sex workers, venue owners as well as clients and acted as a forum through which knowledge, up-to-date information, advertising, marketing and debate could take place.

Including sex workers on this website reflected a wider change in the sex markets as the entrepreneurial sector developed from the mid-1990s through women advertising and negotiating their business entirely through the Internet. Although there is no statistical evidence, sex workers, owners of establishments and clients suggest that the Internet-based sex market grew rapidly for two reasons. First, many sex workers already in business ditched traditional methods of advertising in local newspapers or specialist magazines (which were costly and required weekly maintenance) for the more convenient web-based marketing format. Second, the Internet sex market grew because women who have entered sex work in more recent years decided to use the Internet from the outset to organize their business. Some of the periphery industries that supports the sex industry are webmasters, designers and photographers who update and manage websites for sex workers and venues. An increasing number of women with web-authoring skills manage their own websites (and offer women-friendly web authoring services to other sex workers), giving women complete control over content, style and marketing.

Sex workers are actively participating in the online sex work community. It is the arena where their clients congregate and therefore sex workers have vested interests to ensure that men or negative misogynistic attitudes do not dominate the virtual content or culture. The three UK-based websites I have observed as part of this study are all governed by a similar set of rules. One website, that requires registration but no fee, has a comprehensive set of rules, warning that those who break them will be banned from the site immediately. The rules largely cover what topics are acceptable to discuss, what level of detail is appropriate, respecting the privacy of sex workers, parlours and other clients and appropriate language. 'Virtual' aggression or gendered hostilities do not usually surface because the rules of the space 'inspire in users a degree of commitment and emotional investment that makes social continuity and stability possible' (Reid 1999: 130).

Field reports: looking beyond the text

Field reports continue to be a key facility hosted by the Punternet website (see Soothill and Sanders 2005). On 1 August 2007 there were 40,583 field reports available to read online on Punternet which cost men a total of £5,129,615 (the average cost per visit is £127). Here, clients describe their commercial sexual encounters, often in explicit detail (sometimes reading like written pornography), while others state that they 'won't go into detail' so provide vague summaries of the event. All of the field reports contain factual information such as the price, length of time of the service, location and a recommendation of whether the client would return. The number of field reports posted highlights the popularity of this method of communicating information as well as suggesting the prevalence of commercial sexual encounters that take place in parlours and with escorts. The vast number of reports also reflects the commitment to the facility, as each report has been individually written by an author and then moderated for content and appropriateness by the website regulators.

There have been criticisms of the existence, nature and function of the field reports. Anti-prostitution writers have claimed that access to sexualized images of women and descriptive text about sex acts is derogatory: 'viewing and interacting with women in online sex sites causes a loss of empathy for them as human beings' (Hughes 2001: 1). Such observations overlook the active involvement of sex workers in the dynamics of computer-mediated communication and simplifies the etiquette of the virtual environment. The field reports have been criticized as an example of 'cybersexploitation' because some commentators have viewed the written accounts as derogatory as they personify the commodification of individual women for their sexual abilities (Sharp and Earle 2003). This surface-level analysis ignores two key sociological phenomena: first, the role of the field reports as a mechanism in the sex industry; and second, the complexity of the field reports as sexual stories that are produced and consumed by various authors and audiences. These observations will be discussed in turn.

Sex workers I have spoken with who have field reports written about them usually have high praise for the system. It provides them and their

business with regular, up-to-date free marketing from genuine customers who have significant weight in persuading other clients to visit.
Krystal had worked in a flat for six years and had this view of field
reports: 'I don't mind the field reports and recommendations, that is fine.
I know I am good at what I do, so they are always going to be pleasant
and the guys usually ask if it's OK before they do it.' Natasha, an
entrepreneurial sex worker who charges £250 for each service, described
how her business depended on field reports:

> A lot of the people who see me only do after reading a good report.
> They always say I have a written report or I have been recommen-
> ded because obviously they are paying a lot of money and they want
> to know that what they are getting is good. I quite like that because
> they know what they are coming for and who they are seeing.

The Punternet website states that 9 per cent of reports do not recommend
men to visit the sex worker, suggesting that the vast majority of reports
are complimentary. Outsiders who read the reports must be aware that
behind the textual sexual stories are real-time relationships that men
have with sex workers. Some field reports are written by clients who
regularly visit the same sex worker and it has been suggested by both
parties that field reports are part of a 'thank you' or public appreciation
ritual, or even to keep in the worker's 'good books' and facilitate the
regular relationship.

Each field report goes through a rigorous moderation process to check
against slander and unfair comments. These reports are not an unregulated, uncontrolled splurge of pornographic content but are
checked, moderated and form part of a wider set of sexual scripts and
expectations of client conduct. Even though their real identities are
hidden, authors are made accountable as the moderator has an e-mail
address for correspondence. In order for a field report to be accepted by
the board of moderators, a set of criteria must be matched: reports are
rejected if they are malicious or personally vindictive, or they are not a
'legitimate' report because they are considered grandiose self-promotion
by a sex worker or establishment or fantasy tales from men. In order to
post a field report, an author must register as a free member of the site,
so that the report appears next to an identifying name.

Sex workers often praise this moderation process, especially as women
can lodge a complaint with the website host if they are disgruntled by a
report, usually resulting in the removal of the report. In addition, the
field reports play an important function in the socialization of men into
the sex industry. Among the descriptions of sex acts, pleasure and
feelings, essential information is passed on about how to decide what
venues are legitimate and which establishments may leave men open to

potential scams such as financial extortion or physical violence. Issues of nervousness and embarrassment, what to do when sex does not go as planned or condoms break enable novices to learn the intricacies of the commercial sexual transaction. Importantly for both parties, field reports facilitate a sound match between a client's desires and a sex worker's services, promoting a smooth, stress-free and safe commercial interaction.

Men's public sexual stories

The second sociological curiosity of the 'field report' phenomenon is how these textual accounts manifest as sexual stories and become revelations of sexual identities. The field reports are textual narratives of sexual selves and evidence of the proliferation of personal narratives on 'the intimate' which have found both a voice and an audience in cyberspace. Intriguing is how men express their masculinity and reflections on their own sexual performance through self-constructed narratives of their sexual encounters. For example, one poster with the pseudonym 'The Godfather' had written 142 field reports, totalling expenditure of £16,895 by 15 January 2007. These perfunctory explanations of basic sex acts, physical and social features of the sex worker and the venue are generally not explicit. Instead they are mundane records of commercial encounters that show the poster's own desires, affirming sexual virility and masculinity by 'going public' with his personal testimony. For 'The Godfather' who has posted up to six descriptions a month of his commercial encounters since 2003, the reader can track the sexual relations, attitude and habits of 'The Godfather' and his constructed persona. These public performances of intimate sex acts promote self-narratives of the sexual performance through a medium that is open for all to read.

The impression given is that the sexual account is of a 'real'-life encounter between the writer and a sex worker. There is obviously no way of knowing if these accounts ever took place, and even if they did, the report represents an interpretation of events by one actor, at a certain time and place, with a specific audience in mind and reputation to maintain.

From accounts of sex workers about their sexual performance and acting routines (Sanders 2005b), the sex workers' 'sexual story' would be very different from that of the client. The reliability, accuracy and even authenticity of the field reports were often brought into question by interviewees:

They're not infallible. There was one woman I saw – she had lots of field reports. They were all genuine I think. I mean there are ways of picking out obviously fake ones. And they all said she looked more attractive than her website pictures and they all said she was very slim. And she was actually neither of those things and I thought – am I seeing this woman through different eyes?! And just before I went to see her I noticed there was a field report that said something quite – completely different from the others, so obviously a field report is based on what you want and what you expect. (Tom, 60, widower, social care)

The process of sexual storytelling that the field reports represent is understood and accepted by the male readers as constructed sexual accounts, yet is still considered a valuable resource for decision-making. The field reports are produced through the eyes of the writer, doctored by the criteria of the moderators and also written with the scrutiny and expectations of fellow punters and sometimes the sex worker in mind. The role and identity of the client is performed through the field reports both at a personal level (re-enacted through the textual process of writing one's sexual encounters) and through a public performance of the sexual self (writing sexual stories for others to consume). As Kibby and Costello (1999: 352) evaluate from adult video conferencing websites, male sexuality displayed in cyberspace acts as both 'affirmational community performance and an individual erotic display'. The field reports as sexual stories are mirrors into many different sexual lives and sexual identities across the spectrum of the imaginary and the real.

One report, multiple authors and audiences

There are several 'producers' of field reports and the 'readers' are not a homogenous group. Storytelling through field reports is successful as a medium to express versions of the sexual self because there are several receptive audiences: the system is (largely) supported by sex workers and owners of establishments and the motivations mean that there is a steady flow of new reports on a daily basis. The process of producing field reports reflects Plummer's (1995: 24) wider observations: 'Story production and consumption as an empirical social process involves a stream of joint actions in local context, themselves bound into a wider negotiated social world.' Dean, a 34-year-old, single, sales manager, recounts how he is conscious of the sex worker when writing a report: 'If I'd had a particularly good experience I would write to say "yeah this girl deserves some work" and you know you feel quite happy about doing that. But if a girl said please don't then I wouldn't, I would never do a report on her.' The negotiated process of these specific forms of sexual stories goes beyond the individual writer and can reflect the relationships that clients have with sex workers and venues.

When we ask 'What role do the field reports serve?', we need to look beyond the simplification of providing men with additional sexual gratification through confessional tales. No doubt this is one function. But the field reports are a significant part of the mechanisms of normalization that clients use to understand their behaviour not as 'deviant' but as acceptable, non-threatening and in many ways reflective of normal male heterosexual sexual scripts. Plummer (1995) argues that sexual stories are not evaluations of unproblematic truths and, in the case of field reports, they are examples of complex personal lives, multiple authorship and wider dynamics of the sex worker–client relationship.

The field reports are surface narratives of tales of sexual sorrow, excitement, forlornness, pleasure, shame, stigma, romance, experimentation, danger, disappointment and thrill. Plummer (1995: 34) notes how people turn themselves into 'socially organised biographical objects' by constructing tales of the intimate self to be read by others as testimonies of complex life worlds where their sexuality is subject to constraints, control and condemnation. Again, Dean explains the attraction of writing field reports as self-affirming: 'You can create your own little world sort of thing but also just the fact that there's my name, you know there's me, I did that. That's just to say that I did it.' The desire and need to create one's own world where recounting sexual behaviours is accepted suggests the process and production of a report goes far beyond recommending or warning others of good or bad experiences. But for some, the field reports are one of the few mechanisms for sifting out the 'good venues' and workers from those that are dubious. As reported in Chapter 3, men have had nasty experiences of robbery, clipping and physical violence where they have walked 'blind' into a situation. The field reports act as part of the wider mechanisms of regulation whereby benchmarking and evaluation of 'good' and 'bad' parlours takes place.

Those who avidly read field reports as part of the 'research' and planning process were clear that the reasons why other men write out their sexual experiences were somewhat selfish and indeed far from altruistic: 'I think some guys must write a field report about every single experience they have because they've got hundreds of them, so it's a way of – perhaps a way of boasting. Perhaps it's a way of diarizing it' (Tom, 60, widower, social care). Plummer describes how some movements that have formed around the telling of sexual stories have used textual testimonies to gain a voice and have their experiences heard. In an area of sexual behaviour that lies at the crossroads of legality, legitimacy and 'deviance' and involves a powerful group of men who have no political power as 'punters', cyberspace has provided a 'safe' and anonymous space for clients to lay bare their intimate selves for a range of reasons, both personal and political. For some, the field reports are permanent and public testimonies of their masculinity, affirming their engagement in the sexual world and abilities to perform as a sexual being. Equally, the majority of men do not contribute field reports (but perhaps read them), as their need to 'go public' is not as compelling. The overall function of the field reports as a mechanism of self-affirmation and shared narratives act as social cement to bind a 'community' in the virtual and real world.

Accessibility and intimacy in the virtual arena

Theorizing on the broader picture as to why sexuality and cyberspace are so compatible, Cooper *et al.* (2000: 522) describe the 'Triple-A-Engine' that makes 'the virtual' so attractive for sexual pursuits. These attractions of accessibility, affordability and anonymity are clearly what encourage men who are thinking of buying real-life sexual services to use online facilities to explore the commercial sex industry. As the sex industry is usually a secret area of men's private lives, the Internet has been a crucial facilitating tool whereby men have control over when and where they access information about the sex industry. Browsing websites, observing interactions as a 'lurker' and participating on message boards can take place at a time and place of their convenience. There are no longer real-time constraints that limit opportunities to explore different markets, meet sex workers and make informed choices about who to visit and what service to buy. Time boundaries have been entirely abolished as all the information on the Internet is available at any time and in any place. For men who take overseas work trips, their connections to sex workers and ability to continue making arrangements, contributing to message boards and keeping up e-mail contact is not diminished. Equally, the facilitation of the Internet means that they are not dependent on waiting for the real-time availability of a sex worker. Men can send e-mails to sex workers, asking questions and proposing meetings, at any time of the day and night without breaching the real-time rules of etiquette. In this respect, using the Internet to learn about, negotiate and participate in the sex industry for male clients has been permanently shifted to 'leisure time' at their convenience, whether this be 'sexual surfing' in their lunch break at work, after working hours in the office before the commute home, or in the privacy of their own home. In addition, another hook that attracts both sellers and buyers of commercial sex to the Internet is the lack of law enforcement. Although most sex workers advertise as 'hostesses', flagging websites with disclaimers about their customers paying for their time, it is most unlikely that law enforcement agencies would enforce solicitation and advertisement laws against those that explicitly advertise services and prices. The police appear to have heeded Soothill's (2004a) message that heavy-handed tactics through message boards would be counter-productive and force activities underground.

A middle-class medium for middle-class clients

Technological fluency is determined by socio-economic groupings: some social groups have more access to information and communication technologies than others. This access is determined by occupation, the opportunity to learn and actively use Internet facilities in private, and pragmatics such as the space and economic resources for computers and fees for broadband connections. Web-based advertisements for escorts, saunas and sex clubs are most likely to reach middle-class men because of the availability and ordinariness of Internet facilities at work and home. Men in higher socio-economic groups are also targeted by entrepreneurial sex workers and business bosses. The communication between sex workers and their clients is not simply one where the men actively 'hunt' or take the lead in finding commercial sex. Entrepreneurial sex workers make conscious business decisions to work from the Internet in order to attract higher fee-paying customers. They design their marketing websites and construct their availability and prices for men with higher levels of disposable income. If women charge £250 per visit then they will expect only men from professional occupations, who have access to that level of disposable income, to make bookings. Targeting clients with money has other benefits for their safety: some women create a working persona that has the refinery of the type of woman they consider a middle-class man would pay to spend time with (Sanders 2005b). This not only means looking the part and being able to engage in discussions about culture, art and politics, but sex workers also ensure the physical surroundings are safe, clean and appropriate in style (sometimes luxurious), easy to find (with parking or near a train station), with limited risks and maximum discretion for the customer. In addition, as I have described before as the 'prostitution trust game' (Sanders 2005a: 53), sex workers consider men who contact them through the Internet to be 'good customers' (relatively low risk in terms of violence or non-payment), because such men have more to lose if they did not fulfil the contract. Sex workers make rational calculations about targeting a certain type of client to reduce their chance of encountering violence or other scams that are more prevalent in massage parlours and on the street. For both the client and the sex worker, the Internet enables informed choices to be made, resulting in less time wasting and unprofessional behaviour.

Racial exclusivity online?

The unequal access to technologies between countries across the world, what is known as the 'digital divide', is also widely applicable to inequalities of access and use among social groups within nations. Privileged groups, who enjoy multiple opportunities and life-chances, are more likely to be switched on to computer-mediated communication. It is an observation that computer-mediated communication between sex workers and clients may be distinct not only in terms of socio-economic group but also ethnic group. This was an original hypothesis from my interviews with entrepreneurial sex workers who advertised and negotiated with clients entirely online. Esther, a 34-year-old escort who works from a rented apartment, manages her own website and negotiates only through e-mail, explained that the majority of her clients were white, middle-class men and that this was probably because of her advertising methods:

> I tend to mostly see white men but that's basically more down to who contacts me. Through the Internet I have never been contacted by a black man. I would say maybe 5 per cent might be made up of Asian or Chinese. Maybe sort of different race groups of men do it [look for sex workers] in different ways.

An implicit consequence of targeting a middle-class UK-based clientele is that the ethnic backgrounds of clients may be less variable. If men are tending to use the Internet to learn about and enter the sex industry then those sectors of society which are less inclined to have ready access to the Internet in their homes or work space will be under-represented in the client base. Men from Asian or African-Caribbean backgrounds may be more inclined to seek out sex from the local area where sex venues are physically visible and easily accessible. For instance, Fazel, a 22-year-old Asian man who had visited a massage parlour in a nearby town a couple of times a month for the past three years, did so because he was aware of the parlour's presence and it was convenient to his everyday routine. He did not use the Internet to explore the sex industry because the only times he was online was in a public computer room at university.

Online–offline dynamics

Observing the banter evident through threads on message boards, individuals do not simply use the Internet to communicate with others, but the interactions are heavily contextualized in the everyday negotiations of selling and buying sexual services as an eventual real-life experience. The social construction of the sex work community exists in an online format, but it is supported by the expectations of real-life interactions, in particular the sexual etiquette and social organization of the commercial sex liaison. The micro relationships in real life are in part affected by the interactions online and also what happens in the online forums is transferred into real life negotiations and dynamics. This connection between online and offline appears to be a common feature of certain 'work-based' virtual arenas. From their in-depth study of a professional medical forum, Fox and Roberts (1999) conclude that interactions online are best understood as extensions of wider social relations in the world of medical general practice. In the sex work virtual forums, online discussions are based on real-life encounters, expectations, rules and regulations. One interviewee recounts how the online discussions of sex without a condom reflect real-life confrontations and disagreements between sex workers and clients:

> I mean there's something on Punternet at the moment about that, you know, bareback [sex without a condom]. The other day there was a hell of a commotion and one of the girls was throwing somebody out because I think he'd asked for bareback sex. And I thought perhaps he'd tried to take the condom off which was obviously the justification for throwing him out. But no, she'd thrown him out very forcibly, shouting at him and you know, door slamming, just because he'd asked for it! (Benny, 70, widower, retired trucker)

In some instances, there is little separation between real life and the virtual arena, but instead people interact and reinforce codes of conduct, points of contention and mechanisms of regulation that are apparent in real time. These findings echo Hardey (2002: 583) who concludes that 'virtual spaces are shaped by and grounded in the social, bodily and cultural experiences of users' and are 'grounded in pre-existing social and economic processes'.

Learning to be a 'punter'

What is evident from observing Punternet and other similar websites is that they become a new space where men who are novices can learn about the sex industry from other men and other players in the sex markets. Websites that facilitate communication between male clients that engage in commercial sexual encounters have been described as an 'anonymous network of support for perpetrators' (Hughes 2001: 2). Indeed, the website I studied could be considered as a training ground for men who are pondering buying sexual services or are new to the activity, as well as thòse long-standing clients. Contrary to what anti-prostitution commentators suggest, these training grounds are not necessarily a forum for perpetuating misogynistic, derogatory attitudes about women but instead such space and communication provides a set of standards and reinforces expectations of the 'sexual script' that men adopt in their role as purchaser. One respondent replied to the Home Office (2004) consultation by setting out the educative nature of the websites, demonstrating the responsible attitude of many clients:

> The Internet has transformed part of the paid sex industry. There are websites with message boards where punters can exchange information. These message boards have an educative function, and among other things do set benchmarks. To give examples: Any mention of unprotected sex (bareback) will be met with a barrage of both criticism and informed argument. Just before the law was changed regarding sex with under 18 year olds someone attempted to advertise the availability of a sixteen year old; despite this being technically legal at that time strong negative responses were expressed, leaving any possible user in no doubt as to what others would think of him. Message boards often contain links to Crime Stoppers or similar resources, encouraging users to report illegal activity such as the use of those under-age. Boards often contain sections where both punters and service providers can warn others about dangerous people or practices.

The benchmarking referred to by this client (see Chapter 3) indicates the strength of the virtual community to positively influence the real-life sexual interactions between sex workers and clients, and ultimately set the norms of the subculture and the sexual scripts of clients within an agreed set of guidelines and practices.

Mentoring, encouragement and support

Just as Rogers (2005) identifies how the function of men's magazines is to offer shared meanings about sex and intimacy to a fragmented male community, the Internet provides the same function of virtual bonding. Alongside the daily banter that occurs on the message boards there are permanent online guides for men to consult and find out about the expectations of being a 'punter'. For instance, the Punternet website hosts a 'Beginners Guide to Sauna and Massage Parlours' which details advice on how to find a parlour, how to pay, what to expect in the communal lounge and bedroom, and the general manner in which a man should conduct himself with a sex worker. The guide also explains the 'dark side' of prostitution to the novice client which warns of women who are exploited and trafficked and scams aimed to exploit men. A set of 'Frequently Asked Questions' about the London sex markets imparts information about the protocol for the 'walk up' flats of Soho (a rather different scene from the rest of the country), the legalities of being a punter and the dangers of scams such as 'clipping'. Men are warned: 'Avoid any woman who approaches you on the street. Not only is this illegal, but more often than not is a blatant ripoff – the girl asks you for a "deposit", then disappears never to be seen again.' Introducing men to the pitfalls of an unregulated market is again motivated by the desire for a safe and legitimate sexual services environment.

Message boards: dialogues of play, politics and performance

The message boards are the most obvious example of how the virtual communities for patrons of the sex industry are a 'live' entity. They are constantly changing and updating, providing an expansive amount of detail and opportunity for interaction. From observing the types of discussions and the functions of the message boards and chat forums dedicated to the sex work community, three types of interactions can be suggested based on the functions of play, politics and performance.

Playfulness

There is a light-hearted element to the 'chat' that takes place in cyberspace among clients, sex workers and third parties. Some websites have divided up message boards based on different functions, stating which are for general issues and which are specifically about the sex industry. Billy, a 43-year-old married man working in manufacturing, looked at message boards most days for social reasons:

> I enjoy them and they are not centred around commercial sex or you know have you seen so and so. Just chatting in general. But it is interesting because it's almost like you have exposed the most intimate parts of yourself to these people and then you are putting up barriers as they don't know you.

General chat is often permeated by sexual banter and humour in the everyday exchanges. The sexualized nature of talk is not necessarily directed towards sex workers or women in general, as some of the sexual banter takes on the 'locker room' type of male joking about their own sexual performance and experiences. Again, feeding into the public sexual stories that cyberspace attracts, the playful element of the message boards have serious undertones relating to emotions, friendships, relationships and stigma.

Politics

A significant proportion of 'chat' on the message boards relates to real-life events. Commentary on everyday politics is evident as people interact and exchange ideas and opinions about the state of the world, everyday problems and the complexity of modern-day living. Dialogue is also exchanged on the politics of prostitution from a client's perspective, discussing prices, services, quality, safety, new establishments, changes in the local scene and different sex work sectors available in the UK. The discussions online, between virtual strangers, are somewhat different in quality from those that may be encountered in everyday settings. Andy, a 31-year-old sales executive in a long-term relationship, commented:

> Well you get to have quite intense discussions online because the normal kind of social barriers, which prevent you talking about such intimate things, which you would find embarrassing, aren't there.

The politics of the Internet message boards involves comments on real-time events, gossip and rumour, discussions about real-life meetings, or planning events and parties. Outsiders can identify groups of posters who have familiar offline relationships that appear exclusive to others. Long-term members of message boards sometimes colonize the space and show territoriality over the use of virtual space. This can create board politics, divisions between posters, even manipulative game playing and 'flaming'.

Performance

The third visible function of the message boards where clients congregate is that of performing the role of the client and also asserting sexual performance and identity. Benny, a 70-year-old widower, saw the message boards as a communal 'agony aunt' facility:

> I think you can put your problems on it or your thoughts or concerns. I mean I've had concerns recently and I've put my thoughts on. And a couple of times I've not got the answers that I would have liked to have had, but I've been glad to have received them and they've made me think. And helping people out in terms of, I suppose advice; educating people. I mean some people have got some very silly, silly ideas.

> I think the Internet is a very important, a medium I guess for that kind of information. Because it does make you feel a lot less like you are doing something that's the worse thing in the world. (Adam, 32, long-term partner, media)

The message boards become intimate storytelling boards about the sexual self. Message board dialogue is a function to express emotions, but equally there is a sense of airing personal emotional and sexual experiences as a way of asking for advice and affirmation:

They just make me feel I am not alone in what I am doing. There are other people out there with the same desires. I mean some of these people are highly educated people but not in a stereotype, I don't think. Some of them are quite caring and sensitive from some of the postings on the Internet that people put up various problems. (Daniel, 41, single, teacher)

An example of sexual storytelling on the message boards that stood out because the post gathered approximately 60 responses was of a thread a man had started titled 'My Very First Punt'. He disclosed by stating 'I had my very first punt today and am left with mixed feelings.' What followed was a string of responses, all very supportive, from men revealing empathy and sharing their own 'first encounters' as well as comments from sex workers on the emotional reality of buying sex. The discussion was in-depth and insightful, revealing the emotional aspects of having sex with a stranger for money, the struggles that men have with their feelings about buying sex and why men seek out sex workers as solutions to gaps in their life. This discussion between twenty people, most of whom would have never met each other, was an example of the collective nature of the message boards as a function of public testimony on sexual intimacy and emotional fulfilment. These cybertextual practices of telling sexual stories are borne out of individual sexual selves shrouded in silence and secrecy. As Plummer (1995: 13) explains, there are complex social processes involved in telling sexual stories that go beyond the content. The process of 'telling' is equally as important as 'doing', and whether stories are told through asking advice or explicitly retelling sexual encounters through field reports, who is telling and who is listening represents a window into the place of commercial sex and online communication in men's sexual and social lives.

There are strong expectations that by becoming a member of the message board you will take part in and contribute to in-depth 'baring of the soul' type conversations with virtual strangers in a virtual place. During the long thread referred to above, one poster commented 'Now this is what I signed up for Punternet for – straight up discussion on punting and its effects, thank you'. Smith (cited in Rheingold 2000: xxviii) uses the concept of 'collective goods' that bind people together in cyberspace to form communities. The emphasis on a balance between posting and reading is encouraged in order for the message board to maintain its functions and not become monopolized by a few. The disclosures are treated with great respect and other contributors and lurkers are often motivated to reveal their own experiences as a supportive gesture. These interactions are usually in the spirit of helping someone to come to terms with different emotions that are sparked by commercial sex experiences.

The self-disclosure and self-presentation through posting is a mechanism for gaining intimacy with the other members of the community. By posting messages of an intimate nature in a virtual environment, Schnarch (1997: 17) identifies how these interactions are without risk, exposure or being known. However, in the online sex work community, the relationships often go offline, and men meet each other in real social spaces.

Doing your homework

In many of the threads and comments that develop on the message boards regarding sex work, finding a compatible business transaction and avoiding disappointing or unreliable experiences are key concerns for men:

> There's a whole script of stuff on there, all the terms and this, that and the other; because it's all double Dutch. If you've never looked at it before like I hadn't a few years ago. It's a way of educating yourself and you certainly pretty much know how things should go. (Ali, 27, long-term partner, manufacturing)

> It's got a lot of information in there and if you are not sure about something or what have you then sometimes a thread comes up that can answer your question but obviously the main sort of source for it is the field reports that are on there and that is quite important really if you want to choose the right person if you like. (Jonny, 51, married, IT)

There is a consistent theme that it is the individual's responsibility to make sure they do their research in order to avoid unpleasant situations and find compatible service providers based on venue, sexual desire, physical attraction, personality and sociability. Making an informed and 'accurate' decision is also in the sex worker's interest so that 'disappointed' clients can be avoided. The vast amount of information on different sex markets, sex workers, types of services and prices provides men with all the information they need in order to make an informed selection regarding which sex workers they visit. Those men who post messages appear to only visit women they have learnt about through field report recommendations, rather than go on a 'blind' visit where no information has been gathered:

The message board is my route in, and seeing what they say on the message boards and what they say in their websites, and you can tell a lot from that I think. And a lot of guys are pretty careful about who they choose. (George, 58, married, IT)

It can be a bit soul destroying at times but like I say nowadays I don't get those sorts of feelings because I have got the opportunity to do research beforehand and, so the chances of having a bad session or a bad experience, I wouldn't say they've gone completely but they are minimized. (Howard, 49, married, academic)

The emphasis on 'research' is motivated by several objectives: not wasting money, being safe and finding a compatible sex worker and venue. In addition, as much of the excitement and thrill of engaging in commercial sex is the planning and preparation (Peng 2007: 324), the Internet, with an infinite amount of information and specialist features such as the field reports, extends the time spent researching potential sexual liaisons. 'Reading FRs is vital if you want to find out what exactly is on offer and at what price without the embarrassment of ringing up and asking' (Tom, 60, widower, social care). The virtual availability of a huge amount of in-depth detail from those who have experienced individual women and venues first-hand has become a priceless resource for men who can be intimidated by the traditional processes of seeking out a sex worker.

Community, identity and friendship

Groups of people who interact through networked communications have been studied through the sociological lens over the last decade.[2] These studies have drawn out similarities and discrepancies between virtual online interactions and face-to-face dynamics. Still, the term 'virtual community' that refers to repeated online interactions between those who have common interests or identities remains contested (Rheingold 1993). Fox and Roberts (1999: 644) note how the absence of geographical proximity can weaken claims that networked communication is similar to real-life community and that, at best, the Internet can offer possibilities of an 'imaginary community'. There were limited, if any, sex work communities in the UK which facilitated interactions between sellers and buyers of commercial sex before websites such as those under analysis became available. The collective decision among male patrons that such a space was needed provided the ingredients for a virtual community as defined by Rheingold (2000: xx): 'Virtual communities are social aggre-gations that emerge from the Net when enough people carry on those public discussions long enough, with sufficient human feeling, to form webs of personal relationships in cyberspace.' The ease of accessibility and affordability on the Internet has provided a virtual meeting place that enables men and women to interact in a 'safe' arena, whereas before interactions existed only on an individual level and were based entirely around the real-time sexual encounter. Through the presence of key websites, men looking for commercial sex and female sex workers found common ground to form a community, where their interactions could continue beyond the private one-to-one liaison but among others who were involved in the secretive world of commercial sex.

So, why was this virtual space needed? Jones (1995: 16), although sceptical of the 'community' capabilities of cyberspace, notes there are attractions that transcend landscape. First, there is recognition that there are others who share the same experiences, and second, that there is a 'safe' space where communication can take place without having to hide, downplay or deny their involvement in the sex industry:

> It's an opportunity for a conversational exchange in a very different way from what you would normally do because this sort of habit is not something you would talk about among even intimate friends because you know, when you're married you tend to have married friends and they know your wife and so on. I mean there are one or two people that I perhaps would tell that I have known a long time but I'd feel uncomfortable telling. I suppose the message board is rather bizarre because everybody is sort of already exposed themselves as I say as a 'user'. (Paulo, 54, married, property developer)

Building on Anderson's (1983) idea of 'imagined communities', Jones (*ibid.*) argues that if the community feels significant to the participant then Internet communities have the capacity to become parallel to human communities. Tom, a widower working in the social care profession, had contributed to the virtual community for a year at the time of the interview. He commented on the ordinariness of the virtual interactions that mirror everyday communities:

> The message boards have a supportive function. For example, the death of a regular client, or the death of a regular escort, can be as devastating as any other bereavement, with the added complication of it usually having to be secret. There is definitely a sense of community on such occasions.

This sense of 'knowing' individuals, even if there has been no physical contact in real time, suggests that relationships can be strong and supportive even when the interactions are confined to posting messages.

As Rheingold (2000: xxxi) states: 'community is a matter of emotions as well as a thing of reason and data'. Andy, a single, 31-year-old sales executive, comments on the intimate nature of online communication:

You tend to kind of talk about things which you wouldn't talk about if you just met someone first time in the pub. Then once you have sort of developed those sorts of relationships, meeting kind of seems easier and more natural.

An inner sense of security is gained when interacting with people with whom there are no pretences, shame or secrecy about their identity as a client. On the websites, among all patrons, there is an acceptance that the men, for whatever reason, seek out commercial sexual liaisons outside the confines, propriety and acceptability of conventional intimate relationships. This acceptance and mutual ground remains the attraction for most people committed to online networks whether the bond is fighting an illness (Muncer *et al.* 2000) or sexual identity (Nip 2004). The online communities represent a 'human corner of cyberspace' (Rheingold 2000: 1) in a world that can be isolating and disenfranchized for many.

Motivated to explore online networks to find others who share similar identities, the message boards and chat rooms provide a confidential matching of like-minded people who are not going to react negatively or condemn behaviours as strange or wrong. While this can provide opportunities for sex criminals to congregate and interact (Durkin 1997), the online community facilitates self-acceptance for those who are sexually disenfranchized by a society that is still troubled by accepting sexual difference among consenting adults. The virtual provides a space where those who normally feel 'the odd one out' or disenfranchized in their everyday communities can come together in one space and be the majority.[3] It would be very difficult outside the sex markets to find other men who are also clients because of the intensely secretive nature of buying sex. Virtual meeting spaces overcome these physical barriers and societal judgements that produce shame and embarrassment, allowing individuals to gain support in a non-stigmatizing environment. From this coming together of identities, without pretence or deception, contributors and observers can gain freedom from the constraints placed on their sexual expression and identity by everyday expectations of sexual prescription. From these online connections, 'quasi relationships' (Cooper *et al.* 2000: 523) have the strength and capacity to move into real-time physical meetings and friendships. This is evident when some of the board contributors meet up for social events:

I was looking at Punternet most evenings and even when I wasn't contributing I was certainly seeing a lot of the same names coming up and I thought well it would be interesting to actually see who these people are. I mean there were a couple of people there that I was chatting to that I thought were absolutely lovely people and you know they were at the time quite big on the board as well so that was quite nice to see that the people who seem to be quite nice on the board are also quite nice in real life. Because obviously you are creating a bit of a character whenever you do anything on a chat room or a forum on the Internet you can become somebody else. But it's quite refreshing to see that people weren't really changing that much in real life. (Stuart, 38, single, media)

The virtual communities formed through the common connection of the sex industry are not superficial or shallow. The characteristics of this Internet community meet the requirements of a typology of social support that constitute social companionship, informational support, esteem support, and instrumental support (Muncer *et al.* 2000). These different types of support exist to answer the questions, queries and consolations of those who meet online.

Male real-time networks

Early questions about the validity and consequences of computer-mediated communication were raised by sociologists in relation to issues of community. Would the virtual interactions produce what we desire in offline relationships? For instance, would the Internet provide spaces where individuals could develop friendship, community, connectivity and a sense of belonging (Jones 1995)? Rheingold (2000: xxvii) describes how one of the levels in which computer-mediated communication has the power to transform our lives is through 'person-to-person interaction where relationships, friendships and communities happen'. The Internet as a mechanism to improve communication beyond time and space constraints unleashes the potential to be a great sticking plaster to mend the fragmentation of social ties caused by late capitalist consumerism and production (Bauman 2005). This is evident from other research that establishes how virtual communities have real-life currency as relationships transfer from the anonymity of the message board to real-life interactions. Turning the virtual companionship into real-life relationships is perhaps particularly attractive to those who have a hard time finding like-minded people or who are adversely affected by stigma in their local communities. Shaw (1998) describes how gay men congregate on a website and engage in Internet Relay Chat as a first stage before forging real-life friendships with people who live locally. Like-wise, evidence suggests that the stigma attached to buying sex and the secrecy surrounding the identity of a 'punter' encourages some men to seek out other men and make the transition from online to real relationships:

> There is definitely a punter community. Well it's a cyber-community primarily although there are plans afoot on various boards to try and have physical meets. I contribute, I don't contribute very much actually, I tend to read a lot but there was a meeting last year that somebody tried to organize saying: 'I'll be in such and such a parlour at 1 o'clock on Saturday afternoon, anybody wants to come along and say hello please do.' I was going anyway that same day, same parlour. I know the guy now, I have met him a couple of times and we exchange e-mails on a fairly regular basis. (Howard, 49, married, academic)

It is also the case that people who are regulars on the message boards are involved in socializing in the real world at exclusive non-sexual social gatherings. These events involve clients, sex workers (and sometimes their spouses) meeting in small groups for socializing. These offline social interactions between male clients are popular among men who consider themselves frequent 'punters' and are driven by the need to communicate with peers without having to hide their activities or cope with the fear of being stigmatized or ridiculed for their behaviour: 'It's staggering that you know, people have this urge to kind of share their experiences. But the community is just so vibrant. They have their own – they have these kind of social parties and they all meet up outside' (Kelvin, 36, single, charity worker).

The cyber-community for men who buy sex shows the need for a social space that transgresses the virtual into the real, and provides a forum for men to interact without the constraints of social stigma: 'I meet up just for the social thing. I mean to talk to people who have the same interests. I mean, it's [buying sex] a big thing in my life really. It's an interest I have, it's something I do and I can't talk to anyone about it. None of my friends, family – it's a shame really' (Craig, 38, single, sales).

Given the secretive nature of buying sex, and the lengths that some men go to conceal their involvement in the sex industry and ensure that no one finds out, it is not entirely predictable that male clients want to meet peers.[4] Despite an intense desire for privacy (see Chapter 6), all of the interviewees who were actively involved in contributing to specialist websites had met at least one other male contributor in real life. Half of the interviewees had introduced other people (both male and female) to message boards, suggesting that the websites and the usefulness of the virtual community are promoted as much by word of mouth as they are stumbled across when searching the Internet. Broader male friendships and social networks are established which take relationships beyond their commonalities of buying sex:

> *TS*: So do you meet up with them for more social occasions?
> Murphy: Yeah. About a couple of times. It's just like you generally talk to somebody like, and you make up like a friendship out of things. You meet up and say all right, let's meet up for a drink, for a meal and – I mean when you get there you're not talking about punting, it's just – it's like different things. It's like – it's basically when you get to know like know somebody, like basic friendship. (Murphy, 28, single, sales)

> I do research with the Internet because these message boards, I mean people, you know there are people who've been punting for 35 years . . . I know one bloke well: I went to Manchester with him. He gave me a lift and we went together because he is from near where I live. He is in his 50s now, nice bloke though. You can find out what's good and what's bad and on the site they rate the parlours. (Jeremy, 24, single, student)

It can be argued that the Internet and virtual sex work communities are places where men build social capital and support networks which are both reliant on and separate from their common identity as patrons of sex workers. Some online interactions between male clients develop into real-time friendships. Cyberspace is a place that unites people who have specific interests and oversteps differences to match common characteristics:

> I have met up with the people from the website on three occasions. We've had social events where we've gone to a bar and then back to one of the ladies hotels just for drinks and they are the most nice, friendly people you know, the girls, the guys. I mean I would consider some of them good friends and one of the ladies I e-mail privately and good friends. I mean I wouldn't be interested in seeing her as a client. I mean she is a lot old, I think she is in her forties but she is a good friend you know? I e-mail her all the time. I was e-mailing her last night. (David, 46, divorced, social care)

Like real-life communities, it appears that the online communities are not static in their form or nature. Dependent on both the website host maintaining the online facilities and individuals' motivations to contribute to a forum, virtual communities change when people move away from them. The fragile nature of one particular online community is noted when one aspect of the website was deleted and there was no longer a space for people to communicate. One interviewee, who contacted me several months after the initial interview to impart his experiences of stopping being a client, explained that one reason was related to the reduction of networks that were previously facilitated through the Internet:

> Another minor feature of the last year has been the demise of the XXX message board. Subjectively that really seems to have frag-mented what was a community. I hardly contribute to the Boards now, and know of several other regulars who no longer contribute. XXX seemed to be the only board which had the critical mass to feel like a major meeting place rather than the private club of a few cronies and sycophants.

The virtual networks are reliant on those who provide the websites and also the enthusiasm of the community. Where social ties may be fleeting as individuals 'just pass through' as 'explorers' or 'yo-yo-ers' (see Chapter 3), their flirtation with the virtual sex work community fades with the click of a mouse.

Theorizing Internet usage by male clients

Castells's (1996) significant contribution to understanding how the new information technology paradigm is changing the shape of all aspects of society and human interaction can be applied to the reshaping of the socio-sexual structures and sexual behaviour in late modernity. Castells (1996: 429) writes how the transformation of time through technology has altered all kinds of practices, including social practices, as a new society based on information technology and computer-mediated com-munication becomes less dependent on clock time. The socio-sexual patterns of human sexuality have been transformed through this new temporality. Access to infinite amounts of information through the timelessness of Internet advertising, marketing, testimonies and message board 'conversation' produces a seductive industry that is built on strong scaffolding: the emptiness of modern-day man or what Bauman (2005) calls 'togetherness dismantled'.

There is evidence that the pull factors for men congregating in virtual spaces stem from the need to make connections with like-minded people, to build social ties both of a virtual and real nature and to combat the disconnected or weaker social networks in their everyday lives. As all aspects of modern industrial culture are mediated through information technologies, it comes as no surprise that the sex industry has graduated into an online medium and that its functions go beyond that of facilitating commercial sex. Identity and sexuality are constructed, expressed and reshaped by virtual networks. Cybertextual practices reveal sexual stories and act as a mechanism of public testimony of sexual, emotional and social behaviour. Chat rooms and message boards are a place where culture emerges amid the freedom to experiment with persona and identity, providing a fertile ground for the telling of sexual stories. As Plummer (1995) explains about all sexual stories, the field reports have a social role: the stories are both a symbolic and a political process when we uncover how they are produced, what they do, the role they have among fellow 'punters' and the work they perform at an individual and collective level. As written accounts of sexual and intimate closeness, albeit commercial, the stories make sense of the world not only to the individuals who write them, but to the community of men who think about buying sex, and do so occasionally, regularly and prolifically. Field reports have a special and powerful significance in that they shape expectations in the 'real' world. Field reports are part of the 'pull' factors (see Chapter 3) that feed into men's decisions and fantasies of what type of sexual and emotional encounters they want to experience.

The client–sex worker relationship is determined partly in cyberspace at both an individual and a collective level. By this I mean that through one-to-one online interaction between a sex worker and a client (typically through e-mail), the parameters of the exchange are set and the contract is determined and agreed before a real-life meeting takes place. At a collective, community level, there are benchmarks regarding behaviour, attitude, etiquette and general standards of sexual interaction in the commercial exchange. Online benchmarking that has real-life effects happens in other communities (here I am thinking of medical practices, parenting guidelines). In the unregulated world of commercial sex, these mechanisms take on additional importance because they represent one of the few means whereby sex workers and clients can collectively congregate and regulate the industry. For example, although there are constant disputes among patrons (and some sex workers) regarding the use of condoms, the online community has been consistently vocal in promoting safe sexual health practices. The Internet has a self-policing facility, a natural tendency for collective regulation, and in the case of a sexual activity which in the UK is outside the realm of state regulation, this benchmarking has overwhelming benefits for the safety of sex workers and clients.

There is also political power evident in the strong presence of communication and community among some sex workers and their clients through cyberspace. The Internet enables people to resist the social controls of real time that are placed on sexual interactions through legal constraints, policing strategies and moral campaigns that preach what is and is not acceptable adult sexual conduct. Communication technologies have a profound role in terms of challenging existing social structures and democratic systems as cultures evolve and take new shapes. It is clear from the massive amount of flow through the websites that traditional mechanisms of social control are beyond adequacy in their capacity to control or stem commercial sexual activity. The 'technologized' sexual exchange has become a dominant pattern of sexual commerce which produces communities and networks that provide solidarities and business opportunities that do not necessarily reflect gender inequalities but are a key mechanism for constructing safe and responsible sexual services.

Notes

1 The Internet is, of course, a medium for male sex workers to advertise to men and women, and for couples, transvestites and various kinds of sex clubs to advertise sexual services, but this will not be included in this discussion due to lack of space and the complexity of the subject.
2 Various studies of virtual communities are available. For example, Wang and Fensenmaier (2004) explore an online travel community; Pleace *et al.* (2000) look at self-help groups on the Internet; Yang (2000) researched how gay men use the virtual arena; Fox and Roberts (1999) examine how GPs use virtual forums for work-based information sharing.
3 The role of the Internet for disenfranchised communities based on sexuality has been described in relation to the gay, lesbian, bisexual, transgendered and rape survivor communities (see Cooper *et al.* 2000).
4 See Soothill (2004b: 49) for a discussion of clients avoiding each other in parlours to the extent that such privacy is required for some men that they would prefer a separate reception from the waiting room in parlours.

Chapter 5

Buying intimacy: pleasure, commerce and the self

Sociologists have explored the centrality of intimacy as the core of a meaningful personal life. The 'transformation of intimacy' (Giddens 1992) as a product of late modernity and its impact on personal relationships has been a preoccupation of sociologists in recent times (Jamieson 1999; Roseneil 2007). Generally, however, commentators on intimacy have not considered commercial sex as a site where intimacy is sought or exchanged because the primacy of the sexual aspects of the relationship have been privileged over any complex understanding of the sex worker–client relationship (Jamieson 1998: 107). This chapter argues that in this particular phase of modernity, commercial sex is increasingly part of the 'transformation of intimacy', and a personal choice in the lifestyles of often middle-class men who seek out relationships with sex workers. This chapter has three objectives. First, by examining the meanings men apply to their relationships with sex workers, I highlight that a form of bodily and emotional intimacy is achievable in commercial relationships between men who become 'regular' clients to the same sex workers. Second, the sex worker–client relationship is not necessarily different in content from that of non-commercial sexual relationships where emotional and physical intimacies are produced and consumed. This argument will challenge the false dichotomies between commercial and non-commercial relationships by drawing on theories of intimacy and commerce (Zelizer 2005). Third, from the empirical findings I draw out the range of emotions that male clients experience through the commercial sex experience, including heteronormative male sexual scripts, vulnerabilities and pleasures. The conclusions draw on Giddens' (1992) concept of the 'pure relationship' and 'plastic sexuality' as mechanisms for understanding processes of self-reflexivity and the restructuring of the personal life.

Intimacy meets the sex markets

What is intimacy? Jamieson (1998) speaks of 'disclosing intimacy' as a type of mutual listening, sharing of thoughts and expressing of feelings but also describes how there are several types of intimacy. 'Deep knowing' and 'close association' can be achieved on a spectrum in different types of relationships and can mimic the 'disclosing intimacy' which is an expectation of the relationship between significant others. Jamieson (1998: 13) states that 'disclosing intimacy must include close association, privileged knowledge, deep knowing and understanding and some form of love, but it need not include practical caring and sharing'. Zelizer (2005: 14) in her advanced theorizing of intimacy and commerce expands what is meant by intimate 'knowledge' as shared secrets, interpersonal rituals, bodily information, awareness of personal vulnerabilities and shared memory of embarrassing situations. Further, Zelizer extends the manifestation of intimacy to include 'attention' such as terms of endearment, bodily services, private languages and emotional support.

It is not easy to locate emotional intimacy in the research on sex worker and client relationships. For instance, Mansson (2006) summarizes 14 Scandinavian studies on motivations of male clients since the mid-1980s and reduces men's motivations to five factors: the whore fantasy, another kind of sex, image of the kind-hearted comforter, sex as a consumer product, and fantasies of another kind of woman. In this summary, Mansson underplays the desire for emotional as well as sexual consumption. 'Mass produced images about sexuality in pornography, advertising and other media' (Mansson 2006: 90) are attributed to forming men's views of the ideal woman and sexual partner. While this is certainly one influence, discourses of intimacy, love, romance and courtship, which are equally strong in late modernity (Illouz 1997), are not considered as influential on the desires of male clients and their motivations for seeking relationships with sex workers. Picking out only negative cultural manifestations and ignoring a whole range of important defining narratives in contemporary gendered relations reduces possible understanding of why men desire commercial sex to a narrow essentialist position that does not move beyond the male sexual urge and expression of power.

Emotional intimacy and other types of sociability have more recently been researched as part of the commercial sex dynamic as the psychopathologizing theories of earlier theorists have lost significance. Over fifty years ago it was recognized that men were not only motivated to buy commercial sex because of sexual needs but had emotional needs that were satisfied by sex workers. Winick (1962) concluded from a snowball sample of 732 clients in five major cities in the USA that the motivations for buying sex are complex and that there was never one defining reason: 'emotional meanings and overtones' were more important than the desire for sex. From her covert observations of 1,242 sex worker–client interactions, Stein's (1974) nine behavioural patterns that categorize clients into types includes those who act as 'lovers' and 'friends', seeking out a fuller, emotionally based sexual relationship. Hoigard and Finstad (1992: 95) note from a study of men in Norway the complexity of intimacy in commercial sex because economic boundaries of the market merge with emotional needs as some clients want unemotional sex but at the same time also want 'intimacy and understanding'. The psychological reasons for seeking out sex workers for intimacy is a significant push factor for a group of clients. Australian research by Xantidis and McCabe (2000) described one group of clients as those with 'low social-sexual effectiveness' who displayed an interpersonal need for intimacy, compared to a group of clients who were seeking novelty and variety in commercial sex.

The emotional reasons why men seek out commercial sex have inevitable consequences for the work that sex workers perform. The emotional labour performed by sex workers who directly recognize the emotional needs of clients and even construct their businesses to pander to these needs is now well documented in the literature (Brewis and Linstead 2000b; Sanders 2005b). Lever and Dolnick (2000) interviewed 'call girls' who explained that clients both expected and received emotional services in the form of intimacy, and that sex work was indeed one of the 'listening occupations'. Empirical findings from both sex worker and male client studies suggest there are some men who buy sex who do not want a distant, perfunctory sex encounter but an emotional experience within the boundaries of a commercial exchange. Bernstein (2001) is one of the few scholars who has probed the meanings of what is being purchased in commercial sex. In the West there is a paradox between the problematization of male sexuality (through punitive laws and moral messages) alongside what Bernstein (2001: 389) calls 'the unbridled ethic of sexual consumption' as expansion and demand for sex industries reaches unprecedented levels. This paradox of the sexual exchange can be understood through the transformation of culture and sexuality and, I would argue, the complexities of male sexuality and the desire for intimacy and emotional connectivity which can be found through forms of commercial relations. Changing relationship formations in contemporary society are manifest through the 'regular' client–sex worker relationship which is predicated on the same content of non-commercial relationships but mediated through a monetary transaction.

Becoming a 'regular' client

There are differences between 'one-off' visitors who sporadically experience the sex industry, 'repeat' customers who buy sex from different women, different markets and different venues periodically without building up familiar relationships and 'regular' clients. Regulars return to the same sex worker (or potentially two or three) consistently over a long period of time. Egan (2003: 277) describes how the regular customers form emotional and erotic bonds with dancers, viewing them as lovers and girlfriends. In my study of 50 men, 28 defined themselves as currently a 'regular' client to one sex worker (in six cases two or three sex workers). A further four interviewees said they had previously been a regular client. Sixteen other participants described themselves as 'repeat' customers; six clients described their habits more as 'one-off' engagements.

There may be no real differences between the frequency of 'regular' clients who visit the street compared to the indoor markets (see comparison in Lever and Dolnick 2000), but I surmise that the nature of the 'regular' relationship between indoor sex workers and clients is qualitatively different based on the development of 'deep' intimate relations. Although there is evidence that long-term sexual relationships exist between clients and street sex workers (see Freund *et al.* 1989), they rarely include the spectrum of intimate acts, emotions and connections that have been documented among indoor sex workers and clients (Frank 2006). Empirical findings from my study demonstrate that the desire for emotional intimacy as well as physical intimacy leads men to become regulars to the same sex worker and develop a relationship that mirrors heterosexual male romantic scripts (Wyatt Seal and Ehrhardt 2003).

Seeking intimacy, closeness and individualism

Frequently, the 28 men who were regular clients described their relationships with sex workers as significantly based on emotional fulfilment: 'I mean in a way the sex is almost secondary. It is someone who accepts me as I am and, for a period, you know, fusses me and pays attention to me' (Alan, 59, divorced, retired). Although the sex was considerably important, and often the initial reason for seeking a regular commercial relationship, Jeremy, a 24-year-old single student, summarizes how relationships with sex workers go beyond the physical: 'I think it's about companionship as well as sex. It's being able to talk to people. It's just the whole thing.' Both the motivations for being a regular client and the positive outcomes were tied up with self-esteem, self-worth and the construction of men's identity. Benny (70, widowed, retired trucker) describes how being a regular to the same sex worker in a parlour provided a deeper sense of self through the feeling of belonging: 'I like the sense of belonging, being somebody's regular.' The characteristics of the sex worker–client relationship that were founded on emotional closeness appeared similar across the life-course for men of different ages.

The characteristics that sociologists have described as intimacy or 'deep knowing' are evident in the narratives of clients when they reveal the content of their relationships with sex workers. Communication through talking and conversation was a general feature of the desired closeness:

> I like to be able to talk to somebody. I like them to be human beings and I like to be able to have a conversation with them at the same time. I don't particularly like to be, what I call hurried. To me it's an experience. I am not going there just to empty me tanks. (Trey, 24, single, student)

Patrick, a 39-year-old working in social care with a long-term partner, described himself as a 'semi-regular': his behaviours demonstrated an awareness of the emotional attachments that could develop with sex workers and this was something he wanted to avoid:

> I've chosen to only be a semi-regular, because I think it slightly worries me about if you see someone two or three times a month then I think it becomes quite complicated. I know it's sort of a defining line, what is regular and semi-regular? But I think that could be a bit tricky because for me, you're kind of then delving into girlfriend territory and I think that'd be a very tricky area to negotiate really.

The regulars did not typically want non-emotional sexual encounters but specifically sought out sex workers who provided a more holistic service. Andy (31, long-term partner, sales) explains how continuity and familiarity were more attractive in sexual partners and therefore the long-term commercial relationship was preferable:

> I don't actually like having sex with strangers very much. Sex is obviously quite an intimate act and it feels a bit funny just walking in with somebody you have never met before, having sex with them and then walking out again. While as seeing someone regularly it feels more like a proper human interaction.

The benefits of being a regular client were a combination of physical satisfaction that extended beyond just sex acts but included emotional connections through exchanging life information and demonstrating interest and 'care':

> It's when the girl sort of kisses you and it's sensual as opposed to being just physical sex between two people. So it's more an overall experience . . . .when you do get to know them and you can be that much more intimate for want of a better word. They know a lot about your life, and you end up knowing quite a bit about their life. (Ross, 54, single, engineering)

Lever and Dolnick (2000: 96) describe how intimacy in some sex worker–client relationships is achieved through a range of interactions such as non-sexual massage, conversation, caressing, kissing, hugging, sensual touching to relax and/or arouse, and both 'small' and 'deep' talk. Some clients described how they spent hours doing their research on the Internet to find a sex worker whom they consider will provide a high-quality emotional and bodily intimate service: the 'girlfriend experience'.

Finding the ultimate girlfriend experience

In the sex work community, particularly on the message boards, the concept of the 'girlfriend experience' (GFE) has been coined to express a commercial experience that combines physical and bodily ecstasy and emotional nourishment:

> For me a GFE has got to build up over some time so if I go and see somebody for the first time let's say, I mean I've seen women in their thirties and it just hasn't worked and I never see them again. It's almost indefinable, you see somebody and if there is a rapport or if you develop a rapport, whether it's her meeting my needs or occasionally me meeting hers, I'm trying not to use the word chemistry. (Ron, 51, separated, teacher)

The GFE was described using concepts such as 'rapport', 'chemistry', 'passion', 'connection'. Interviewees found it difficult to put this experience into words as they would defer to a 'feeling' of intimacy. John (58, divorced, sales) describes how intimacy is sought that mirrors conventional relationships and disguises the commercial element: 'You're with someone who is really friendly and nice and you get on with and you've had sex and it hasn't felt like a paid encounter.' There is a sense of caring and consideration in the girlfriend experience that the men appreciate and use as a benchmark for the quality of the relationship: 'In the girlfriend experience you get a cup of tea and a chat and a glass of wine and it's not interpreted by the hour but by the service' (Richard, 56, separated, media). The perception of these relationships overrides the commercial element which acts as a technique of neutralization that prevents commerce colouring the experience of the relationship.

For regular clients, kissing was highlighted as important in defining intimate relationships with sex workers as kissing symbolized bodily intimacy that was the product of emotional connections:

> That when the girl gets very sensual possibly kissing. Some girls don't kiss, some girls do. And trying to make you enjoy your time while she's there. Whilst some girls are definitely into you know they want to go through the physical, sexual act without giving anything in return as such. You know its 'sack of potatoes' are the sort of phrases that come to mind. (Craig, 38, single, sales)

In the narratives there were frequent comparisons about commercial sexual experiences where the sex worker was not emotionally involved, but 'clinical' or 'distant'. In contrast, interviewees described their preferred experiences which were more like a 'girlfriend' where emotional sincerity went alongside sex. Through acts such as kissing, intimacy is experienced in the flesh enabling men to experience moments of suspended commercialism. From my research with sex workers who do provide kissing in the service, they are consciously providing an 'all round' service that looks and feels like a 'girlfriend' encounter and therefore enables them to charge the appropriate price for this level of 'intimate' service (see Sanders 2005b). However, some participants recognized that the 'girlfriend experience' was perhaps emotionally dangerous as it created attachments and ties that could lead to confusion and upset. Matthew (39, married, teacher), who was once a regular client for several years, spoke about the GFE as a fantasy that men seek out: 'If you get to believe it then that becomes dangerous emotionally, because that's where the emotional entanglement comes.' Other clients were more satisfied with finding normalcy and ordinariness in their commercial relationships despite the risk of emotional involvement that spilled across boundaries.

Doing intimacy: traditional sexual scripts

Key features of the traditional heterosexual male sexual script are prominent in commercial sexual relationships between regular clients and sex workers. The role of communication, courtship rituals, sexual familiarity and the development of friendship and emotional connections were important for regular clients.

Being a regular offers the thrill of courtship and the romance of a conventional relationship, perhaps involving an overnight stay, dinner, dancing, kissing in public and being considered a 'couple'. Even if the escort service is not as sociable, being a regular still enables the client to act out the rituals of courtship: typically bringing gifts of chocolates, perfume, flowers and lingerie, which promotes the feelings and pleasures of courtship, romance and 'winning the heart' of the desired woman:

> I find pleasure in the kissing, probably take a bottle of wine and we'll sit and share a bottle of wine or sit, cuddle, talk about what I've done since I saw her last. She'll want to tell me what she's done 'this has happened, that's happened', you know, back home. It's something of normality of life. I don't want to go and be sexually processed, for me it's like dating. I prefer the girlfriend experience. (Paul, 56, married, retired bank manager)

Responding to a radio programme, where one female commentator was describing clients as 'sexual predators', a man wrote a lengthy e-mail to me, resisting this broad brush generalization. Describing his own 'script' as a client which drew heavily on behavioural characteristics and expectations of courtship, he wrote:

> I always like to arrive early so that I can chat to the receptionist and as many of the ladies as possible. I always take a small present for the receptionist and all of the ladies and then a personal present for the lady. These are only small gifts. They are not given in any attempt to acquire special favours, it is simply that I like to do this because I know that such gifts will be appreciated. Is this the action of a 'sexual predator'? I do not think so . . . I am absolutely sure that like me, the vast majority of men also CARE about the ladies they visit.

The traditional heterosexual male script was a set of rules and behavioural expectations that some clients relied upon to resist stigma and accusations of exploitation. The client script therefore was not necessarily different in form or context from normative heterosexual male scripts.

Communication by e-mail, phone and text message were all used as media through which courtship was exercised, boundaries were explicitly or implicitly negotiated and contact was maintained in between visits. The 'regular' relationship had a context outside the bedroom activity and the physical site of commercial sex. Relationships often had continuity over time and place through communication that permeated ordinary life:

I've known her for nearly two years and we've probably exchanged several hundred e-mails in that time. I probably only see her every couple months but in the meantime we still communicate a lot about a lot of different things and talk about all sorts of stuff that are completely unrelated to the punting side of it. (Terry, 68, married, lawyer)

The 'commitment' and sexual fidelity that is the assumed bedrock of conventional long-term relationships was transferred by some regulars to the commercial setting. Steve, a 47-year-old IT specialist who is divorced, expressed how 'monogamy' featured strongly in his interactions in the sex industry: 'For the past two years I have only seen the same girl. I wouldn't see anybody else now. I am monogamous in my perversion.' Commitment was important for some men as part of the commercial relationship because it simplified their fantasy of the 'girlfriend experience' and provided them with a pseudo-security.

More than sex: friendship and trust

Many of the critiques of the sex industry start from the premise that in commercial sex women's bodies, emotions and sexuality are commodified and objectified as sexual entities for the purpose of male pleasure (see Scully 1990). The conclusions to this argument are that the female body becomes devoid of individualism through the process of objectification and therefore it appears as normal and legitimate to acquire the female body for a fee. The process of objectification is a necessary part of the separation between emotions, intimacy and sex. If the sexual partner (e.g. sex worker) is an object then it is possible to avoid feelings or be concerned with any wider issues of emotions, exploitation or ethics. There are two accounts on which this simplification of what happens in the sex industry can be challenged. First, the argument of objectification ignores that there are emotional aspects of the client–sex worker relationship, and second, some men give a low priority to sex and a higher status to emotional connectivity, therefore resisting objectification.

First, regular relationships with sex workers are not necessarily based on objectification but are emotional in both content and form. Clients do not always distance their emotions, desire only bodily contact or prevent feelings of 'care' or admiration developing. Hart (1998: 124) describes sex worker and client relationship in the barrios of Spain through 'friendship'. Friendship, according to these anthropological interpretations, takes on different meanings in different commercial sex contexts. Hart distinguishes three types of friendship: the sales pitch, where friendship is used by either party to negotiate a better deal; 'genuine' friendship;

and friendship borne out as 'property rights' or fidelity within the sex work relationship. Friendship is a useful lens through which the emotional aspect of the relationship can be further examined.

In my study, the concept of 'friendship' was used by several participants to describe the level of intimacy and express fidelity: 'It's important to see the same girl. I still see one of the girls regularly, I mean every week. We're friends' (Jeff, 57, married, senior management). John (58, divorced, sales) described his relationship with a 40-year-old escort whom he had visited for three years by saying: 'We are actually friends now as well as if you like business associates.' Relationships that were built over time suggested a familiarity and connection that went beyond cursory arrangements. For some men, the commercial nature of the relationship meant that some aspects of the relationship were not dissimilar to those with close work associates who were more than colleagues, actually friends.

Vernon (50, divorced, teacher) described how he had a relationship with a regular sex worker that operated on several different levels. He sometimes visited for non-commercial reasons, for instance to assist with household jobs or other manual tasks that were outside the commercial relationship but were acceptable as part of the mutual friendship: 'After a while, especially when you have been seeing someone for so long, they actually become friends like your other friends.' Several interviewees commented on the importance of 'trust' as an emotion that produced some level of security in the relationship, which resulted in quality bodily intimacy: 'The awkwardness vanishes over a period of time. It would, when you meet anyone new. You would trust them. You would develop a degree of interest in them. They would develop a degree of trust in you' (Mitchell, 49, married, managing director).

Second, the argument that commercial sexual relationships objectify the sex worker so that sex and emotions can be separated falls short when we consider that some men are not overly concerned with the sexual but desire emotional closeness. Male clients were not always looking for sexual adventure but sexual stability that led to intimacy. Kelvin (36, single, charity worker) had seen the same sex worker for 18 months and stated that the basis of the relationship went beyond the physical: 'I don't see it as just a sex act. The reason I go, it's for the emotional connection.' Howard (49, married, academic) started visiting escorts after a marriage sexless for ten years and found that the reason for his relationship with one particular escort was emotional and not physical:

I thought I was looking for sex, and in a sense I was because I missed that, I never had much when I was younger, I certainly hadn't had any for a long time. But as I got into it, I mean I met somebody who was pretty magic. The sex became less important and the friendship became much more important.

Jamieson (1998: 107) asks: 'Are we witnessing the decline of macho-male masculinity with its predetermined sexuality which ritually denies intimacy?' The middle-class men in this sample who sought out regular relationships in the commercial arena displayed a non-traditional form of masculinity. A form of masculinity was on display that included emotions, the need to feel nurtured, the need for 'ego-massaging' and the desire for emotional closeness. In addition, the commercial sexual interaction was not free from anxieties around male sexual performance or pleasuring a woman (discussed below). Some clients described how the commercial sex setting made them feel pressurized to prove their masculinity through sexual abilities and created anxieties about perform-ance and embarrassment at their own sexual histories of inexperience, impotency and sexual incompetence. Sex workers were not epitomized as the targets of sexual conquest, excessive fornication or constructed simply as bodies. Finding a 'special' sex worker, usually with assistance from the Internet (field reports, sex workers' websites, advice from fellow clients), can cause these fears and anxieties to subside.

Mutual enjoyment, delusion or just a good service?

Achieving 'reciprocated' intimacy, where clients believe that sex workers are experiencing emotional and sensual closeness as well as sexual pleasure, are props that turn the commercial act into what some clients considered to be an egalitarian experience based on 'private', individual-ized (rather than routine or standardized) intimacy, similar to that expected from conventional relationships. O'Connell Davidson (1998: 158) suggests that this is the contradiction of 'clienting': 'Clients often want to believe that, although the prostitute is a paid labourer, in their particular case she enjoys her work and derives sexual and/or emotional satisfaction from her encounter with them.' Some clients in my study did not sign up to any discourse of mutuality: 'I always take it with a pinch of salt what they tell you. You know. And maybe, I always half believe and I don't believe. And again that helps to build that distrust, helps to keep things at arm's length' (Darren, 38, long-term partner, customer services). But for the majority of the regulars, delusion played a significant part in understand-ing their interactions with sex workers. This is not surprising given that the research into long-term heterosexual couples suggest that doing 'sex work' and 'performing the couple game' were ordinary strategies used to aspire to expectations of mutual sexual satisfaction (Duncombe and Marsden 1996). Mutuality, whether real or illusionary, formed an essential ingredient of the regular client–sex worker relationship.

Other commentators have noted how the discourses of mutuality in clients' narratives are important, but their conclusions dismiss the sex worker's position in the creation of 'mutuality'. Plumridge *et al.* (1997: 178) comment on the reality of mutual enjoyment: 'Sexual reciprocity or mutuality is highly problematic. It is undoubtedly a self-serving interpretative schema leaving men who pay for sex free to enjoy it on their own terms.' Below I argue that the 'contradictions of clienting' are more complex than delusion as mutuality occurs in different guises, usually within the control of the sex worker's routine and emotional labour skills.

Mutuality and its many guises is intriguing and reveals complexities about the sex work relationship, the relationship between commerce and intimacy and the nature of sex work as a performance. The 'confusion' or belief that some men have regarding the mutual pleasure (I refer to mutual pleasure in this case as both sexual and emotional) of the relationship can be understood in various ways.[1] There are at least three explanations of how and why mutuality is experienced by the male customer:

1. *The 'authentic' delusion of mutuality.* Acting (i.e. not pleasure) by the sex worker is necessary to provide the illusion of mutual pleasure yet is experienced by the client as genuine mutual pleasure, holding their own sexual and intimate abilities in high esteem.
2. *The 'authentic-fake' delusion of mutuality.* The client understands that the sex worker is acting as part of the service (she is a sexual and emotional labourer) but he still experiences the interaction as mutual and authentic even though both parties are aware it is fake.
3. *The 'genuine' mutuality.* 'Real' mutual pleasure is experienced by both parities either inside or outside the professional boundaries of commercial sex.

The authentic delusion of mutuality

Referred to by Plumridge *et al.* (1997) as 'the myth of mutuality', clients present an inflated and exaggerated ideal of the sexual interaction which the sex worker does not experience: 'I know it was satisfying to her. Trust me it was more satisfying to her than it was for me but it was one of those things that I'm just glad if being with me can satisfy someone because in a way that validates me as a male' (Alan, 59, divorced, retired). There is a level of naivety among some clients who were adamant that the sexual pleasure is two-way: 'I personally would say she's not acting with me. She says she's not' (Howard, 49, married, academic). The desire for the sexual experience to be pleasurable on both sides was a recurrent theme in the client's narrative:

I'm not saying it's always pleasurable for them but it's not as horrendous as some people think. You know, some people think well, it must be wrong. It must be a terrible situation. Well, it's not. It can be pleasurable on both sides. Not all the time but on many occasions it can be. (Patrick, 39, long-term partner, social care)

For men who had sexual difficulties, sexually pleasing the sex worker took on extra importance because it verified their ability to perform sexually and fulfil a traditional masculine sexual role: 'I do have problems which mean it doesn't always work and I don't always get satisfaction. So knowing that I can give pleasure, um, at the same time as getting it, that is ultra important to me' (Liam, 70, widower, retired academic). In these cases, there was blind acceptance that what happened in the bedroom was a 'real' pleasurable experience or that the 'care' shown by the sex worker was because she had genuine feelings. Here, the skill of the sex worker and her ability to fake and act out the encounter as pleasurable is not considered. Bernstein (2001: 402) notes that certain men purchase a 'bounded authenticity' which convinces them of genuine mutual pleasure. It is most unlikely that these scenarios of delusion in sexual pleasure are confined to the commercial but are more likely to mirror the absence of mutual pleasure in conventional heterosexual sex lives. Dunscombe and Marsden (1996) identify that in long-term relationships, sex and pleasure become complex, often not mutually satisfying and an area of married life where lies and deception are commonplace (also see Litzinger and Gordon 2005).

The authentic-fake delusion of mutuality

Other men who described emotional liaisons with sex workers were fully aware of the business contract that framed the sexual exchange. Among regulars, despite the overt desire for intimacy and closeness, many were aware that the woman is a sexual labourer and that the relationship exists within the context of a professional job:

I think that one has to look upon it like a lot of other service industries. I mean obviously if women are being exploited, that's terrible, if women are doing it under pressure or duress or whatever, then that's not right. But I think certainly the vast majority of women that I've met are doing it not only because they're comfortable doing it but they've actually made a conscious decision to do it for a period of time, for – to give themselves some economic independence or whatever. And they're completely comfortable with it. (Paulo, 54, married, property developer)

Sex workers were constructed as 'business women', 'service providers' and choice-makers who were opting to apply their bodies, sexuality and femininity to make money. The sexualization of the work through both bodily services and emotional labour was acknowledged by men who admitted that the mutuality that they may have experienced, or convinced themselves of, was in fact an extension of the sex worker's ability to provide a 'good' service. When describing close intimate relationships, caveats would be added such as that by Craig (38, single, sales): 'Remember at the end of the day it's just a business transaction, albeit a very pleasurable one.' Some participants defined a 'good worker' as someone who provided a service that masked the economic exchange to create a scenario where the marketplace was not visible at an emotional or physical level:

> Not all the girls that I've known, are all good actors. It's a job. I recognize it's a job to them. But for the hour or couple that you're with them, a good escort will make you feel that they are not prostitutes, they're you know, girlfriends. (Jeff, 57, married, senior management)

> Some of them are very good actresses shall we say. You do believe them, but you obviously can't take it totally to heart but yes, you can believe that you are there and they do enjoy your company. (Ross, 54, single, engineering)

These 'authentic-fake' experiences were considered to be mutual experiences of pleasure *in the moment*, although rationally clients were fully aware of the performance of the commercial liaison. Commenting on the trusting relationship he had with a sex worker, Mitchell (49, married, managing director) commented: 'There is some kind of bond even though it's not real.' It was evident that some men bought into and believed the illusions of mutuality that the sex worker, with her sexual skills and emotional labour, constructed. Contrasting the quality of the 'authentic-fake' experience between parlours and escorts, Steve (47, divorced, IT specialist) commented: 'What I go for is when you are treated like a friend whether you are or not. As I say it's all theatrical. It's an act she's putting on and it's just far nicer than "wham bam thank you mam" down the parlour.' Men who were realistic about the authenticity of the relationship were aware that acting was a necessary part of the service and were prepared to pay more money to receive a service that accounted for this fantasy.

The 'authentic-fake' delusion of the mutuality is most interesting because of the various competing dynamics and objectives at play. For the sex worker, there are preventions in place, also known as emotional management strategies, to avoid feelings of intimacy in a work situation.[2] Stein (1974: 17) concludes from her observations of hundreds of 'call-girl–client' interactions that 'creating and preserving illusions is perhaps the call girl's most important and personalized skill'. Such skill, Bernstein (2001: 403) notes, involves the 'rigid emotional boundaries' and 'de-eroticized category of identity' that sex workers apply to their own interactions with clients that rarely, if ever, transcend the professional. Sex workers are often 'successful' as entrepreneurs because of their ability to 'deliver' intimacy in the commercial context, without breaking their own boundaries or putting their own emotional management strategies under strain. Elsewhere I have written about the acting, 'manufactured identity' and performance skills that sex workers craft to provide the 'girlfriend experience' (Sanders 2005b). There is evidence that sex workers often do not experience sexual pleasure from clients, but instead pretend and fake sexual excitement and orgasm (Brewis and Linstead 2000b; Weinberg *et al.* 1999). These skills are very often intentional, precise and an art form that sex workers learn can be used to make profit and maintain a regular client base.

In these relationships, both parties are content if the customer feels intimate at the time of the encounter. 'Authentic-fake' mutuality is still a process through which intimacy is experienced for the client because 'intimate relationships do not necessarily have to be mutual' (Zelizer 2005: 15), but instead one party (the client) can experience intimacy without the other. In regular client relationships the sex worker has to perform mutuality at the levels of communication, courtship, sexual familiarity, friendship and other emotional levels in order to convince the customer that what they purchased was mutual intimacy. This delusion was not necessarily manipulative or contrived in the sense that the worker was tricking the customer as his experience of emotional closeness and physical pleasure was not fake for him while he was with the sex worker. Paulo describes how some sex workers encouraged regular custom through personable, flirtatious communication which pushed the boundaries: 'She actually encouraged it I think, if anything. She would text and e-mail and ask when I was visiting next. Very professional but gave the impression of being very attached and very detached at the same time.' Men were usually aware of the complexity of the service, how emotions were constructed as part of the commercial interaction and ultimately accepted mutuality as a delusion and the sex worker's displays of pleasure as fake.

Genuine mutuality

Another scenario is that pleasure and mutuality are genuinely experienced by both the sex worker and the client. It is not conclusive (and very unlikely) that sex workers are always faking the pleasurable aspects of the relationship. Accounts of sex workers' views on genuine friendship and mutual pleasures with clients are needed in order to compare their narratives of mutuality with those of the clients. Some sex workers have described how they enjoy interactions with clients on both a sexual and psychological level (Sanders 2005a: 145–6). Frank's (2006) auto-ethnographic accounts of erotic dancing and her relationships with clients identifies how sex workers often have mixed feelings about their clients as emotions blur between the commercial and non-commercial.

If client–sex worker interactions start to occur outside of the initial strictly commercial setting, then the boundaries of the relationship start to become hazy. Take, for example, the case of George (58, married, IT). When the relationship he had with a parlour worker moved out of the clear confinements of the commercial setting to become 'out-of-hours' meetings, the relationship became distorted:

> I mean we went out to the theatre a few times and that sort of thing, off hours. And you know, she seemed to enjoy that enormously. And we'd go out for about six hours on many occasions over a couple of years – which is a lot of hours to expend purely on what you might call customer relations. And it gets very dubious you see. It's very hard to read these sorts of things. How do you weigh up the fact that somebody's spent say 12 hours with you in their own time and only about 10 hours' paid time in that year, say. It's very hard to make those judgements, and you're continually trying to judge whether somebody really likes you and wants to spend time with you.

Outside the strict boundaries of the commercial setting, the relationship sat in the hinterland between commerce and non-commerce, creating confusion but also enabling real genuine relations to develop. In my previous research, sex workers have described scenarios when they began 'dating' a client, no longer taking money for sexual services and eventually having a full non-commercial relationship with an ex-client (Sanders 2005a: 146). On a few occasions this transgression resulted in marriage. In other business relationships where commerce and intimacy are merged, for instance lawyer–client or doctor–patient, the professional relationship is set aside while a personal, intimate and mutual relationship flourishes and is interpreted as 'time out'.

Vulnerability and emotional attachment

Clients explained a range of uncomfortable and sometimes negative emotions as a result of experimenting with the sex industry. At the extreme end, these include 'falling in love' or futile emotions for individual sex workers that could not be realized. More common were feelings of embarrassment, anxiety and emptiness.

Nerves, anxiety and emptiness

Men described initial encounters in the sex industry through a range of emotions such as disappointment, intense nervousness and anxiety. After describing the emotional fallout from his first encounter with a sex worker one man posted on a message board: 'I was left with this kind of empty feeling. Not in my wallet but inside.' In response, another more experienced client summarized the types of emotional reactions from having 'one-off' commercial sexual encounters:

> There are two types of emptiness ... there's the kind of 'broad sword through your soul and dragged out again leaving a heaving gap' type and the more natural type that is inherent with these types of liaisons. In nature sex is a ritual of bonding and mating. People have sex and get so hooked up in the emotions that they stay together for a lifetime. So it's not surprising that your emotions are a little out of tune when one minute your spending an hour of absolute passion with a girl and the next minute you are hardly more than strangers who may never cross each other's path again.

The thread continued in a supportive manner to reassure the first-timer that his experience of emptiness was usual and that the only way to improve the situation was to become a regular client:

> I was very nervous my first time and didn't really enjoy it that much. I was still nervous for about a year or so (25 punts) but now it's more of an excitement to either meet someone new or catch up with some of my favourite ladies ... if you do your research properly then no doubt you'll find someone who you click with (sexually as well as socially).

Sexual dissatisfaction is not uncommon in commercial sexual liaisons. Sawyer *et al.* (2001) found that a third of a sample of men who buy sex said they did not enjoy sex when purchased. These intense emotions can sometimes halt men's involvement in seeking commercial sex as their emotional tensions produce unwanted side effects.

Falling in love, confusion and upset

If intimacy is a desired and experienced outcome from regular commercial sexual relationships, it only follows that there are further issues relating to over-attachments and vulnerabilities experienced by men in commercial sexual relationships. Accounts have been described of men falling in love with sex workers (Peng 2007: 327), usually when the feeling is not reciprocated. The desire to achieve 'deep knowing' and 'close association' in intimate commercial relations brings emotional risks. Graham (52, divorced, public sector) explained his intense relationship with an escort that left him feeling confused:

> For a couple of years I was on this thing of never quite knowing whether there was anything there or not. I'm cynical in lots of ways, I'm not gullible I don't think, but you know, to actually try – to actually measure something and weigh that something up is quite difficult. And the financial angle does corrupt everything.

Some men felt safe because of the boundaries of the commercial relationship whereas other men, when intense emotions became involved on their part, were confused about the boundaries of the relationship and could not assess whether the relationship had 'crossed a line' into something genuine and non-commercial:

> I have just been seeing this girl for 18 months now and she's just got under my skin. She's let me in. I mean she does have a reputation for being a very, very giving person. She gives herself a lot in a sexual way as well. But whether I am confusing that with something but there is definitely a chemistry between us and she says that. (Vernon, 50, divorced, teacher)

Clients expressed deep emotions they had felt for sex workers: 'You get some very complex emotions. And there was a Lithuanian girl who I got very close to and again I would actually go and we wouldn't have sex' (Dean, 34, single, sales). Unrequited emotional attachments normally ended in complete disassociation:

> I just had that feeling. And I then I started to lose sleep over her and lost a bit of weight because I wasn't eating . . . You know, I couldn't see anyone else. I went to another parlour and had to leave. In the end I wrote her a letter to tell her why I had to stop going . . . I've never seen her again. (Benny, 70, widowed, retired trucker)

Of the 50 men interviewed, 16 men who described themselves as 'repeat' customers were clear that they did not want to be become a 'regular' client because of the potential emotional attachments with unavailable women. These men were motivated by the sexual desire to have liaisons with many different women and have sexual relationships without emotional obligation or commitment. Despite visiting the same sex worker once a month, Craig identifies how sticking with the commercial boundaries of the relationship prevents any attachments forming that could be problematic: 'I mean I know some people get involved as I am sure you know and it all becomes very hopeless. I don't think I've, you know I've always I think had my eyes open' (Craig, 38, single, sales). Others were well aware that the attractions of buying a fantasy could become a compulsive process: 'I can see how it can be addictive and there can be a danger of getting emotionally attached to girls' (Jeremy, 24, single, student). Some clients had altered their behaviours because emotions became too intense: 'There are a couple of women I've stopped seeing because I was getting too fond of them' (Alan, 59, divorced, retired).

Emotional consumption and exploitation

Men I interviewed were aware of their somewhat vulnerable status in terms of their economic generosity towards sex workers to whom they were particularly attached. George, a 58-year-old married IT consultant, claimed he had spent £10,000 in gifts for a particular 35-year-old parlour worker he had been visiting regularly for three years. His feelings for her were described as intense but he also felt he had been manipulated by her material demands:

I know I've given her far too much. The money doesn't mean anything to me really. She wants some cosmetic surgery. But what I said to her was, 'but I won't do it until July.' I said part of it will be sort of like a reward for being my regular for another year. And the other part would be a sort of incentive for her to keep me as a regular.

Spending money, buying gifts and responding to the sex worker's financial demands were tied into maintaining a relationship that is framed by commodification and can never be anything other than commercial and not mutual. Egan (2005: 95) describes the contradictions of the consumption of love and emotion in the commercial context as: 'Regulars want something that is almost impossible in a scene of commodification – real connection (love), something other than the relation of commodity in which they are situated.' It could be argued that having the financial capacity to buy a woman's attentions for a long period of time and create some form of obligation in the commercial sexual relationship is an expression of economic and social mastery and a harmful micro-relationship that mirrors the structural patriarchal power of men over women. Yet equally, where women exploit the emotional attachments that men form for financial and material gain, the agency of the woman in determining and controlling the relationship needs to be considered. The two sides of the relationship, one of emotional vulnerability and the other of emotional power, highlight the contradictions of the commercial relationship. Such scenarios of mutual exploitation are clearly not confined to commercial relationships but are regularly evident in relationships sanctified by society where financial gain and emotions are swapped.

The contradictions of marriage

The public story of marriage is as an intimate dyad where understanding between husband and wife is permanent and implicit and expressed through emotional and bodily intimacy. Half of the men I spoke with who were regularly involved in purchasing sex were either married or in long-term partnerships that they considered committed like a marriage. Men who were married yet frequent buyers of sex often had no desire to end their marriage but displayed strong commitments to the caring and sharing duties for their wife and children. When asked about their relationships with their wives George and Terry replied:

> Well, there's no real connection really. I had no sex with my wife for donkeys' years. We had very little intimacy at all. But at the same time I've got a daughter of about 14 who makes it very difficult to actually wade out. I would have waded out – I think I should have waded out a long time ago, been married over 30 years – but there is virtually nothing there from that point of view. We operate as business partners. There's no sex, there's no intimacy, there's no human contact at the lowest level if you like. (George, 58, married, IT)

> It all really started off because sex at home just didn't work at all satisfactorily and I didn't want to break up the marriage. I didn't want to leave the kids and so on and I discovered that I could actually make good the shortcomings without affecting the relationship . . . I like to think that keeping my marriage together is a less bad thing to do than cause it to fall apart. (Terry, 68, married, lawyer)

Marriage was not described as emotionally intense, but was considered an institution that prioritizes care and obligation rather than intimacy and personal fulfilment. The contract of marriage was upheld because of financial obligation to provide for the spouse and children. The commercial element of marriage was often devoid of intimacy, rendering these relationships reminiscent of pre-modern unions based on economic circumstance. As Stein (1974: 58) found, the relationship between marriage, prostitution and the helping professions is that clients visit sex workers for needs that should be met by marriage. Sex workers become part of the helping professionals through their restorative and therapeutic skills.

Clients' stories about 'empty marriages' where intimacy was no longer found became a reason for seeking out sex and intimacy from other women in commercial liaisons:

> It's probably got to be quite a reasonably sort of well argued justification for going and having sex elsewhere that I wasn't getting it in my marriage. And in some ways I think it's even more OK that I'm going elsewhere for emotional support because I'm not getting it in my marriage. (Matthew, 39, married, teacher)

Several clients lived in fear of the consequences if their wives found out about their sexual habits:

> I suppose if my wife found out then it would probably destroy our marriage actually and I really love my wife and I wouldn't want to upset her. Which is why I've never actually talked about it to – I wouldn't discuss it with anybody, at work or anywhere else I don't think apart from here. (Tony, 55, married, pilot)

Deep knowing was not necessarily absent from some men's marriages. After many years of marriage, the connections between emotional and bodily intimacy had faded but men were still satisfied with the emotional content of the relationship: 'The sex side of the marriage has all but gone but I don't miss it, it's just a cuddle or something like that but we love each other and I am quite happy with it' (Billy, 43, married, manufacturing). A good relationship may not always be defined by mutual sexual pleasure. A British sex survey by Wellings *et al.* (1994) asked respondents to comment on the statement: 'Sex is the most important part of any marriage relationship'; only 16–17 per cent of men and women agreed with this statement, suggesting that sex is not an overwhelming priority in marriage. Mutuality and romance are postwar narratives built around marriage, compared to the traditional social and religious obligations that made marriage the norm. Heterosexual marriage symbolizes several contradictions that still retain its superficial but central position in the social order (Giddens 1992: 154). For instance, sex and intimacy are no longer wedded to marriage and the changes in the use of marriage do not mean that there is a collapse of family life or commitment.

Married clients who had no intention of changing their status but were at the same time committed to commercial sexual relationships identified a 'separation between public stories about personal life and the life that is lived' (Jamieson 1998: 10). Some of the clients' public accounts they presented to the researcher and other external audiences such as their friends and colleagues, particularly the eight married participants who had been visiting sex workers for over twenty years, were at odds with their private 'story'. The 'front stage' of their lives, that which is evident to the outside world, protected the institution of marriage and presented the public 'face' of respectability by being a good husband, father and citizen (see Chapter 6). The 'back stage' of their lives, an area that the researcher has privileged access to through the interview process, highlighted the contradictions between public values and private stories and practices. Married clients were adept at maintaining one story – that of marriage, commitment, fidelity – while living another story both emotionally and physically. The privileged social and economic position of men meant that they could maintain the facade of marriage and respectability while finding intimacy in a commercial relation shrouded in taboo and secrecy. For married clients, emotional reliance, co-dependency and public accountability were still achieved through marriage while a combination of sexual and emotional intimacy was achieved through commercial relationships with sexual labourers.

Commerce and the 'transformation of intimacy'

These empirical findings move the debate from an oversimplified one that regards sex workers as only providing sex and male clients as only wanting sex to a more evolved understanding of desire and pleasure and the motives for seeking them through the commercial exchange. The place of intimacy and 'deep knowing' at both an emotional and physical level between some sex workers and clients, whether deluded or genuine, suggests that the somewhat constructed boundaries between commercial and non-commercial relationships are further eroded by a realization that the parties move in and out of these two spheres. Seidler's (1992) dichotomous perspective suggests that men separate sex from intimacy to maintain a sense of masculinity or to avoid it being threatened. This separation process is not necessarily one that happens in commercial sex for clients who become regulars. Regulars do not separate sex from emotional connectivity with sex workers and therefore the commodification process is not necessarily part of the client–sex worker relationship. A false dichotomy is maintained between commercial and non-commercial relations. Instead, heterosexual male scripts, the desire for intimacy and romantic emotional connectivity, are evident within the commercial setting.

Understanding the relationships between intimacy and commerce in the sex industry can be positioned within contemporary sexuality. If men are indeed seeking out commercial sex more than in previous stages of modernity this may be explained by Giddens' (1992) concept of 'plastic sexuality'. Giddens charts the rise of a more creative form of sexuality which discards any pre-given way of being sexual or preconceived patterns or expectations for sexual behaviour. Sexuality and sexual behaviour are freed from reproduction and expectations of typicality. Plastic sexuality encapsulates the ability to create ourselves without being beholden to tradition, religious expectation or long-term obligations. To achieve this reflexivity, Giddens (1992: 7) goes on to describe how the individual becomes preoccupied with developing the project of the self: 'Where large areas of a person's life are no longer set by pre-existing patterns and habits, the individual is continually obliged to negotiate life-style options . . . life-style choices are constitutive of the reflexive narrative of self.' Commercial sex and what it provides becomes a realistic choice which can be combined with marriage and is not diametrically opposed to the obligations of marriage. As contemporary relationship formation undergoes a radical transformation represented by non-conventional sexual relationships (Roseneil 2007), commercial sex as a site where intimacy can be found becomes ever popular.

Regulars who experience intimacy with sex workers achieve a 'pure relationship' because the explicit boundaries of commerce are freed from the strains placed on conventional relationships. The delusions of mutuality that take different forms provide the emotional sustenance alongside sexual pleasure that result in the desired intimacy. Clients engage in reflexivity of their own emotional life, auditing their desires and measuring levels of satisfaction and fulfilment. 'Plastic sexuality' enables men to find commercial relations that are fulfilling while at the same time holding on to, and benefiting from, the public story and private security of marriage. Through the principle of autonomy, personal life can be democratized by continuous engagement in commercial sex as 'the possibility of intimacy' is realized (Giddens 1992: 188). As men become increasingly influenced by the ideals of romantic love, departing from traditional historical masculine roles, the emotional and sexual relations sought through commerce are evidence that intimacy has become an organizing principle of personal life and a key element in the construction of self-identity. Male clients, particularly those in marriages that are devoid of intimacy, become choice-makers, seeking out the 'pure relationship' in other contexts of sexual expression. Male clients undergo a process of restructuring their intimate life through continual self-reflexivity (such as engaging in research and information gathering) as emotions such as guilt, anxiety, pleasure and romantic love are reconciled.

Psychological stability is achieved through intimacy and contributes to the overall project of the self where individuals gain 'ontological security'. However, I would argue that for those clients who maintain the security and public face of marriage, the autonomy to move away from traditional ties is not as emancipating as Giddens suggests. Men who were still married and in long-term relationships felt bound to the contract of marriage (as well as feelings of commitment to their wives), but at the same time underwent a process of restructuring their intimate personal lives through commercial relationships. While commercial relationships were frequently acknowledged as more fulfilling for men, they still lived out their lives according to the expectations of middle-class respectability.

Exploring the 'project of the self' is the privilege of those who have the economic, social and personal capital to engage in activities that are seen to contribute to personal development. Middle-class men are in the privileged position of being able to explore the self and their own 'plastic sexuality' yet are still constrained by the ties of tradition. They must be all things to all people: good husband, good father, good neighbour, high achiever and model citizen as well as finding space for the 'project of the self'. Other social thinkers, such as Bauman, have criticized Giddens for not examining the project of the self in late modernity as the epitome of individualism and consumerism that threatens intimate relationships. Bauman's take on the rise of commercial sex would be that divorcing intimacy and sexual pleasure from the stability of long-term relationships commodifies these special emotions and connections, putting pressure on everyday relationships. While late modernity could be corrupted by the proliferation of commercial sex as an extended aspect of the 'sex as culture' frenzy that infiltrates our lives, the natures of commerce and intimacy do not necessarily conflict (Zelizer 2005). Instead, as I discuss further in the final chapter, intimacy and commerce may turn out to be stabilizing features that maintain 'normalcy' in a web of complex and often contradictory social and emotional relationships in contemporary society.

Notes

1 I am grateful to Michael Goodyear for his comments and suggestions on this subject.
2 As I have written elsewhere (Sanders 2002) the place of the condom is central to the sex worker's repertoire because it prevents any closeness or contact of a physical or emotional kind.

Chapter 6

Against respectability: stigma, secrecy and the self

Although the 'whore stigma' that is attached to women who work in the sex industry is a far more powerful and pervasive discourse that runs through the institutional structures of capitalism and gendered relationships (Hallgrimsdottir *et al.* 2006; Pheterson 1993; Roberts 1994), men who buy sex are increasingly under fire from a set of stereotypes that stem from the official disapproval of the sex industry. The stigma attached to men who buy sex has more recently appeared in government policies, but social science literature has, for some time, promoted an image of 'the john' as a man who is driven to sexual deviance because he is physically, psychologically and/or socially inadequate (Holzman and Pines 1982). Psychological and psychoanalytical theories locate the client as the troubled sexual defect (Ellis 1959; Gibbens and Silberman 1960). Yet these theories of psychological pathology are incongruent with what is known about the 'ordinariness' of men who buy sex. Demographics and interview accounts of men who buy sex suggest the average customer is a 'typical' man (Holzman and Pines 1982: 91), and that there are no signs of 'abnormality' among the population of clients (Monto and McRee 2005; Stein 1974). Clients are usually not interested in bizarre sexual acts, do not act violently and generally stick to the conditions of the commercial contract.

The discrepancy between the image of the 'punter' and the reality of who they are and how they behave has resulted in a series of consequences including stigmatization. Research shows that stigma is a common social and psychological factor experienced by men who buy sex. Peng (2007: 320) identified a moral stigma in the narratives of clients as well as a stigma that was derived from media portrayals of those who engaged in buying sex, which in turn affected the way that men interpret their experiences and ordered their lives. The consequences of social disapproval is that men live 'double lives' where commercial sex activities are consigned to a separate part of their lives, minds and emotions. For example, Campbell (1998: 156) found that only five of 28 interviewees had informed someone that they purchased sex, but even these clients still concealed behaviour from people, especially their partners. Secrecy born out of stigma and a sense of shame, fear of their partner's reaction, fear of being labelled strange or sexually perverted were all findings from Campbell's study.

This chapter explores the exact nature of labels and stereotypes attributed to men who buy sex that lead to stigma. I explore the negative emotions of guilt and shame and the secrecy that is born out of managing stigma. Examining how men who are involved in the sex industry as purchasers confront the stigma attached to buying sex, how they make sense of the stereotypes, the need to keep their activities hidden and the consequences of secrecy in their lives identifies processes of compartmentalization and strategies of stigma management that lead to the construction of the self. These 'multiple realities' that contribute to a subjective understanding of the self are influenced by social processes, particularly the 'discourse of respectability' (Skeggs 1997) that regulate sexuality and the social order. Before presenting these findings, it is important to clarify exactly which processes and social constructions have singled out 'the client' as being different and categorized as 'deviant'.

Human difference and the origin of stigma

'Stigma,' although criticized for its vagueness, is a useful conceptual tool available to analyse the meanings male clients attach to their lives. The starting point for this analysis is Goffman's (1963: 3) definition of stigma as the relationship between an attribute (or characteristic) and a stereotype. Tracing the process of stigmatization, how attributes become defined and linked to people, is the link to finding out how men who buy sex have become a group who face labelling, prejudice and criminalization in Western society. Link and Phelan (2001) note that the first component of stigmatization begins with distinguishing differences in human behaviour and then labelling those differences as 'deviant'. For most of the time human differences are irrelevant, remain unnoticed and form no basis for social categories. The case of sexual difference (for instance 'straight' or 'gay') identifies a process of 'social selection of human differences that will matter socially' (Link and Phelan 2001: 367). Through a social selection process, men who buy sex are singled out as different in comparison to men who have multiple non-commercial sexual partners or men who are protected by the state sanctioned institution of marriage.

The components of stigma need more fertile ground on which to move from recognition of difference to a rejection of the difference. The categorization of human differences requires intense simplification (for instance, Black and White people) and is also dependent on time and place. Cultural conditions create social constructions and categorizations of groups. Foucault, in *The History of Sexuality* (1979), traces how sexuality has been produced differently at specific historical moments through social meanings and discourse. He identifies how medical, moral, religious, political, educational, welfare and scientific discourses have contributed to the prevailing stories produced about sexuality. Men who buy sex have, fairly recently, been singled out from an array of sexual differences and have received social intolerance through a social and political process that crosses boundaries and discourses. For example, the process that led up to the criminalization of the buying of sex in Sweden happened because a strong women's movement, both inside and outside the political machinery of policy-making, marked out this group of men not as sexually diverse, but as perpetrators of violence against women and a destabilizing force against gender equality (Svanstrom 2004). This group's sexuality has been transformed from 'different' to 'deviant' through the process of social construction.

This book identifies the role of powerful institutions and machineries that oversee the categorization of 'difference' to 'deviance' that separates out men who buy sex, particularly those who engage in the street market, from other aspects of male sexuality. The law and policing practice (Chapter 7), the social construction of moral panics (Chapter 8) and the powerful labelling effects of the media are pivotal structural and cultural institutions that contribute to stigmatic dynamics. The power of institutions to construct categories was evident in the interviewees' responses. Dean, a self-confessed *Guardian* reader and BBC Radio 4 listener, echoed the thoughts of a further 14 men who commented on the misrepresentations in the media that influenced stereotypes about the sex industry:

> I think that the problem is that whenever you see anything on the local news or in the newspaper, it's ninety-nine times out of a hundred they are talking about the street scene and all men that purchase sexual services are tarred with that brush. There are two types of story. Whenever you hear about stories they're either horribly abusive on the street or it's the kiss and tell celebrity hooker on a £1,000 a day. You don't really hear anything about what's probably the majority of the thing, which is really the girls who work in flats or saunas or whatever . . . I think a lot of it is down to the papers. Reactionary papers such as the *Mail* or the *Express* and then you get the real hypocrites like the *Sun* and the *Star* who like

sell their papers through sex and titillation and then when something happens it's 'Oh that's terrible'. (Dean, 34, single, sales)

When describing society's views about the sex industry, twelve men referred specifically to the unique British attitude towards sex, suggesting the present-day attitude involves a myriad of social constructions that draw on national legacies of history and modernity:

It's the British stereotype about sex, we don't talk about it do we? We're British. If you go back to the 70s and 80s, wasn't there a play on in the West End called, or a film called *No Sex Please We're British*? And it's as though sort of talking about things like that are things the continentals do. We sort of buttoned up, British can't do that. (Alan, 59, divorced, retired)

Cultural and religious ideas about the place and role of sex in society have also been integral to the process of categorization and a powerful force in defining 'good' and 'bad' sexual behaviour: 'The whole of Christian society has majored on the importance of marriage as keeping the family unit together and the whole social fabric evolved round the family as a stable unit and it's [commercial sex] potentially undermining that' (Terry, 68, married, lawyer). Popular labels bestowed on men who buy sex are taken from those that also refer to the images and discourses surrounding the working classes: vulgar, unkempt, unruly, disrespectful and unrefined.

Labelling: misfits, perverts, and loners

In order for a stigma to occur, dominant cultural beliefs must produce labels which are then linked to stereotypes. Labels are a set of undesirable characteristics. When I asked Trey, a 24-year-old student, to define the labels that society attached to men like him, he responded: 'Stereotypes such as dirty sleazy men. Desperate men. Men who don't respect women. Men who just see women as sexual objects. Sort of men who have perverted interests in sex.' Adam, a 32-year-old media specialist who had been spending a £100 a month visiting parlours for the previous six years, relayed similar perceptions: 'I think probably loners and those with weird sort of sexual habits . . . Generally not part of society . . . Fairly unfair generalizations. And the same in terms of the stereotypes that sex workers get laid at their door.'

Interviewees discussed a distinct set of labels that constructed the image of 'the punter'. The labels spanned a wide spectrum of undesirable characteristics: sexual dysfunction or incompetence, social misfit, ugly, reclusive, unfashionable and incapable of attracting a woman, an inadequate sexual partner, an irresponsible father, a deceptive lover, an adulterous husband, a sexual fantasist, sadist or just insatiable and out of control. As Norman (50, married, engineering) summarizes: 'People who choose prostitutes are men in dirty raincoats and they're all fat and they're all bald and they all smell and what have you ... it's the roots of the stereotypical image.' These intricacies of human differences were bundled together in society's perceptions of the 'punter' which attacked the core of men's perceptions of their masculinity: 'People tend to think you're paying for it so you're less of a man than I am, probably, but I am not paying for it for the reason that I can't get it anywhere else. I am paying for it because I want a specialist service' (Arthur, 50, married, Army). The labels produced a multitude of stigmas derived from assumptions about inadequacies and non-normative behaviour which were internalized in the construction of the sexual self.

One strong aspect of the stigma related to conventional, gendered expectations about the 'right' type of sex. Contrary to the acclaimed sexual promiscuity and virility of the alpha male, men who buy sex are often considered to be acting against their role as the sexual instigator, accomplisher and satisfier. For example, Patrick felt that other men as well as women made different types of moral judgements about why men paid for sex based on what convention suggested were the 'normal' routes to sex:

> I still think it's taboo to sort of pay for it. The men will sort of think, well, god, why are you paying for it? You know, get a life. Most women would probably think it was morally wrong. So therefore you've got two sets of values coming in. You've got the men who say 'Well, go to a night club for god's sake, you don't need to pay for it'. And then you've got the women who would probably condemn it as something which is wrong. So I think that's where the two different values come in which is why you might wish to keep it quiet really. (Patrick, 39, long-term partner, social care)

Other interviewees pointed to how commercial sex surpassed expectations about the sanctity of sexual relations, the 'specialness' of sex that should only be found in 'relationships' and the general distaste for sex outside a conventional, monogamous commitment: 'I expect some people think you're sad because you've got to pay for sex. I expect they may well feel it devalues sex because sex should be within marriage or a loving partnership/relationship and is meaningless without' (Mikey, 38, married, IT). Different sexual lifestyles and behaviours became polarized and compared to the vision of social purity upheld by the heterosexual dyad. This process, where differences are marked out, known as separating 'us' from 'them' (Link and Phelan 2001: 370), facilitates the categorization of 'normal' and 'abnormal', 'respectable' and 'unrespectable'. The birth of the 'deviant' male punter is secured in the categorization of 'faulty persons'.

Status loss and social class

Goffman traces the process of social stigma to the construction of the 'faulty persons' who cause others to be ill at ease with their own behaviour. Men who buy sex can fall into the category of the 'discredited' when they become visibly connected to the sex industry (for instance, by being spotted entering a brothel, caught out by the wife, arrested for kerb-crawling or outed by the media). More likely, however, considering relatively few men are arrested, buying sex is not against the law and most spouses probably remain unaware, the stigma status of men who buy sex remains at the level of a 'discreditable': the stigma is invisible, known only to a few and the 'character blemish' is easier to hide. The men in my sample were mostly 'discreditables' in their everyday lives: they were affected by stigma but it was of the type that is not observable or easily identifiable but a result of internal knowledge about the self and identification as a rule-breaker and a 'deviant'.

Link and Phelan (2001: 370) note that an essential fourth component to the process of stigmatization is the experience of status loss. Even the possibility of status loss creates stigma anxiety for this group of men as their preoccupation with defending their class and status position became a defining narrative. Matthew, a 39-year-old teacher who was married and had visited massage parlours over the past five years, was acutely aware of how his social status and employment as a teacher could be affected if his identity as a client was revealed:

> As a teacher you've got to be fairly respectable and, as I say, even though I'm not ashamed other people might regard it as a subject of shame and I wouldn't bring it up in a work context at all with colleagues and certainly not with students.

Likewise, Boris, a retired accountant, engaged in his daily interactions knowing that his colleagues and bosses would frown upon his commercial sexual behaviour: 'I still work for a firm of solicitors and if they happened to know that they wouldn't be happy at all. People have been sacked for less than that. So I'm conscious.' Occupation was an important peg on which 'respectability' hung for the middle-class men in my sample. Men referred to their occupations to signify their social status, while at the same time used their social status and inferred class position to separate themselves out from others. Among the male clients there was a status hierarchy based on the types of occupational cultures where buying sex was more acceptable. Jobs were assigned a degree of 'normality' in relation to the acceptability of buying sex, concluding that some men 'risked' less and other men had more to 'lose' based on their class and status position. Steve, a 47-year-old divorced IT specialist, used occupational hierarchies and cultures to explain why 'someone like him' in a 'respectable', serious profession was breaking the rules compared to other manual jobs where sexual frivolities were expected:

> There are certain environments where you do expect they're all doing it. I mean if you were in the Navy for example or something like that – all sorts of sub-groups – you would visualize them in that world. But people like me who are sort of dullards and scientists type people, you know, living in a respectable world, you wouldn't expect it, to be honest. I mean computer programmers are not like salesmen.

Those in higher status jobs or responsible positions in society were more concerned with managing information about themselves because they did not want the discrepancy between their 'virtual social identity' (that which they presented to others), and their 'actual social identity' (their real self) to be known. The concern with hiding the discrepancy between these two forms of social identity was usually more acute among men who were protective over their marriage, their family life and their occupational status:

> I think that if I was found out that would be devastating. I think that it would most likely spell the end of the marriage. I'm quite sure that my wife would be appalled because she is a very upstanding person. She's also quite religious. I think that she would be absolutely appalled and certainly wouldn't want me near her in the future if she was contemplating resuming relations with me. But more than likely it would mean that I'd have to leave home. I think it would be as bad as that. (Tony, 55, married, pilot)

> I certainly wouldn't tell anybody because it's far too big a risk. It's still looked down upon by a large number of people – most people probably – and as I say I live in a world which is thoroughly respectable and I think I'd be hard pushed to even guess at anybody who might be a punter. (George, 58, married, IT)

The fear of losing 'respectability' was a fear of rejection, of bringing disgrace upon their own character and shame on their family and spouse, and of losing the moral authority they exercised through social, cultural, economic and symbolic capital.

To understand the process of stigma for men who buy sex, 'discourses of respectability' (Skeggs 1997) are central to the production of categorizations and the labelling of 'deviance'. The middle-class men that made up this sample of clients fiercely defended their status and 'respectability', reinforcing that 'respectability is one of the most ubiquitous signifiers of class' (Skeggs 1997: 1). This was evident in several ways. Men would distance themselves from the street market that was associated with disease, contagion and vulgarity. Middle-class clients did not want to be associated with working-class characteristics such as threatening behaviour and conducting oneself without respect and decorum. Most interviewees made statements that distinguished the 'respectable' and 'safe' brothels, parlours and escorts they visited, to the 'dangerous', 'unhygienic', 'pimped' streets: 'There is a big divider between street prostitution and the more straightforward brothels and parlours . . . they're more organized and more, they're more legit really, and they're cleaner and safer' (Richard, 56, divorced, media). The street market was no place for the respectable client to do business (also see Chapter 3). For the individual, the hierarchical sex markets translated into defining characteristics of the type of man that visited each market.

Men recounted feeling 'uncomfortable' and 'ill at ease' when their identity was connected with the vulgarities of the uneducated, uncouth pursuits of the working classes:

> I've been buying the *Star* recently. Buying the *Star* bothers me actually. Somebody saw me buying the *Star* at the newsagent near where I worked. That bothers me . . . People expect me to be a certain type of person. I think the *Star*'s associated with like . . . well people not like me. You see the sex ads and they assume that you're some sort of pervert or something. And you're not. And that bothered me as much as anything. (Vernon, 50, separated, teacher)

Some men who were not in a conventional relationship looked down on those who 'cheated' and 'deceived' their partners, describing such behaviour as disgraceful and not the 'right' way to behave (see below). The classification of 'respectable' and 'unrespectable' was reinforced by men's own hierarchies and perceptions of the sex industry. There were clear definitions of 'respectable' forms of purchasing sex and 'respectable' sex workers, and those that were unacceptable and warranted control. The defence of 'respectability' took many forms, but what was defended was a social position that infiltrated all parts of their personal, social, familial and emotional life.

Guilt and 'crossing the line'

While there were varied responses to the threat of one's social identity being affected by the stigma of buying sex, the influences of social disapproval on the self were expressed by all of the participants. What Goffman termed 'ego or felt identity', the feelings a person has about their own identity, was often affected by the 'discreditable' stigma. Dealing with harsh images and the misunderstanding of others about their lives and relationships produced a range of negative emotions, most notably guilt.

Goffman (1963) pointed out simply that where there is any change in role, status or relationship, there may well be an alteration in the person's self-conception. Where rules are broken, guilt or remorse may result, and guilt may turn to shame. The guilt can manifest as a form of personal disorganization as rule-breaking jolts with the expectations of behaviour. Problems occur for the individual's interaction order when social disadvantages develop through stigmatization.

Moving from the status of non-stigmatized to stigmatized was expressed repeatedly by interviewees by the phrase 'crossing the line'. This idiom was used by several participants and is also one I observed in threads on message boards. Such a phrase referred to a boundary that had been broken because the intimate act of sex had been merged with the world of commercial monetary exchange. The extract below is taken from an online message board. A man explains his first experience of buying sex, revealing the stigma he confronted:

> I did feel mixed up and weird for a bit because I had crossed a big line. I was now one of those evil men who frequents prostitutes – scum of the earth, all the papers say so. It took me a while to realize that my instincts were right and the papers were wrong. I walked in there a decent bloke and I came out still a decent bloke. Once I got that, there was a huge sense of freedom and relief. I had been trapped in a life with no sex, and suddenly I was living a life where I could have it again, and without having to try and get somebody drunk or persuade them I'm worthy.

A fellow client responded to this thread by describing why engaging with sex workers often brought with it difficult feelings because of the hidden and secretive nature of the activity:

> . . . for most people punting is something you do on your own. Generally, it is not something you bring up at a dinner party, or discuss with your boss or work colleagues, friends and family. It can

therefore take some time for it to settle comfortably in your mind. That empty feeling is vulnerability.

In several interviews there was a comparison made between the acceptability of other parts of the sex industry, such as buying sex in the entertainment districts of Amsterdam, sexual services as part of stag party rituals and the mundane everyday-ness of lap dancing bars. Anthony (31, long-term partner, customer services) describes how 'prostitution' breaks rules of acceptability despite the dismantling of barriers around commercial sex through the commonplace occurrence of erotic dancing:

> On many a company's night out we've ended up in a lap dancing bar. And it's a bit of a laugh. It's all lads together. Whereas, prostitution is that one step further. It's more, more acceptable nowadays, but it's still, it's still that extra step. It's just crossing that boundary, you know.

This feeling of 'crossing the line' became a less prominent emotion, fading over time, as men became more comfortable with their identity as a 'punter', secure in their strategies of managing the stigma and concealing information to protect their 'respectability'. Those who were in long-term committed relationships were faced with irreconcilable negative consequences of rule-breaking.

Adulterous guilt and felt identity

Of the 18 men who were married, 13 said their wives did not know about their extra-martial sexual behaviours and that there would be serious consequences if this information was to be found out:

> If she ever found out, then of course that's it, I don't think I'd be in a relationship any more, but yeah you do, I do feel guilty, especially if it's on TV or people make comments about it then you are in a bit of a – well, my dark side is that I have engaged in that myself. (Morris, 55, married, academic)

Terry (68, married, lawyer) had been married for over forty years and for the last twenty had been buying the services of escorts regularly, spending on average £500 each month. Terry had made a decision to stay in his marriage and defended his double life, based on secrecy, charades and lies, which in turn produced difficult emotions:

What I feel guilty about is not the infidelity bit because I think the alternative could have been the marriage to end but the lies that are necessary to keep it confidential. I think its absolutely essential if you love your wife as I do, not to let her find out because I think the people that decide to bare their soul and tell all are doing the cruellest thing they could possibly do. But going down the route that I have chosen to go down you have an absolute duty to do everything you possibly can to avoid discovery and it's the deception that is the bit I feel least happy about.

Of the eight interviewees with long-term partners, two said their partners knew about their relationships with sex workers. Even in liberal relationships where men suggested their partners were relaxed about multiple sexual partners, there were other family commitments that induced guilt: 'On the monetary side of it I – I've got two children who live with me. And I do feel sometimes guilty about spending a hundred and twenty pound an hour and not spending the money on them' (Darren, 36, long-term partner, customer services).

The majority of men (8/12 single, 6/9 divorced or separated, 4/4 widowed) in the sample who were not in a committed conventional relationship said they would stop buying sex if they developed such a relationship. These men only engaged in the sex industry because they were not in a conventional relationship and maintained that, for them, buying sex was incompatible with a steady, loving relationship:

It would cease because the reason for me to punt would cease to exist. I would have companionship, maybe I would have more regular sex. Also I'm a traditional kind of person, I could never envisage cheating on a woman. I know there are probably punters out there and the vast majority of them are probably married, that disturbs me. I'm a single person, I know what my reasons are and they're fairly rational ones and to most well-adjusted rational people they would be okay. But as for the married men, I sometimes think that really what they should be doing is sorting out their own relationships with their wives. Don't get me wrong, if they want to do it they'll do it, I won't condemn them for doing it, but at the end of the day I think they really should be looking at themselves. (Michael 45, separated, public sector)

Not being in a conventional relationship often meant that any guilt about buying sex had weakened as there was no third party to consider, and the sneaking around was not as pronounced. Vernon (50, separated, teacher) had started visiting parlours over the past three years after he separated from his wife five years previously: 'I made a decision I wanted to do it. And I made the conscious decision. And I can live with that decision. I don't have any problem about it at all. I have no qualms about what I do at all. And nobody else knows.' Paulo (54, married, property developer) had been buying sex for thirty years and said that he and his wife had an agreement about additional sexual relationships. As a result, Paulo was able to describe his engagement in the sex industry as 'guilt-free':

> Maybe I ought to feel guilty but I don't, I don't. I don't feel guilty. I mean maybe I should feel guilty about spending the money but it's something that I can afford. If I didn't spend it on this I'd spend it on something else. So I don't feel guilty about the money, I don't feel guilty about you know, the – the nature of my relationship with my wife is such that this wouldn't make any difference if you see what I mean. I mean if I felt guilty, it's not because I felt guilty in the sense that I'm cheating on my wife if you see what I mean. I'd feel much more guilty if I started having a relationship with someone than if I was doing this.

For men like Vernon and Paulo, despite an absence of guilt, their 'felt identity' was still affected by the social disapproval attached to buying sex. Despite Paulo's account of 'guilt-free' sexual consumption, his behaviours and strategies for 'being careful' suggests the stigmatic dynamics influence his everyday interactions and the presentation of the self:

> I do all my web browsing from my office. So I'm quite fortunate because I've got my own office and I'm self-employed – I mean I have a secretary but I'm self-employed, so my PC is in my office. I don't do any of it at home. I have a separate mobile phone. I have separate e-mail accounts and I just try and be as careful as possible.

While Paulo displays 'good adjustment' to the stigma, the reality may be a 'phantom normalcy' (Goffman 1963: 122) which intersects with the politics of his own identity. Although buying sex was acceptable in his marriage, Paulo continued to be stigmatized as a 'discreditable' because of social disapproval. Paulo, like all the men in the study, designed their purchasing habits through stigma management strategies, taking great care not to be identified as a 'punter' in the physical world. Subjective reactions to one's own 'blemishes of character' reflect what the individual feels about the stigma and influenced the strategies men employed to manage the information.

Managing stigma

Controlling the flow of information for the 'discreditable' is the basic interactional problem. Goffman (1963: 42) summarizes this predicament in the statement 'to display or not to display; to tell or not to tell; to let on or not to let on; to lie or not to lie; and in each case to whom, how and where'. Such a quandary of disclosure can become a life-long preoccupation for anyone involved in the sex industry, even after they have quit (Sanders 2007a). Similar to the passing off strategies of sex workers (Sanders 2005a: 124/136), men who engage in the underworld economy of commercial sex are masters of 'passing off' one identity while concealing another.

The concealment of information through the management and control of personal information about the stigma was a significant aspect of men's lives. How they researched, negotiated, prepared for visits, decided on a location and market, chose an individual sex worker or parlour and organized their daily events incorporated the concealment of information and the management of stigma. Minimizing the evidence of stigma was performed through 'covering' (Goffman 1963: 103). For instance, fake business trips, meetings and colleagues were invented for a variety of audiences to mask the real activities of engaging in the sex industry. Terry (68, married, lawyer) takes his regular sex worker on short city breaks several times a year and masks this with his ordinary professional and social calendar and routine. A forthcoming weekend away with his regular was covered by a golfing holiday with old friends:

The nature of my work meant that I was away quite a bit. Even now the work determines I can invent a case in Manchester if I need to but for quite a while I was getting lots of invitations to retirement parties and retirement dinners and I could invent another retirement anytime I wanted ... But I have always been aware of the need to plan. If it was something I'd planned in advance I'd put a note in my wife's diary, like this trip to Spain, when I was going to be away and where I was going to be. I even put the golf clubs in the boot of the car.

Passing off was closely tied to the importance of maintaining a respectable identity and keeping up appearances with different audiences. While the day-to-day involvement in the sex industry could be concealed through passing and covering strategies, there were mental strategies to manage the stigma that affected the thought processes of the clients.

Compartmentalization

The importance of keeping information hidden and the role of secrecy to balance and control information divided the front and back stages of men's lives. One of the most prolific paths to personal adjustment to the stigma of buying sex was that of separating out different forms of sexual and intimate relations. Living a 'double life' both physically and psychologically was described in several ways: 'I suppose I sort of create a mental partition' (Edward, 38, long-term partner, engineering); 'I have got my life in two parts. I have got my punting life which I keep completely separate from the other life' (Sol, 58, widower, self-employed); 'I regard what I do, seeing escorts, that's my private life, that's my private little area which is mine and mine alone' (Howard, 49, married, academic); 'I differentiate my life into different categories' (Alan, 59, married, retired). Discourses of privacy, separation and distance between activities were strong strategies that enabled men to move in both worlds without either of them colliding or causing psychological chaos or repercussions for normative relationships.

Through various processes of separating off their commercial relationships from marriage, family, work and 'normal' life, men were able to continue the double life without the two worlds overlapping:

> I think I have got this sort of area of my life quite boxed off if you like and I know why I am doing it and I am not looking for anything sort of extra if you like, so I think I have got it under control I suppose. (Murphy, 28, single, sales)

> I usually compartmentalize my life anyway to the extent that, sometimes, I will go home with like one or two important work phone calls to make and forget all about them once you get home. So actually having that sort of mind means it is reasonably easy to maintain, for the want of a better word, a double life. I suppose keeping the secret hasn't been a problem and you know occasionally just issues of guilt and disappointment on behalf of my partner sort of do come to the surface. (Paul, 56, married, retired bank manager)

Despite these stringent methods of separating out the 'deviant' activities from the rest of their everyday lives, there were other social settings where men were able to disclose their 'discreditable' status, acknowledge their 'difference' and not be chastised or judged.

Social solidarity and the construction of stigma

Phenomenological sociology explores the meanings that social actors place on their lives through the individual subjective reality that is produced through their engagement with and understanding of the socio-cultural world. Subjective realities intersect with objective realities which form the individual's interpretation of reality. Through this process of interpretation, reality becomes a social construction (Berger and Luckmann 1976). Holzman and Pines (1982: 96) draw on a phenomenological framework: 'The structure of the shared reality of the social world is held together by continual exchange of meanings held in common.' This way of understanding the world is a useful lens when understanding how men who buy sex interact with each other. How men interact with each other in the sex industry shows partly how their shared realities and subjective interpretations of their identity are constructed.

Revealing of how clients construct their socio-cultural world, one finding in my study that was different to Goffman's assessment of how people manage stigma is that 'discreditables' do not always display ambivalence to others like themselves. Solidarity and loyalties among men who buy sex is visible in certain social settings. Norman, a 50-year-old, married engineer who had bought sex for the past 25 years, directly links the Internet community to a reduction in feeling stigmatized:

> Just makes me feel I am not alone in what I am doing. There are other people out there with the same desires . . . Like I say in the last six or seven years Internet time, yes I've felt a lot better about it whereas before I used to feel a bit dirty, grubby, ashamed and worried about the stigma. I am less concerned about that now.

In the face of adverse publicity about the morality of buying sex and the type of men who buy sex, new sexual cultures of communication are forged. Chapter 4 explains how virtual spaces on the Internet have become a central meeting place where stigma becomes dissipated and connections are made with others who experience similar marginalizations. Virtual relations demonstrate how male clients come together online and face to face to create solidarity. Durkheim's observations of how rituals create social solidarity among members of an 'in group' that reaffirm shared values and a shared reality are clearly evident in the online sex work community:

> I think the Internet is a very important medium I guess for that kind of information. Because it does make you feel a lot less like you are doing something that's the worst thing in the world, which if you read say the *Daily Hate* oh sorry the *Daily Mail* or any of its ilk you know you'd think these people had never had sex wouldn't you? (Alistair, 30, long-term partner, IT)

Because of the ability to plug into what's happening online, otherwise you're just an isolated person who has nothing but their fantasies and assumptions about what's going on. You can't ask a mate, so it's just you on your own, standing in the cold in the street looking at something that's – a sign saying 'sauna' or whatever. Or perhaps going to Amsterdam, to a window or something which is – you know, I just wouldn't want to do that kind of thing. (Tom, 60, widower, social care)

Yet in many ways, the safety of Internet communication where there is a definite reduction in stigma is a false world which is protected from the heavy weight of the taboo surrounding buying sex. There is another objective reality in the physical world that influences men's meanings and processes of being 'a john'.

When men meet in person in sex work venues, the shared reality of the taboo and social disapproval is reinforced by their mutual silence and absence of communication: 'The guys that I have seen in communal lounges, apart from the guy who I knew that I went with they are very quiet, they don't make conversation or eye contact. When there is another guy in, it is awkward, you know they don't, the guys they don't like to speak' (Brian, 37, married, manual worker). A strong taboo persists that means men politely ignore each other in saunas and massage parlours despite the Internet developing new methods of networking. Hart (1998: 107) describes how in the barrios in Spain, the venue is both a sociable environment (men will drink at the bars, play cards, pass the time of day together) and a place to buy sex, yet the group remains fragmented. There are several reasons why men may not communicate with each other in a commercial sex setting:

- *Competition*. Men are visiting the same sex workers and there is a silence around having sex with the same woman.
- *Preserving the illusion*. Conversing with another client who has had a similar experience and routine with the same sex worker threatens the illusion, 'authenticity' or fantasy of the sexual encounter, or the belief that the client–sex worker relationship is intimate or special (as described in Chapter 5).
- *Taboo*. Men who buy sex are very aware of the taboo surrounding the sex industry and encroaching on the privacy of others could perhaps be disrespectful. Not engaging in conversation acknowledges the desire for secrecy and anonymity in a face-to-face scenario.
- *Stigma*. Men who see each other in sex work venues are sharing in the knowledge that they are both 'punters' and both carry the stigma. Acknowledging each other in the venue is drawing attention to the 'discredited' status of the stigma as their character blemish becomes

visible: 'On two occasions I have met people in parlours whom I knew. But the men were there for the same purpose as me so I said "hello" they said "hello" and that was it'. (Billy, 43, married, manufacturing)

The silence and lack of communication in the sex work venues between clients is both a recognition and expression of social solidarity while at the same time reinforcing the stigma surrounding non-normative behaviour and resistance against the (sexual) value system. In other social settings, values and etiquette also induce social solidarity among men about the taboos of buying sex and engaging in paid extra-marital sex. Outside of the venues, men who engage in buying sex do have access to meeting each other through certain work cultures where buying sex is acceptable, if not normalized. Jeff (57, married, senior management) described how international business meetings often came with the additional services of a sex worker sent to the hotel room whether requested or not: 'Guys that I work with, other senior managers, when we are away we're all men of the world . . . It's not unusual. I think that holds up no matter where I've been in the world, whether it's in Europe or America.' Work colleagues often understood the nature of the 'entertainment' on such business trips and it was described as normalized in this world of corporate business. The examples of sharing in the knowledge of being a 'punter' while at the same time maintaining silence and distance demonstrates the 'in-group' mentality of clients and how the stigma frames their face-to-face interactional order. Clients operate in what Schutz (1967) calls 'sub-universes' or 'multiple realities' that feed directly into their own subjective realities and are cultural resources that are drawn upon when constructing the self.

Coming out to friends

To reveal information about the stigma has major implications for how different audiences will react to one's personal identity. The strategic management of information is important for 'the discreditable': choosing who to tell, when, how and the possible consequences can be a long-term preoccupation. A third of the men in my sample had decided to tell someone close to them about visiting sex workers:

I told one person who's my oldest friend and his reaction was – he said 'well, obviously when you say that, I've got a lot of prejudices come up but also what comes up is what I know about you and I know whatever you do, you do it effectively. So I'd rather go with what I know about you than the prejudices'. It was quite a big decision. I felt I needed to tell at least one person as a kind of witness in a way. It's almost a spiritual thing to be known for who you are to at least one other human being. To be straight with that one person so at least they know. (Tom, 60, widower, social care)

Tom describes the weightiness of the decision to tell someone very close to him about his sexual habits and the importance of others bearing witness to his self-exploration. Yet at the same time, the decision to 'tell all' was met with prejudices that needed further explanation. Others described how they had attempted to investigate the reactions of their male friends:

> I told them to test them. I told them a bit of information, as a bit of a tester really. Just to see what was said and just laughed it off really. I know them quite well. And I – I thought I wouldn't have a problem with them. But I was still a bit dubious as to what their perception would be. And they knew my circumstances and knew how I felt and you know and accepted it really. (Daniel, 41, single, teacher)

'Coming out' to their close male friends about their non-normative sexual antics is a process interviewees described as burdensome. Moving their status from 'discreditable' to 'discredited' among significant people in their lives was pondered upon throughout the career of the client. As Tom acknowledged above, something that becomes significant in one's personal life often needed to be witnessed by others as a form of acceptance and normalization. The burden of secrecy and the desire to tell was integral to the 'felt identity' of some men who were uncomfortable with the silence and deception and were driven to 'reveal all' as a process of self-acceptance as well as gaining some form of social acceptance.

The normal deviant

Stigma is something that the majority of people experience in some way, leading Goffman to suggest that stigma is about difference and not deviance. Goffman preferred the term 'normal deviance' to describe the processes of social categorization that take place because the majority of people will be affected by the consequences of rule-breaking, as 'rules' and the norms of behaviour change over time. Goffman (1963) concluded in the epic *Stigma* that the commonplace status of those who participate fully in the social order but also rule-break is that of both normal and 'deviant', therefore the singular category of 'deviant' was not a helpful concept through which social processes could be understood. Experiencing stigma is a result of resisting convention and not necessarily breaking formal laws but a manifestation of wider social change. The acknowledgement of sexual differences without constructing sexual 'deviance' has historically been problematic as conservative institutions such as religion and the state have sought to reinforce a set of common sexual ideals. For instance, even where homosexuality (and prostitution) was accepted as private moral practice by the Wolfenden Committee, the public displays of such sexual difference was outlawed as indecent and morally unacceptable. Half a century ago, social policy accepted homosexuality in private as it was considered a 'self-regulatory, harmless, assimilable and accidental difference' while public displays were considered 'a flaunting, danger-ous, unassimilable and supplementary difference' (Smith 1994: 207, cited in Carabine 2004: 20). The annual celebrations of gay pride and the increasing openness of gay culture in the West has seen the private and public acceptance of gay sexualities assimilated as the 'threat' of homosexuality declines as a result of increased acceptance, understand-ing and social movements around sexual politics (see Kates and Belk 2001).

Stigma dynamics are part of a wider process of change. The 'punter' experiences a stigma related to his sexual behaviour that is one manifestation from a broader spectrum of sexual stigmas. Sexual difference is perhaps one of the most common experience most of us can relate to. Our sexual experiences, lives and feelings have not gone according to 'plan' but have in some way deviated from or not lived up to the norm. Whether it be losing one's virginity, learning how 'to do' sex, attractions to the same sex, being cheated or being a cheater, not following the expected relationship trajectory, or simply not having sex, social and cultural constructs around sexual 'difference' readily merge into social sexual stigma. The ideal templates of sexual conventionality are often something that we all wrestle with at some point in our histories.

Where sexual stigmas differ is in the qualitative nature of the label, categorization and the consequences of the stigma. For instance, having a sexually transmitted infection and seeking medical attention brings with it momentary stigma which quickly dissipates when removed from the setting of the stigmatized 'clap clinic' (see Pryce 2004). With 'the punter' stigma, being found out or 'named and shamed' in the media can bring untold devastation which is sanctioned by the state. Even without being 'found out' the 'discreditable' stigma influences the construction of the self and persists long after men have stopped buying sex. Stigma is reinforced through legal, state and moral doctrine despite the limited difference between 'normals' and 'stigmatized' because they are from 'the same standard cloth' (Goffman 1963: 131).

Against deviance

The origin of the social disapproval against buying sex is deeply rooted in the construction of sexuality in late modernity. Dominant social discourses of heterosexual monogamy and customary sexual behaviour continue to place commercial sex at the margins of acceptability, framing the purchase of sex as a 'deviant' sexual practice outside the moral framework. Men who pay for sex are portrayed as social misfits, personally and psychologically inept and often a potential danger to women, children, family life and the broader moral fabric of society. The construction of men who pay for sex is a product of the labelling process. Becker (1963) argues that deviance is not in the act but in the categorization and construction of the behaviour through an interactive process between those labelled and agents of social control. Deviance is created by those who label certain behaviours as unwanted. The labelling process takes precedence in the construction of deviance producing consequences such as stigma, marginalization and criminalization. The nature of the definition of deviance and how certain behaviours are labelled depends on the social reaction. The social reaction is reliant upon what information is available to the public, what information is withheld and what finally becomes the dominant story. The media becomes a significant informing agency and promoter of certain types of knowledge. Many people do not have first-hand experience of men who buy sex or the street sex work environment, so their opinion of the 'deviant' behaviour, in particular kerb-crawling, is derived directly and only from the distorted media image. This populist understanding becomes the social explanation.

The processes of categorizing 'difference' and defining 'deviance' has become utilized by the state in types of criminal justice policies. Shaming is an integral part of some forms of criminal justice punishments, and the 'kerb-crawler' has been the target of state sanctioned stigmatization. Individual insecurities about 'respectability' are targeted through criminal justice campaigns, notably the 'Kerb crawling costs more than you think' warning messages promoted by the Home Office (May 2007) (see Chapter 7). In this poster and radio campaign the threat of being outed by the media and shamed in public was the core deterrent and sanction. The message that 'kerb-crawling' is wrong, and implicitly that buying sex is generally unacceptable and will be punished in several humiliating ways, attacks the 'respectability' of middle-class men, threatening to reduce their status at a personal and community level. Just as working-class women's sexual 'deviance' and lack of 'respectability' has historically been reproduced through linking their sexuality with the street (Skeggs 1997: 47), middle-class men's fears of losing 'respectability' have become the new target for civilizing the classes with a view to restoring the sexual and social order. Within this objective lies the rhetoric of the 'deviant' sexual predator, who is a threat and danger to the community and the moral fabric of civil society. The justification for criminalization and 'othering' a sexual difference is performed through the construction of stigma and the false construction of the sexual 'deviant'.

Chapter 7

Criminalizing the customer: moral messages

This chapter provides an up-to-date examination of how men who buy sex have crept onto the political and criminal justice agenda over the past two decades. The chapter examines how and why there has been a re-emphasis of who is 'the problem' within the broader conceptualization of prostitution as a social problem. After briefly considering the history of recent legislation, I critique the Home Office consultation documents, *Paying the Price* and the *Coordinated Prostitution Strategy* specifically in relation to how men who buy sex have been positioned, the partial information used to develop policy and the implications of the criminalization agenda. The anti-kerb-crawling marketing campaign and police operations in 2007 are examined and made sense of in light of the zero tolerance policy on street prostitution. Examining why kerb-crawler rehabilitation programmes have been favoured as a viable solution to eradicating street prostitution, I present a review of the effectiveness and limitations of these court diversion schemes. In this critique I identify how 'the user' has been constructed and how the government has overtly used middle-class 'respectability' as the benchmark for criminalizing male sexual behaviour and scapegoating men's sexuality for the existence of prostitution.

Re-emphasis on who is the problem

Any analysis of the history of men buying commercial sex from women demonstrates that, until fairly recently, social and legal discourses, norms and values were predicated on 'privileging male sexual desire' (Brooks-Gordon and Gelsthorpe 2003: 438). Brooks-Gordon and Gelsthorpe document how, from early civilizations through to Victorian times, there has been a historical legacy of acceptability and even encouragement of men seeking out commercial sex as a means for sexual initiation, preferable to the unhealthy self-abuse of masturbation (see Miller 1999), and largely in keeping with middle-class male sexual lifestyles. During the Victorian period of the eighteenth-century men were considered to be powerless to the advances of women and the punitive legislation of the Contagious Diseases Acts in the 1860s focused on containing the 'prostitutes' and protecting the male customers from diseases such as syphilis (Self 2003). Men were assumed to be 'innocent' in their submission to the predatory nature of 'fallen' women who lured them into their dens of inequity. Brooks-Gordon and Gelsthorpe (2003: 441) describe how the post-Second World War saw a decline in the acceptability of engaging with commercial sex as knowledge of public health, a focus on the sanctity of marriage and the 'sexual revolution' changed ideas about sex and the values attached to sexual interaction. While Chapters 8 and 9 discuss the profound cultural, political and social changes that have reignited the sex industry, I will discuss here how the law is a powerful mechanism that frames how men who buy sex are treated.

Drawing the client into the law

The 1956 Sexual Offences Act remains somewhat of an influence on the current-day legal regulation of prostitution. This Act was pushed through Parliament as a consolidation Act during the time the Wolfenden Committee was still debating what should be done about 'prostitution' and 'homosexuality' (Self 2003). This Committee demonstrated a desire from the libertarians to prevent the state meddling in the private morality of sexuality and it was only the visible street prostitution that the Wolfenden Committee found an irritant and worthy of legislation. Protecting the public from the nuisance of street walking was the main intention of the Wolfenden Report (1957) as there was no inclination to make the sale or purchase of sex illegal. Indeed, a loophole was left open in the law to allow an individual woman to legally sell sex alone from her own premises.

While the domain of commercial sexual services, albeit out of sight, was preserved there was a gender bias in both the debate and the application of the law. The Wolfenden Report (1957) left the men who sought out sexual services completely out of the picture, instead favouring the criminalization of women involved in street prostitution by creating the offences of soliciting and loitering. The term 'common prostitute' was written into the law in the 1959 Street Offences Act, which presupposes that women charged with this offence are guilty. Contravening international human rights laws, this term still influences how women are addressed and treated in court and labelled by society. The Criminal Justice and Immigration Bill 2007, proposes to amend the Street Offences Act 1959 by substituting the term 'common prostitute' with 'person' for the offence of loitering and soliciting. However, the gendered term, 'prostitute', has historical legacies in law, religion and culture that will no doubt supersede any change in legal jargon.

At the time of the Wolfenden Report, men who were looking for a commercial liaison were duly considered to be pursuing their 'natural' biological urges and indeed 'rights'. The Archbishop of Canterbury, at the time of the debate, boldly took 'the old-fashioned view ... that men have every right to a reasonable supply of prostitutes and should not in any way be restrained from resorting to them' (Hansard, House of Lords Debates. 206. 4 December 1957 – quoted in Haste 1992: 174). The view taken that men were to be exonerated in their pursuit of what is only 'natural' while women are the conniving profiteers drew on long-established theological and medical ideologies of the natural sexual urges of man. A Royal Commission report in 1871 stated firmly who the culprits in the exchange were:

> We may at once dispose of [any recommendation] founded on the principle of putting both parties to the sin of fornication on the same footing by the obvious but not less conclusive reply that there is no comparison to be made between prostitutes, and men who consort with them. With the one sex the offence is committed as a matter of gain; with the other it is an irregular indulgence of a natural impulse. (Cited in Goodall 1995: 47)

Historically, men 'who consort with prostitutes' were absent from moral debate, political agendas, social policy intervention and policing practice until the 1980s. As the sex markets changed in shape and form, leading to a reduction in the traditional street prostitution market as women became less visible and more sophisticated about advertising and negotiating with their clients, the 'problem' or 'target' also shifted. Since the 1980s, there has been a repositioning of men who buy sex as 'the problem'.

Repositioning the client

The changes that occurred to the prostitution laws, and specifically the introduction of the campaign to criminalize the client, can be understood within the wider political ideological vision of reinstalling conservative morals, citizenship duties and a specific code of behaviour based on conservative values. Sawyer *et al.* (1998) note that the move towards arresting the client came as a result of three separate processes. First, the feminist movement campaigned for equity in law and critiqued laws that blamed women for their own situation, preferring to shift the blame to the men who were providing the 'demand' for sexual services. This radical feminist agenda has had success in some Northern European countries. In Sweden, the radical feminist philosophy that prostitution is violence against all women has successfully infiltrated government thinking and has been the main argument for changing the laws to make the client the criminal.[1] These discourses have not been found in other European countries such as the Netherlands (see Pakes 2003) that lifted the ban on brothels in 2000 and Germany where a 'sex as work' discourse was adopted through employment and labour laws in 2002 (Laskowski 2002). In the UK, although there is little evidence for the presence of a strong feminist movement that has called for equal laws, what has been evident is the rejection of the sex industry as a legitimate institution in society. Prostitution has been framed as inherently wrong, damaging and something to be eradicated in recent government policy. While allowing the activity of commercial sex to remain legal, the government have framed many of the activities such as advertising, owning a brothel and soliciting on the street as 'anti-social' that cause only nuisance and distress to local communities.

The second reason for the refocus towards men relates to broader community and police relations. Kerb-crawlers, alongside sex workers, have received the brunt of local activism from upset community residents who claim their quality of life is deeply affected by prostitution on 'their' doorstep. Activism against prostitution is accompanied by media-fuelled stereotypes of clients as sexual predators and perverts warranting increased police attention and official policy response (Hubbard 1998). Evidence detailed below highlights how the voice of the community in some areas has shown abhorrence to both the sex worker and the client in some towns and cities in the UK (Williams 2005).

Third, conservative attitudes towards sex and sexuality have dominated politics since the 1990s, resulting in a shift away from gay sexuality as 'deviant' to other sexualities and behaviours as the target for moralizing. In the UK, there has been increased acceptance of non-heterosexual lifestyles and partnerships. Significant changes such as enabling civil partnerships between same-sex couples and the legal adoption of children by gay individuals and couples are a testament to a shift in tolerance of a spectrum of sexualities and lifestyles (see Carabine 2004; Scott 1998).[2] Acceptance of gay sexuality may have come at the cost of rejecting other forms of sexual behaviour that continue to be cast as abnormal, unpleasant and not to be tolerated but instead controlled. As a result, prostitution has become one of the new 'urban disorders' that is the target of sexual intolerance.

In their wider review of what they term 'the problem of sex' that has been constructed around all aspects of daily life, Phoenix and Oerton

(2005: 3) examine formal and informal methods of sexual regulation that aim to 'keep sex under wraps, to constrain and control what was perceived as its potentially threatening and dangerous aspects'. Analysing documents from official and quasi-official discourses on law and order from a whole range of government, professional and organizational agencies, the authors examine the 'regulatory frameworks' that address 'the problem of sex' in contemporary Britain. Relevant to how sex work has been problematized over the past two decades are the concepts of 'consent' and 'force'. Men who buy sex from those under 16 are rightly considered sexual offenders and criminals as young people cannot be considered of an age where voluntary consensual decisions can be made about involvement in prostitution. Phoenix and Oerton (2005: 94) identify that interpretations become skewed when conceptions of exploitation and abuse are applied to all types of relationships that men have with women who are involved in prostitution. A recent example of this blanket application to all men involved in the sex industry automatically as abusers can be found in the call by ministers to charge men who have sex with women who are trafficked into prostitution with rape.[3] Such a simplistic approach offered as a gesture to protect and stem the abuse of women in prostitution takes no account of the organization of coercion and the control of forced prostitution which may not be evident to an unsuspecting client. In official discourses, men involved in organizing sex work or intimate partners of sex workers are all constructed as abusive pimps, coercers and exploiters. Where men involved in commercial sex are only understood on this extreme level, there is no room for understanding men who buy sex as being anything other than abusive.

Phoenix and Oerton (2005: 76) make the point that official discourse is seen to be doing something constructive about the 'problem of men' who are involved in the sexual and financial exploitation of women and children through prostitution precisely because of the construction of a discourse that frames women as victims in prostitution (also see Kantola and Squires 2004). By rejecting that women can voluntarily choose to be involved in prostitution, men who buy sex are immediately cast as wielding power over innocent, vulnerable women. Academics have also been involved in creating the problem of prostitution. For instance, Matthews (1984: 103) exaggerates the issue by stating that 'kerb-crawling has for some time been a national problem of major proportions', supporting such a statement by referring to only four cities where residents have overtly campaigned against the activity. Critiquing a report, *Prostitution in the Street* (1984) by the Criminal Law Revision Committee, Matthews (1984: 106/108) supports the proposed introduction of further legislation that criminalizes kerb-crawlers but argues for a review of the legislation on soliciting so that the offences surrounding nuisance caused by prostitution are merged to apply to both male clients and female prostitutes. Appealing to arguments of gender equality or neutrality in law to manage prostitution is highly speculative because they ignore the gendered social reasons that mean women enter into sex work. The momentum slowly gathered over the past two decades that has constructed the problem of prostitution around 'dirty and dangerous men' and 'vulnerable female victims' distorts the complexity of relationships and the organization of the sex industry. Reframing *who* is the problem in prostitution has resulted in some significant legal changes that have facilitated the current criminalization agenda.

The kerb-crawler as public nuisance

The role of the law in regulating private sexual behaviour and relationships has been increasing since the reduction of the libertarian views evident in postwar modernity. Kantola and Squires (2004) examine the official discourses that have surrounded the prostitution debates since the 1980s in the UK by looking closely at the rhetoric produced in policy debates. Examining parliamentary debates and newspaper reports, Kantola and Squires conclude that (1) there is an absence of a sex work discourse; (2) the public discourse in relation to kerb-crawling is dominant; and (3) there is a dominant moral order discourse in relation to trafficking. Concentrating on the second finding, the authors retrace how the debate on kerb-crawling during the 1980s and mid-1990s was fuelled by a desire to criminalize kerb-crawlers. The authors document how the media constantly connected prostitution with organized crime, deviant sexual morals and values to form a public nuisance discourse that targeted both street sex workers and kerb-crawlers as undesirables to be removed.

In the House of Commons there were few criticisms of this initial attempt to criminalize men looking for sex on the street, as unfounded statements linking the activity to crime were used to justify why kerb-crawlers should be targeted (see Kantola and Squires 2004: 82). In the 1990s, the English Collective of Prostitutes (1997) set up a campaign against the new proposed legislation against kerb-crawlers (Campaign Against Kerb Crawling Legislation). A small victory was gained as they were successful in getting the law amended to include 'the need to prove persistence, annoyance and nuisance' before any conviction for kerb-crawling can be substantiated.

These debates that promoted the criminalization of the kerb-crawler succeeded in the 1985 Sexual Offences Act that marked the first piece of legislation to include the offence of kerb-crawling. This Act introduced two offences. First, that of 'kerb-crawling' as soliciting another person from a 'motor vehicle' or 'in a street or public place' that is 'likely to

d towards street prostitution, organized crime linked to
the sexual exploitation of young people and protecting
from anti-social behaviour.

sultation document there was no acknowledgement of the
he sex industry, the professionalization of some aspects of
ets or the diversity of men who buy sex and their capability
sibly. In the document it was never recognized as legitimate
ision of sexual services could be considered work for some
en who were working voluntarily under certain circumstan-
the review process began from the stance that prostitution
to all with no room for difference, diversity or agency. As
Oerton (2005: 77) note, five centuries of tolerant attitudes
stitution were quashed with this consultation document as
was framed as a 'problem' in need of state intervention
criminal justice system.

o critiqued *Paying the Price* noted that limited research had
upon and that a vast range of empirical studies, in particular
men who buy sex, had been glossed over or simply ignored
rdon 2005). In addition, there was no acknowledgement of
l backdrop through which prostitution has been managed in
the legacies that were being challenged were not acknowl-
Soothill and Sanders 2004). It was as if the government was
prostitution policy for the first time. Equally, *Paying the Price*
ount of the rapid and radical changes in sexual behaviour,
d relationship patterns or the dominant sexualized nature of
ry Western culture. There was no wider sociological reflec-
commodification of bodies (not just women's but men's and
as a normalized part of consumer culture and leisure time
2006). The wider content of why women sold sex (notably
d exclusion) or why men buy sex, were not investigated or
n any considerations for viable policy solutions. Discussing
l sex and the possibilities for regime change outside the
ntext of sexual behaviour in late modernity ignored the reality
ject and the social relationships and structures within which
especially the desire to purchase sex, occurs.

a contradiction in terms

ltation can be critiqued specifically in relation to its treatment
d understanding of men who buy sex. The language of the
firmly states the position of the government: men who buy sex
d to as 'the user' (Home Office 2004: 16). This suggests that the
ice wrote the report with only condemnation for men who
ex rather than understanding purchasing behaviour as part of

cause annoyance to the person . . . or nuisance to the other persons in the neighbourhood' (s. 1 Sexual Offences Act 1985). The second offence is that of 'persistent soliciting' by a man who solicits another person in a public place for services of a prostitute (s. 2 Sexual Offences Act 1985). This offence only carried the severity of a level 3 fine (approximately £400) and was not arrestable but arranged through a letter ordering the accused to attend the magistrates' court. Case law has demonstrated that simply driving in a 'red light district' cannot be interpreted as persistent soliciting but that further intent to purchase sex must be proven (Brooks-Gordon 2006: 32). However, under the guidelines issued in the *Coordinated Prostitution Strategy*, the burden of proof may well be eroded to less compelling evidence of kerb-crawling.

During the mid-1990s the pace of the public nuisance discourse around prostitution gathered in parliamentary debates, largely due to the persistent community activism that brought the issue to MPs' surgeries. Notably at the time, Birmingham's Balsall Heath street prostitution scene experienced significant community activism championed by a group of residents who formed the Street Watch residents' organization. Hubbard (1997) comments that some aspects of this community resident action turned to vigilantism fuelled by religious doctrines and moral condemnation for those involved in prostitution. The Street Watch group in its form among the South Asian community of Balsall Heath and later the middle-class white neighbourhood of Edgbaston had both social and cultural capital that resulted in a powerful lobbying group, ensuring their moral concerns were turned into political agendas. Williams (2005) studied the same Street Watch group some years later and noted that the spectrum of resident views and actions continued to include vigilantism. Williams described how the police had difficulty controlling the residents who took on a policing role in their own neighbourhoods that was not entirely legitimate but compromised policing authorities.

The concerns raised by communities in the 1980s and 1990s were approached from a multi-agency partnership model advocated by Matthews (1984; 1986). Matthews supported a policy response that adopted a situational crime prevention approach by introducing physical changes to the street environment that would deter both sex workers and kerb-crawlers. Barriers such as road closures, alley-gating and traffic-calming measures were introduced specifically to appease residents yet took no account of the needs of sex workers or the implications this would have on their lives and safety. Such an approach brought the police and local authority together in favour of the demands of the residents but without any attention paid to the women who worked the streets. From a study I conducted in 2000 in the Birmingham area, I observed how the Street Watch campaign targeted men in their cars as they drove through the streets where sex workers walked. The uniformed residents recorded car registration numbers and took photographs of suspected kerb-crawlers and passed them on to the police. There appeared to be no criteria for judging who was a kerb-crawler and who was simply driving through the area. Men who were considered 'undesirable' in the neighbourhood were policed by the privileged, self-appointed residents.

The concerns raised initially by a small group of residents in specific parts of the country were successful in lobbying a handful of MPs which led the government to favour an increase in police powers to apprehend those suspected of kerb-crawling. Throughout these changes, local communities such as those in Soho and Liverpool who do not favour displacement or eradication have not been taken seriously (see Bellis *et al.* 2007). Under the Criminal Justice and Police Act 2001, kerb-crawling was made an arrestable offence. The Powers of the Criminal Courts (Sentencing) Act 2000 gave magistrates the powers to remove driving licences from persistent kerb-crawlers and driving disqualifications were introduced as a sanction in January 2004. After rejecting a bill for toleration zones in 2003, Scotland followed the trend to target men when kerb-crawling was made an offence under the Prostitution (Public Places) (Scotland) Act 2007, sending the clear message that the state will not tolerate the sale or purchase of street sex.[4] It was this contemporary backdrop that saw the shrinking of the libertarian philosophy as the public nuisance discourse gathered dominance and achieved legislative changes.

Strong message, minimal effect?

The message that men who buy sex from the street will not be tolerated has been gaining momentum for several years. In areas such as Middlesbrough and West Yorkshire, the police have fairly regularly (every few months) moved in on the street beats and made arrests of men looking for sex. Continual and sometimes high-profile reporting in local and national media gives the impression to the public that the police operations yield significant success and are apprehending many men through decoys and sting operations to combat a significant social 'problem'. Yet these reports in the newspapers do not provide a fair picture of the policing operations across the country. Table 7.1 identifies that the numbers of men convicted for kerb-crawling offences actually fell from 1996 to 2005. During 2005, the middle of the government consultation period, there were only 635 convictions, the lowest rate for ten years.[5]

Policing practice with regard to implementing the law on kerb-crawling is sporadic and concentrated in a few key cities. The majority

Table 7.1 Convictions for kerb-crawl

Year	1996	1997	1998	199
Number of convictions[a]	1,096	813	700	599

[a]Under s. 1, Sexual Offences Act 1985.
[b]Note that statistics for 2006 were not availab to press).
Source: RDS Office for Criminal Justice Refor

of police forces have not engaged i the past ten years. In 2005, less thai cautioned a total of 269 men for ofi police forces convicted 629 men of t conviction rates were: Metropolitan Midlands (66); West Yorkshire (45). represent the political will of a handi partnerships rather than a systemati policy. Given that a new anti-kerb-cr way since 2007 (see below), the fi probable, due to the resource-inten; ations, that the message will weigh h

The policy and political agenda

Construction of the kerb-crawler and ' gained new strength in recent years un Rarely did men who buy sex feature ii the 1990s. This section charts the rise oi of prostitution policy as a crime reduct

Paying the price: a consultation on prostitution

After calls from campaign lobby groups ting to and legislating for the Sexual Ofi announced a review of the laws and mi in 2004. The management system fo outdated and not relevant to the mod prostitution. This review was based on a set out what the Home Office considered and consultation. From the outset the coi caused by prostitution to both individu;

heavily bia; prostitution communitie

In the coi diversity of the sex mar to act respo that the prc women or i ces. Insteac was harmfi Phoenix ar towards pi prostitutio: through th

Those wl been drawi facts about (Brooks-Gc the historic the UK, ar edged (see deciding o took no ac attitudes a contempo; tion on th children's; (Attwood poverty ai included ; commerci; broader cc of the sul sex work,

'The user'

The cons and limit documem are referi Home O purchase

sexual lifestyles or considering the legitimate functions of commercial sex. 'The user' is described, from research conducted on behalf of the Home Office, as a 30-year-old male who is married in full-time employment and has no criminal record (Hester and Westmarland 2004: 143). This suggests that men who buy sex are ordinary citizens who are upstanding members of the community in terms of employment, obeying the law and fulfilling family obligations. Yet it is this 'type' of man that is clearly in the firing line for their corrupt sexual antics and 'using' women. The contradiction of the policy against men who buy sex was evident from the outset. The characteristics of these men are very different from who the policy-makers think they are.

When discussing issues relating to men who buy sex it must be remembered that it is not illegal to pay for sex, and indeed the commodification of sex was not included in the consultation as something that the government wanted to debate or legislate on. Understanding the realities of why men buy sex and considering the possible place for commercial sexual services was not written into the consultation as a legitimate concern. The Home Office did initiate an Internet questionnaire to try to capture the views of this group but the questionnaire was flawed in the sense that no questions were asked about the motivations to buy sex, the importance of commercial sex in the quality of an individual's life or the way that men act when they purchase sex. There is an overall assumption that penetrative vaginal sex is the main reason for visiting sex workers which ignores the literature on preferences and motivations (see discussion in Chapter 3). In particular, the role of emotional, psychological and social support and intimacy gained through visiting sex workers is without acknowledgement in the whole of the review process (see Chapter 5).

In the *Paying the Price* document, men who buy commercial sex are conflated with those who perpetuate criminal activities, evident in the statement: 'going to a prostitute can mean supporting the illegal drugs industry' (Home Office 2004: 12). These same views are promoted on the Home Office website in 2007, justifying the campaign against kerb-crawlers because they 'indirectly support[ing] drug dealers and abusers while, perpetuating a market fraught with violence and abuse'.[6] This simplistic assertion ignores many facts relating to the social and gendered reasons why the sex industry exists, the motivations for men seeking commercial sex, the diversity of the sex industry and the rules upon which some sex markets are organized. In the consultation document there was no attempt to differentiate between the many different types of sex markets or acknowledge that men who do not go to the street market may be fully aware of the relationship street workers often have with drugs. Those who visit indoor premises or reputable establishments are often attracted by the 'drug-free' rules that are enforced by receptionists, managers, owners and sex workers themselves (see May *et al.* 2000: 26; Sanders 2005a: 15). It is established that class A drugs are not prolific in the indoor markets (where most sex is purchased) and accounts from men suggest that drugs are not frequently offered in massage parlours. The differences between the markets and consequently patterns of behaviour among male clients should influence policy.

The public consultation period ran until November 2004. There were 861 responses to *Paying the Price* as well as a range of consultation initiatives that sought to gather the views of interested parties. There is little evidence that consultation activities were focused on obtaining the views of clients, although informants in my study did contribute lengthy responses both on an individual and collective basis. Some information about 'men who solicit women' was gathered from the evaluation studies conducted by Hester and Westmarland (2004: 143) but this remains at the level only of socio-demographic detail and numbers of arrests. The scant and ill-informed nature of the consultation document and lack of direct consultation with the so called 'demand' side of prostitution meant that any policy recommendations made from this platform would not reflect the reality of commercial sex liaisons or the complex organization of the markets. By the end of the consultation process, prostitution was redefined as a social problem, with sex workers as victims or undeserving criminals if they failed to take steps to 'exit' and those on the 'demand' side as simply sexual predators and 'users' to be controlled through the criminal justice system.

The Coordinated Prostitution Strategy: 'tackling demand'

What resulted from the consultation was a philosophy and map for the police, local authorities, community safety partnerships and other related agencies to follow when tackling prostitution in the community. The *Coordinated Prostitution Strategy* (Home Office 2006, hereafter the Strategy) included five areas of prioritization: prevention, developing 'routes out' for sex workers, ensuring justice, tackling off-street prostitution and tackling demand. This critique will focus on the last objective, although there have been several other commentaries that draw out a wider range of concerns about the intentions and impact of the Strategy (see Boynton and Cusick 2006; Brooks-Gordon 2006: 62–71; Sanders 2005c; Sanders and Campbell 2007a, 2007b).[7]

The overriding emphasis of the Strategy is to 'disrupt the sex markets' (Home Office 2006: 1). This objective has produced a two-pronged approach: to criminalize sex workers (by supplying avenues for 'exiting' alongside the criminal justice system and endorsing prosecution and sanctions such as the use of ASBOs) and a re-emphasis on enforcing laws against kerb-crawlers. There have been no new laws introduced through the Strategy; instead the existing laws outlined above against men who buy sex have been highlighted as the backbone of the enforcement strategy.[8] The tone of the Strategy is one that seeks to change attitudes: 'It is crucial that we move away from a general perception that prostitution is the "oldest profession" and has to be accepted. Street prostitution is not an activity that we can tolerate in our towns and cities' (p. 1). The Executive Summary states that the priority of 'tackling demand' is driven by 'responding to community concerns by deterring those who create the demand and removing the opportunity for street prostitution to take place' (p. 2). Communities who have voiced concern at the presence of prostitution are represented while those who coexist with diversity within their communities are not (see Pitcher et al. 2006).

To achieve a change in both attitudes and behaviour the government has favoured the Swedish model of criminalizing the purchase of sexual services without actually changing the law to make buying or selling sex illegal. The Swedish model has not been adopted entirely: the government has rejected the decriminalization approach that does not make criminals out of sex workers because of the 'magnitude and complexity of street prostitution' (p. 7) in the UK compared to the relatively small numbers of sex workers in Sweden. Despite enhancing the criminalization of sex workers, a key objective of the Strategy is to shift the focus of enforcement 'onto those who create the demand for prostitution' (p. 7) as an effective way to disrupt the sex markets. The enforcement strategy is to follow a three-staged approach: informal warning, court diversion, and prosecution.

Informal warning

The Strategy states that the first stage of the enforcement against kerb-crawlers should be an informal warning by means of a letter. By identifying car registration numbers in known 'red light districts' through the use of CCTV, warning letters about possible prosecution will be sent to men's homes. There are several issues with this initial step. It is assumed that the driver of the car is looking for sex; women may be driving the car or the car may not be owned by the driver. There may be legitimate reasons why a man is looking for a sex worker; for instance, if she has called for assistance or regularly gets a lift with a male friend or partner to and from the area. Significant assumptions are made about the 'type' of boyfriend that street sex workers have, associating only coercers and abusers as possible partners of sex workers. Finally, the implications of a husband receiving a letter about kerb-crawling when he may well be innocent could cause serious family upsets. The Strategy bases this approach as a successful deterrent only on anecdotal evidence.

The Strategy suggests that the deterrence message should be promoted through the media as well as naming and shaming individuals.

Court diversion

The second stage of enforcement is 'kerb-crawler re-education pro-grammes' funded usually by the arrestee. The Strategy states that the content of such programmes should make the individual aware of the criminal sanctions and the impact of street prostitution on local communities and women. It is stated that this option should only be available to those who are arrested for the first time. Alongside attendance at a programme, a caution will be granted which could also include an ASBO, preventing the 'offender' returning to that particular area. Evidence that these rehabilitation programmes deter men from kerb-crawling in the future is not substantiated in the Strategy, apart from brief mention of the 'Change' programme in Hampshire. This one-day programme described by the Strategy (p. 35) is based on a sex offender or violent offender model of behavioural change whereby the aim is to change behaviour by challenging actions and beliefs about the behaviour. The Strategy professes this 'Change' programme as a success solely on the basis of a low reoffending rate: of the 304 course attendees only four have reoffended. The discussion below critiques the promotion of kerb-crawler rehabilitation programmes and the problems of measuring effectiveness by reoffending rates. No account of the evaluation evidence from other rehabilitation programmes is presented by the Strategy, resulting in the government backing an intervention that has no track record of success.

Prosecution

For those already with offences for kerb-crawling or sexual offences, and those who refuse to attend a programme, prosecution is the third and final stage in the enforcement strategy. The full range of penalties will be considered and the Strategy favours disqualification from driving as a solution to stop men from reoffending. Claims that magistrates' courts inconsistently sentence kerb-crawlers are to be addressed by sentencing all similar cases on one day. The Strategy heralds New Labour's policy of public disclosure as shaming sanctions by calling for the 'naming and shaming' of men arrested for kerb-crawling to be announced through the local media. The public shaming rituals are considered to be a useful reinforcement tactic that acts as a deterrent and publicises the tough actions of the criminal justice system on any form of 'anti-social behaviour'. Although given little commentary, Anti-Social Behaviour Orders and Acceptable Behaviour Contracts are suggested as a useful tool for persistent kerb-crawling and the former have since become a regular part of the enforcement process.[9] This prioritization of enforce-

cause annoyance to the person . . . or nuisance to the other persons in the neighbourhood' (s. 1 Sexual Offences Act 1985). The second offence is that of 'persistent soliciting' by a man who solicits another person in a public place for services of a prostitute (s. 2 Sexual Offences Act 1985). This offence only carried the severity of a level 3 fine (approximately £400) and was not arrestable but arranged through a letter ordering the accused to attend the magistrates' court. Case law has demonstrated that simply driving in a 'red light district' cannot be interpreted as persistent soliciting but that further intent to purchase sex must be proven (Brooks-Gordon 2006: 32). However, under the guidelines issued in the *Coordinated Prostitution Strategy*, the burden of proof may well be eroded to less compelling evidence of kerb-crawling.

During the mid-1990s the pace of the public nuisance discourse around prostitution gathered in parliamentary debates, largely due to the persistent community activism that brought the issue to MPs' surgeries. Notably at the time, Birmingham's Balsall Heath street prostitution scene experienced significant community activism championed by a group of residents who formed the Street Watch residents' organization. Hubbard (1997) comments that some aspects of this community resident action turned to vigilantism fuelled by religious doctrines and moral condemnation for those involved in prostitution. The Street Watch group in its form among the South Asian community of Balsall Heath and later the middle-class white neighbourhood of Edgbaston had both social and cultural capital that resulted in a powerful lobbying group, ensuring their moral concerns were turned into political agendas. Williams (2005) studied the same Street Watch group some years later and noted that the spectrum of resident views and actions continued to include vigilantism. Williams described how the police had difficulty controlling the residents who took on a policing role in their own neighbourhoods that was not entirely legitimate but compromised policing authorities.

The concerns raised by communities in the 1980s and 1990s were approached from a multi-agency partnership model advocated by Matthews (1984; 1986). Matthews supported a policy response that adopted a situational crime prevention approach by introducing physical changes to the street environment that would deter both sex workers and kerb-crawlers. Barriers such as road closures, alley-gating and traffic-calming measures were introduced specifically to appease residents yet took no account of the needs of sex workers or the implications this would have on their lives and safety. Such an approach brought the police and local authority together in favour of the demands of the residents but without any attention paid to the women who worked the streets. From a study I conducted in 2000 in the Birmingham area, I observed how the Street Watch campaign targeted men in their cars as they drove through the streets where sex workers walked. The uniformed residents recorded car registration numbers and took photographs of suspected kerb-crawlers and passed them on to the police. There appeared to be no criteria for judging who was a kerb-crawler and who was simply driving through the area. Men who were considered 'undesirable' in the neighbourhood were policed by the privileged, self-appointed residents.

The concerns raised initially by a small group of residents in specific parts of the country were successful in lobbying a handful of MPs which led the government to favour an increase in police powers to apprehend those suspected of kerb-crawling. Throughout these changes, local communities such as those in Soho and Liverpool who do not favour displacement or eradication have not been taken seriously (see Bellis *et al.* 2007). Under the Criminal Justice and Police Act 2001, kerb-crawling was made an arrestable offence. The Powers of the Criminal Courts (Sentencing) Act 2000 gave magistrates the powers to remove driving licences from persistent kerb-crawlers and driving disqualifications were introduced as a sanction in January 2004. After rejecting a bill for toleration zones in 2003, Scotland followed the trend to target men when kerb-crawling was made an offence under the Prostitution (Public Places) (Scotland) Act 2007, sending the clear message that the state will not tolerate the sale or purchase of street sex.[4] It was this contemporary backdrop that saw the shrinking of the libertarian philosophy as the public nuisance discourse gathered dominance and achieved legislative changes.

Strong message, minimal effect?

The message that men who buy sex from the street will not be tolerated has been gaining momentum for several years. In areas such as Middlesbrough and West Yorkshire, the police have fairly regularly (every few months) moved in on the street beats and made arrests of men looking for sex. Continual and sometimes high-profile reporting in local and national media gives the impression to the public that the police operations yield significant success and are apprehending many men through decoys and sting operations to combat a significant social 'problem'. Yet these reports in the newspapers do not provide a fair picture of the policing operations across the country. Table 7.1 identifies that the numbers of men convicted for kerb-crawling offences actually fell from 1996 to 2005. During 2005, the middle of the government consultation period, there were only 635 convictions, the lowest rate for ten years.[5]

Policing practice with regard to implementing the law on kerb-crawling is sporadic and concentrated in a few key cities. The majority

Table 7.1 Convictions for kerb-crawling 1996–2005

Year	1996	1997	1998	1999	2000	2001	2002	2003	2004	2005
Number of convictions[a]	1,096	813	700	599	700	775	891	834	760	635

[a]Under s. 1, Sexual Offences Act 1985.
[b]Note that statistics for 2006 were not available until November 2007 (before the book went to press).
Source: RDS Office for Criminal Justice Reform[b]

of police forces have not engaged in anti-kerb-crawler operations over the past ten years. In 2005, less than half of police forces, 20 out of 43, cautioned a total of 269 men for offences of kerb-crawling. In total, 18 police forces convicted 629 men of the offence. Forces with the highest conviction rates were: Metropolitan Police (286); Cleveland (106); West Midlands (66); West Yorkshire (45). These numbers remain small but represent the political will of a handful of local authorities and policing partnerships rather than a systematic attempt to implement the law or policy. Given that a new anti-kerb-crawling campaign has been underway since 2007 (see below), the figures are likely to rise, but it is probable, due to the resource-intensive nature of enforcement operations, that the message will weigh heavier than convictions.

The policy and political agenda

Construction of the kerb-crawler and 'men who buy sex' in general has gained new strength in recent years under the New Labour government. Rarely did men who buy sex feature in parliamentary discussions until the 1990s. This section charts the rise of 'the user' in the broader context of prostitution policy as a crime reduction problem since 2004.

Paying the price: a consultation on prostitution

After calls from campaign lobby groups and those involved in contributing to and legislating for the Sexual Offences Act 2003, the Home Office announced a review of the laws and methods of managing prostitution in 2004. The management system for prostitution was considered outdated and not relevant to the modern-day issues that arose from prostitution. This review was based on a document, *Paying the Price*, that set out what the Home Office considered the prominent issues for debate and consultation. From the outset the consultation focused on the harms caused by prostitution to both individuals and communities. This was heavily biased towards street prostitution, organized crime linked to prostitution, the sexual exploitation of young people and protecting communities from anti-social behaviour.

In the consultation document there was no acknowledgement of the diversity of the sex industry, the professionalization of some aspects of the sex markets or the diversity of men who buy sex and their capability to act responsibly. In the document it was never recognized as legitimate that the provision of sexual services could be considered work for some women or men who were working voluntarily under certain circumstances. Instead the review process began from the stance that prostitution was harmful to all with no room for difference, diversity or agency. As Phoenix and Oerton (2005: 77) note, five centuries of tolerant attitudes towards prostitution were quashed with this consultation document as prostitution was framed as a 'problem' in need of state intervention through the criminal justice system.

Those who critiqued *Paying the Price* noted that limited research had been drawn upon and that a vast range of empirical studies, in particular facts about men who buy sex, had been glossed over or simply ignored (Brooks-Gordon 2005). In addition, there was no acknowledgement of the historical backdrop through which prostitution has been managed in the UK, and the legacies that were being challenged were not acknowledged (see Soothill and Sanders 2004). It was as if the government was deciding on prostitution policy for the first time. Equally, *Paying the Price* took no account of the rapid and radical changes in sexual behaviour, attitudes and relationship patterns or the dominant sexualized nature of contemporary Western culture. There was no wider sociological reflection on the commodification of bodies (not just women's but men's and children's) as a normalized part of consumer culture and leisure time (Attwood 2006). The wider content of why women sold sex (notably poverty and exclusion) or why men buy sex, were not investigated or included in any considerations for viable policy solutions. Discussing commercial sex and the possibilities for regime change outside the broader context of sexual behaviour in late modernity ignored the reality of the subject and the social relationships and structures within which sex work, especially the desire to purchase sex, occurs.

'The user': a contradiction in terms

The consultation can be critiqued specifically in relation to its treatment and limited understanding of men who buy sex. The language of the document firmly states the position of the government: men who buy sex are referred to as 'the user' (Home Office 2004: 16). This suggests that the Home Office wrote the report with only condemnation for men who purchase sex rather than understanding purchasing behaviour as part of

sexual lifestyles or considering the legitimate functions of commercial sex. 'The user' is described, from research conducted on behalf of the Home Office, as a 30-year-old male who is married in full-time employment and has no criminal record (Hester and Westmarland 2004: 143). This suggests that men who buy sex are ordinary citizens who are upstanding members of the community in terms of employment, obeying the law and fulfilling family obligations. Yet it is this 'type' of man that is clearly in the firing line for their corrupt sexual antics and 'using' women. The contradiction of the policy against men who buy sex was evident from the outset. The characteristics of these men are very different from who the policy-makers think they are.

When discussing issues relating to men who buy sex it must be remembered that it is not illegal to pay for sex, and indeed the commodification of sex was not included in the consultation as something that the government wanted to debate or legislate on. Understanding the realities of why men buy sex and considering the possible place for commercial sexual services was not written into the consultation as a legitimate concern. The Home Office did initiate an Internet questionnaire to try to capture the views of this group but the questionnaire was flawed in the sense that no questions were asked about the motivations to buy sex, the importance of commercial sex in the quality of an individual's life or the way that men act when they purchase sex. There is an overall assumption that penetrative vaginal sex is the main reason for visiting sex workers which ignores the literature on preferences and motivations (see discussion in Chapter 3). In particular, the role of emotional, psychological and social support and intimacy gained through visiting sex workers is without acknowledgement in the whole of the review process (see Chapter 5).

In the *Paying the Price* document, men who buy commercial sex are conflated with those who perpetuate criminal activities, evident in the statement: 'going to a prostitute can mean supporting the illegal drugs industry' (Home Office 2004: 12). These same views are promoted on the Home Office website in 2007, justifying the campaign against kerb-crawlers because they 'indirectly support[ing] drug dealers and abusers while, perpetuating a market fraught with violence and abuse'.[6] This simplistic assertion ignores many facts relating to the social and gendered reasons why the sex industry exists, the motivations for men seeking commercial sex, the diversity of the sex industry and the rules upon which some sex markets are organized. In the consultation document there was no attempt to differentiate between the many different types of sex markets or acknowledge that men who do not go to the street market may be fully aware of the relationship street workers often have with drugs. Those who visit indoor premises or reputable establishments are often attracted by the 'drug-free' rules that are

enforced by receptionists, managers, owners and sex workers themselves (see May *et al.* 2000: 26; Sanders 2005a: 15). It is established that class A drugs are not prolific in the indoor markets (where most sex is purchased) and accounts from men suggest that drugs are not frequently offered in massage parlours. The differences between the markets and consequently patterns of behaviour among male clients should influence policy.

The public consultation period ran until November 2004. There were 861 responses to *Paying the Price* as well as a range of consultation initiatives that sought to gather the views of interested parties. There is little evidence that consultation activities were focused on obtaining the views of clients, although informants in my study did contribute lengthy responses both on an individual and collective basis. Some information about 'men who solicit women' was gathered from the evaluation studies conducted by Hester and Westmarland (2004: 143) but this remains at the level only of socio-demographic detail and numbers of arrests. The scant and ill-informed nature of the consultation document and lack of direct consultation with the so called 'demand' side of prostitution meant that any policy recommendations made from this platform would not reflect the reality of commercial sex liaisons or the complex organization of the markets. By the end of the consultation process, prostitution was redefined as a social problem, with sex workers as victims or undeserving criminals if they failed to take steps to 'exit' and those on the 'demand' side as simply sexual predators and 'users' to be controlled through the criminal justice system.

The Coordinated Prostitution Strategy: 'tackling demand'

What resulted from the consultation was a philosophy and map for the police, local authorities, community safety partnerships and other related agencies to follow when tackling prostitution in the community. The *Coordinated Prostitution Strategy* (Home Office 2006, hereafter the Strategy) included five areas of prioritization: prevention, developing 'routes out' for sex workers, ensuring justice, tackling off-street prostitution and tackling demand. This critique will focus on the last objective, although there have been several other commentaries that draw out a wider range of concerns about the intentions and impact of the Strategy (see Boynton and Cusick 2006; Brooks-Gordon 2006: 62–71; Sanders 2005c; Sanders and Campbell 2007a, 2007b).[7]

The overriding emphasis of the Strategy is to 'disrupt the sex markets' (Home Office 2006: 1). This objective has produced a two-pronged approach: to criminalize sex workers (by supplying avenues for 'exiting' alongside the criminal justice system and endorsing prosecution and sanctions such as the use of ASBOs) and a re-emphasis on enforcing laws

against kerb-crawlers. There have been no new laws introduced through the Strategy; instead the existing laws outlined above against men who buy sex have been highlighted as the backbone of the enforcement strategy.[8] The tone of the Strategy is one that seeks to change attitudes: 'It is crucial that we move away from a general perception that prostitution is the "oldest profession" and has to be accepted. Street prostitution is not an activity that we can tolerate in our towns and cities' (p. 1). The Executive Summary states that the priority of 'tackling demand' is driven by 'responding to community concerns by deterring those who create the demand and removing the opportunity for street prostitution to take place' (p. 2). Communities who have voiced concern at the presence of prostitution are represented while those who coexist with diversity within their communities are not (see Pitcher *et al.* 2006).

To achieve a change in both attitudes and behaviour the government has favoured the Swedish model of criminalizing the purchase of sexual services without actually changing the law to make buying or selling sex illegal. The Swedish model has not been adopted entirely: the government has rejected the decriminalization approach that does not make criminals out of sex workers because of the 'magnitude and complexity of street prostitution' (p. 7) in the UK compared to the relatively small numbers of sex workers in Sweden. Despite enhancing the criminalization of sex workers, a key objective of the Strategy is to shift the focus of enforcement 'onto those who create the demand for prostitution' (p. 7) as an effective way to disrupt the sex markets. The enforcement strategy is to follow a three-staged approach: informal warning, court diversion, and prosecution.

Informal warning

The Strategy states that the first stage of the enforcement against kerb-crawlers should be an informal warning by means of a letter. By identifying car registration numbers in known 'red light districts' through the use of CCTV, warning letters about possible prosecution will be sent to men's homes. There are several issues with this initial step. It is assumed that the driver of the car is looking for sex; women may be driving the car or the car may not be owned by the driver. There may be legitimate reasons why a man is looking for a sex worker; for instance, if she has called for assistance or regularly gets a lift with a male friend or partner to and from the area. Significant assumptions are made about the 'type' of boyfriend that street sex workers have, associating only coercers and abusers as possible partners of sex workers. Finally, the implications of a husband receiving a letter about kerb-crawling when he may well be innocent could cause serious family upsets. The Strategy bases this approach as a successful deterrent only on anecdotal evidence.

The Strategy suggests that the deterrence message should be promoted through the media as well as naming and shaming individuals.

Court diversion

The second stage of enforcement is 'kerb-crawler re-education programmes' funded usually by the arrestee. The Strategy states that the content of such programmes should make the individual aware of the criminal sanctions and the impact of street prostitution on local communities and women. It is stated that this option should only be available to those who are arrested for the first time. Alongside attendance at a programme, a caution will be granted which could also include an ASBO, preventing the 'offender' returning to that particular area. Evidence that these rehabilitation programmes deter men from kerb-crawling in the future is not substantiated in the Strategy, apart from brief mention of the 'Change' programme in Hampshire. This one-day programme described by the Strategy (p. 35) is based on a sex offender or violent offender model of behavioural change whereby the aim is to change behaviour by challenging actions and beliefs about the behaviour. The Strategy professes this 'Change' programme as a success solely on the basis of a low reoffending rate: of the 304 course attendees only four have reoffended. The discussion below critiques the promotion of kerb-crawler rehabilitation programmes and the problems of measuring effectiveness by reoffending rates. No account of the evaluation evidence from other rehabilitation programmes is presented by the Strategy, resulting in the government backing an intervention that has no track record of success.

Prosecution

For those already with offences for kerb-crawling or sexual offences, and those who refuse to attend a programme, prosecution is the third and final stage in the enforcement strategy. The full range of penalties will be considered and the Strategy favours disqualification from driving as a solution to stop men from reoffending. Claims that magistrates' courts inconsistently sentence kerb-crawlers are to be addressed by sentencing all similar cases on one day. The Strategy heralds New Labour's policy of public disclosure as shaming sanctions by calling for the 'naming and shaming' of men arrested for kerb-crawling to be announced through the local media. The public shaming rituals are considered to be a useful reinforcement tactic that acts as a deterrent and publicises the tough actions of the criminal justice system on any form of 'anti-social behaviour'. Although given little commentary, Anti-Social Behaviour Orders and Acceptable Behaviour Contracts are suggested as a useful tool for persistent kerb-crawling and the former have since become a regular part of the enforcement process.[9] This prioritization of enforce-

ment against kerb-crawlers is based on anecdotal evidence that actions taken by the police such as warning letters and crackdowns have a deterrent effect (p. 7). The Strategy adopts enforcement against kerb-crawlers without any concerns for the displacement effect.

Displacement

The effects of policing on kerb-crawlers have not been understood in the context of the wider crime prevention literature and what is known about displacement effects. Displacement is a consequence often associated with policing prostitution. Traditionally, police visibility and arrest spats have resulted in sex workers moving to other nearby areas. Often these effects have been accepted as part of the 'not-in-my-backyard' approach to resolving a community issue. Similar effects of police crackdowns on kerb-crawlers have occasionally been discussed but as the policing strategies have only been a temporary intervention few implications have been described. However, if the guidelines from the Strategy are fully operationalized, the displacement effect will be evident among kerb-crawlers. Just as it has been documented how policing affects how female sex workers use public space (Hubbard and Sanders 2003), similar changes are probable with men who buy sex.

To understand the ways in which displacement of crimes take place, Hakim and Rengert (1981) describe four types of changes to offending behaviour. These types can be explained in relation to the displacement of purchasing commercial sex. First, temporal displacement can result in men seeking sex at different times to avoid police detection. Second, spatial displacement would encourage men to seek sex in different geographical spaces which also causes a displacement of sex workers. Third, tactical displacement means that men would still seek out street-based sex workers but they would use other mechanisms to make contact with women. For instance, mobile phones, regular arrangements or visiting women at indoor locations (such as a crack house) or their home are familiar modes of communication in an era of increased surveillance. Finally, the fourth type of displacement is that the target changes: instead of buying sex from the street-based market men will venture into new markets to act out the same behavioural patterns. These different types of displacement taken together will result in the dispersal of male clients and the creation of a more complex, invisible and underground sex industry that avoids any contact with official agencies.

Rejecting managed zones

The proposal for managed areas, where selling and buying sex would be facilitated free from arrest, was rejected by the Strategy. This was despite the successful models in Germany and the Netherlands and support from some UK stakeholders, councils and communities to be given the option to use 'zoning' as a method of management and safety for sex workers (Bellis *et al.* 2007). Closure of some 'tipplezones' in the Netherlands in recent years (Amsterdam 2003; Rotterdam 2005; the Hague 2006) have related to wider issues of criminal activities, trafficking, drug use and a change in the political climate rather than the specific failure of the zones (Van Doorninck and Campbell 2006: 72). Yet these changes have been considered by the UK government as an indication of the failure of alternative management solutions and unsuccessful in terms of reducing the anxieties of residents. Zones are still in full operational order in Utrecht, Groningen and a new zone has opened in Eindhoven, strongly supported by the community (*ibid.*). When all parties (sex workers, local residents, local partnerships, businesses) agreed on managed zones as a pilot scheme in Liverpool, the government blocked the initiative (Bellis, *et al.* 2007).

One argument in support of this decision related to clients not wanting to be identified as 'punters' and therefore the incentive to use a purposely designated public area for commercial sex exchange would decrease. The Strategy promotes 'those wanting to purchase street sex generally prefer to remain anonymous and may be reluctant to visit an area where they are more visible' (p. 8). Men were not fully consulted on whether they would accept managed zones as an alternative to enforcement. The detailed consultation with sex workers in the Liverpool case found that 92 per cent of women said they would work in a zone, suggesting that their clients would follow. The fact that men continue to buy sex in countries such as the Netherlands that host such a system suggests the stigma attached to designated areas is overcome by men wishing to find safe commercial sex. Zoning brings increased safety for men looking for sex, reducing the chance of robbery or a scam, ensuring that they are buying sex legitimately, free from arrest (Van Doorninck and Campbell 2006).

The 'zoning' discourse in the UK has been presented in opposition, rather than as a solution, to the needs of the community and has been dismissed as a viable solution to address the anxieties of residents. O'Neill and Campbell (2006) identify from research with residents in Walsall that perceptions of safety, fears and concerns for children and harassment from kerb-crawlers are real everyday worries. While not wanting to detract from the concerns that residents have, or the implications of street prostitution on local communities, the Strategy has opted to ignore feasible management solutions through zoning which could equally address the concerns of the communities. Equally, not providing the options for local authorities to legitimately explore formal zoning continues to allow narratives about nuisance to be attached to street prostitution and ignore communities where sex workers and residents live more harmoniously. The Strategy makes firm links between kerb-crawling and nuisance behaviour from which communities should be protected (p. 35). Setting up the image of the kerb-crawler as a sexual menace and as someone to be feared and fought against is tantamount to promoting fear in communities about this group of men and increasing the 'stranger danger' myth rather than addressing the practical concerns that community members have. There is evidence that women and young people living in street beats are approached by men looking to buy sex (O'Neill and Campbell 2006: 46–7) which increases anxieties and fears.[10] Concentrating commercial sex activities in specific zones would reduce, if not remove, such concerns. With the freedom for councils to take this option, some stakeholders are taking more pragmatic approaches. In other areas, such as Northampton, Aberdeen and other large towns, informal zones exist based on tacit agreements between sex workers, the police and health agencies (see Matthews 2005; Pitcher et al. 2006).

The role of the community in policing prostitution

The Strategy aims to prioritize communities through the enforcement approach, protecting them from harm and acting to reduce nuisance that disrupts the neighbourhood. Legitimate concerns have been raised by residents about the impact of prostitution in their local area including issues such as noise, increased traffic, low-level crime and litter such as condoms and needles (Pitcher et al. 2006). These environmental issues can all be addressed by prevention measures and strategies to manage prostitution rather than attempts to eradicate the activity through the intimidation of vulnerable women. For instance, traffic calming measures such as alley-gating have successfully reduced the amount of traffic and make communities safer. Other options for controlling litter are available in conjunction with the environmental services and encouraging responsible practice from sex workers. The concerns raised by residents about public sex 'often in gardens' cannot be a generalized concern as outreach projects report consistently across the country that the majority of commercial sex acts take place in cars or in dark and unused streets and alleys, often in industrial areas, away from the public.

Although there is evidence from various consultations with the public that prostitution does cause certain issues relating to the physical environment and elements of concern about low-level crime and the fear of being approached, research also suggests that these community concerns are not necessarily widespread. Pitcher et al. (2006) in their study Living and Working in Areas of Street Sex Work: From Conflict to Coexistence investigated five different residential areas where street prostitution occurred in the UK and found that most residents were not adversely affected by the presence of sex work and their quality of life did not deteriorate. Although some residents expressed fears about using public spaces, there were also views expressed that sympathized with sex workers and did not want them displaced. The conclusions from the study suggest coexistence between sex workers and the community is possible through an integrated response to addressing concerns and comprehensive, long-term provision of 'routes out' services.

The renewed emphasis in policy on the kerb-crawler and enforcing the existing laws through a three-tiered process is a significant change from what has generally been a lacklustre approach to policing prostitution. Matthews (2005) documents some of the changes in policing prostitution over the past decade, highlighting the shift in who does the policing of prostitution from state police agencies to welfare agencies. The police have deprioritized prostitution since the disbandment of vice squads in the 1990s. Research has identified how police involved in kerb-crawler operations hold their own view of sexual morality which influences how prostitution is policed. Sharpe (1998) observed sting operations on kerb-crawlers in the Divisional Enquiry Team in Kingston-upon-Hull in the North East of England. She revealed how police officers believed prostitution to be a permanent feature of the cityscape and that the role of the police essentially is that of monitoring and containing the activity rather than following any strong aims of eradication. Although the current message from the representatives of the police force (see Association of Chief Police Officers 2004) remains stiffly in line with the government's eradication aims, on the ground after the dust has settled and policy focus turns to some other 'Other', order maintenance and urban surveillance of the night-time economy will once again become the focus of policing.

'Kerb-crawling costs more than you think'

Central to the prostitution management policy, a focused marketing campaign to warn against kerb-crawling was launched by the Home Office in May 2007 across England. Seven cities were chosen because of their demonstrated commitment to enforcement: Middlesbrough, Peterborough, Southampton, London, Bristol, Bournemouth and Leeds. The 'marketing message' was aimed at 'potential' kerb-crawlers through posters in the media and radio 'warnings'. Listeners were told that kerb-crawling will result in an arrest, a court appearance, letters sent to their home, a £1,000 fine, a driving ban and shame to their families and employer. Beer mats entice: 'Turn over to find out how much it costs to pick up a prostitute', the answer on the other side replying: 'Your driving licence. Your job. Your marriage. A £1,000 fine'. The slogan 'Kerb-crawling costs more than you think' that punctuates all of these gimmicks is intended as a deterrent and a moral message that in reality is a mechanism of social control.

The context of the anti-kerb-crawling campaign is revealing. The posters consist of three individual men's stories of how their lives were ruined, shamed and disgraced because they were arrested or convicted of kerb-crawling. The story of 'Alan Davis', merges respectable imagery of a hard-working bloke, responsible father and committed husband, who is a popular local businessman:

> Alan Davis has been married for eight years, has four great kids and a vibrant social life which centres on his local pub, the Crown & Goose. In 2002, Alan realized his ambition to set up a courier company. Alan and wife Sandra sacrificed much in order to ensure the success of their fledgling business. They remortgaged the family home, worked 18-hour days and took no holidays for the first three years. Last Saturday Alan was returning from the pub when he was arrested for kerb-crawling.

Two other 'life stories' are also used: that of 'Jonathan Anderson' who was named local businessman of the year after leaving school with no GCSEs, and that of 'Michael Wilson', married to childhood sweetheart Jane, with twin daughters living in a four-bedroomed house. Both have their lives wrecked because of the kerb-crawling conviction. The stories are attempts to speak to the 'ordinary' middle-class man who 'has it all' but is risking it all by engaging in looking for or buying commercial sex. The deterrent message to men who are considering paying for sex warns them of the shame they will bring to their family, friends and employers if they are caught. The examples of the three 'ruined lives' send home the message that there are no rewards in commercial sex, only risks, losses and regret.

The moral messages that are peddled through the 'marketing' campaign are essentially about 'respectability' and ring-fencing what constitutes acceptable behaviour. The three stories of the 'fallen' men illustrate their 'perfect', comfortable lives with caring families, loving wives and valuable contributions to make to the community. The nuclear family and 'family values' have been at the heart of New Labour's policy and practice in the management of street sex work (see Hubbard 2002; 2004). The new strategy to 'tackle demand' relies on solid images of the respectable male as a proficient 'worker'. All three subjects of the stories are responsible men who own their own companies, had worked hard to achieve their status and were now enjoying public and personal rewards. The 'ordinariness' of the middle classes becomes the backbone of these moral messages and is implicitly compared to the 'sordid', 'unruly' sexual frolics of the working classes. Images of civility spew out of the stories of the 'fallen' men whose brief moment of weakness cost them their respectability and everything they valued.

The 'naming and shaming' that is used as a deterrent in the radio adverts is a formal acknowledgement of the role of the media as a third arm of the criminal justice system. Promising that those men arrested and hauled into court will be shamed in the press is reminiscent of the public disgracing tactics against men who buy sex in communist China, where buying and selling sex is illegal. Jeffreys (2006) describes the real case of a male academic who was penalized for buying sex and subjected to a high-profile public disgracing. The case became a national scandal as the academic went from a senior figure in a university to that of a sex criminal. Jeffreys describes how the media was used as the 'disciplinary apparatus' because the press took on a powerful socio-political role in reinforcing social standards.

At a local level in the UK, similar incidents have occurred in the press as men are 'named and shamed'. After convictions in court, men's personal details have been splattered across the newspapers without regard for the impact on innocent loved ones. The *Evening Standard* ran a headline '29 kerb-crawlers to be named, shamed in vice crackdown' (Edwards 2006) stating the full names, locations of residence, age and occupations of most of the arrested. The Strategy celebrates this form of deterrent. For instance, the Local Strategic Partnership in Middlesbrough (Home Office 2006: 17) which has been 'instrumental in the successful "naming and shaming" campaign to deter kerb-crawlers' is heralded as a successful intervention in the war against street prostitution. Frustrations with inconsistent sentencing in magistrates' courts has meant resorting to naming and shaming in the media as this is considered a more effective element of crackdown operations.

The UK campaign against male incivility is reinforced by the political rhetoric around 'safe', 'cohesive' communities and the assumed nuisance of street sex workers. Home Office Minister Vernon Coaker defended the kerb-crawler campaign by regurgitating the discourses of street sex work characterized only as 'anti-social' and 'uncivil', themes that have framed prostitution policy since 2004 (Scoular *et al.* 2007): 'Local communities are fed up with street prostitution, sexual activity taking place in their parks and playgrounds, condoms and discarded needles littering the streets and innocent women mistakenly targeted and abused by men on the prowl. For the residents it is intimidating, unpleasant and unsafe.'[11] Buying and selling sex are painted as inherently dangerous and so are the people who are involved. Emotive language that implies the 'kerb-crawler' is an evil criminal who has unsavoury and abusive behaviours and attitudes is used, creating the justification that these men must be stopped and that criminalization and shaming is an appropriate and legitimate approach. The clearest case of hatred for the kerb-crawler is in a poster campaign issued by Wolverhampton City Council with the statement: 'Kerb crawling belongs in the gutter. Wolverhampton hates kerb crawlers'.[12]

During the police enforcement operations that preceded and followed the national 'marketing' campaign, there was no amnesty on arresting street sex workers. In March 2007 (BBC News, 10 March 2007),[13] Operation Assent in Doncaster cautioned 54 sex workers while only two men were charged with kerb-crawling: as a result three women were served ASBOs and only one kerb-crawler. After the five murders of sex workers in Ipswich in December 2006, the Norfolk police were criticized by resident associations for handing out ASBOs to street sex workers in the same area that the women were murdered. It appears that since the high-profile crimes against sex workers, the Norfolk police have heavily enforced the criminalization strategy for both sex workers and male clients.[14]

The criminalization of sex workers through ASBOs has been repeatedly criticized for doing nothing to achieve policing or welfare objectives (Jones and Sagar 2001; Sagar 2007). Yet throughout the country, a reduction in street sex workers visibly on the street is taken as a sign of successful policing. For instance, 'The Change' re-education programme professes the success of targeting kerb-crawlers by claiming that the numbers of 'known prostitutes in Southampton' has been reduced from 320 (2003) to 89 (2006) (*The Sharp End*, May 2007). Sex workers are targeted at the same time as sporadic kerb-crawler enforcement operations as the urban street is central to the zero tolerance agenda. Whether sex workers leave the streets after heavy enforcement is unlikely – they simply become more invisible. The objective to 'end prostitution in the city' (Superintendent Peter Nicholson, West Yorkshire Police)[15] is proudly advertised by decision makers, barely aware that such an objective is naive, unachievable and outdated within a cultural system that commodifies sexuality and the female body. At the same time as the kerb-crawler campaign, men who cruise known areas looking for male sex workers have also been targeted in Birmingham by a 'yellow card scheme'. Although not written into official policy, the Birmingham Community Safety Partnership has targeted those suspected of kerb-crawling the gay scene warning that reoffending would be met with a ban from the area or prosecution.

The 'marketing campaign' falls short of demonizing men who buy sex because the three poster stories are of 'decent' middle-class men, reflecting the research findings on who actually buys sex. But where the campaign, enforcement strategy and philosophy do the most harm is that men such as those in the stories are being punished in the extreme for a behaviour that is common and is essentially not against the law. The poster campaign initiated by Wolverhampton City Council (see note 12) has the headline 'Kerb crawlers will end up behind bars' giving the entirely false impression that men can be imprisoned for this offence. As no custodial sentence can be issued to men who buy sex from consenting adults, the only other option the state has to fall back on is that of social punishments of shaming, humiliation and the message that men will lose all things of value to them. The men in the stories whose lives have been ruined will perhaps attract sympathy rather than condemnation from their peers.

There are other serious criticisms of the campaign in relation to the safety of sex workers and their increased vulnerability. By persuading 'decent' middle-class men not to visit street sex workers, the subtle message is then that those yobs and women-haters who have harmful intentions and attitudes towards women are freely left to target sex workers in the increasingly vulnerable environments where street sex happens. Secondly, the marketing campaign can be criticized because it is devoid of any safety messages or messages highlighting that harms against sex workers are crimes. As the Coordinated Prostitution Strategy gave considerable time to the issue of 'ensuring justice' for sex workers and taking steps to make sure that crimes against sex workers were taken seriously and acted upon,[16] it seems unfortunate (and a missed opportunity) that the safety of sex workers has not appeared as part of the message to men who buy sex.

Kerb-crawler 'rehabilitation' programmes

The *Paying the Price* document has been criticized for recognizing re-education programmes as a 'coherent approach' when no objective assessment of the programmes was considered or any recognition of the dangers, costs and implications of the schemes (Brooks-Gordon 2005: 436). The first rehabilitation programme in the UK, set up by West Yorkshire police in 1998, was dropped very soon after it started on the basis that it was too resource-intensive and had limited impact (see Campbell and Storr 2001). Lowman and Atchison (2006), in their review of Canadian research on men who pay for sex, note that there has been no verification on the outcomes of John School, leaving little evidence that they are successful interventions. This legacy has not dampened the recent wave of enthusiasm for the programmes: guest editor of the police magazine *The Sharp End*, WPC Emily Crump, describes the Change programme implemented by Hampshire constabulary as 'classroom sessions to cure kerb-crawlers' (*The Sharp End*, 2007). Others are in operation in Northampton and Hull (Mower 2006).[17] The frontline of delivering such programmes is distanced from the body of literature that reports on evaluations and assessments of the re-education programmes in the USA and North America. From these evaluations, it is clear that there is little evidence to support the effectiveness of re-education programmes.

First, the 'reoffending' criteria on which the programmes' effectiveness is measured are suspect. Basic figures are used by the Change project in Hampshire to celebrate its success: of 366 men who have taken the course only six have reoffended (*The Sharp End*, 2007: 20). Without any systematic evaluation of the programme or any consideration of the displacement effects, these figures must be treated with caution. Recidivism in general is proven to be a weak measurement of effectiveness in relation to kerb-crawling. In Portland, Oregon, Monto and Garcia (2001) studied three different groups who were assigned different punishments as a result of kerb-crawling, one being attendance on the 'Sexual Exploitation Education Project'. The findings show there was no statistical difference between the reoffending rates of any of the punishments, but that reoffending remained low for all of the groups. Monto and Garcia conclude that recidivism is not due to the educational programme, but that behavioural changes occur as a result of arrest. Such changes could stem from the temporary involvement in buying sex, a temporary exit, a change of market, a different geographical location or changing the mode of contacting street sex workers. Other evaluations of re-education programmes have concluded that attitudinal changes were made in the direction expected by men who attended the programme, suggesting that more responsible engagement in the sex industry happens after the programme rather than simply not buying sex at all (Kennedy *et al.* 2004; Wortley *et al.* 2002).

Second, the police crackdowns that are necessary to feed 'offenders' into the programmes are resource-intensive. As Table 7.1 earlier demonstrates, the numbers arrested for kerb-crawling have never exceeded 1,096 (1996) in any year over the past decade. Using female police officers as decoys and setting up undercover operations is intensive in terms of planning, risk assessment and execution for a small number of arrests and perhaps explains why smaller police forces have not bothered with such enforcement campaigns. With reduced budgets, government targets for everyday street crimes as well as specific, complex international crimes and issues (such as terrorism and organized crime), local police do not have the resources to target minor offences in any persistent fashion.

Third, the content of the rehabilitation programmes is significantly biased towards the extreme view that prostitution is violence against all women and provides only very cursory information that can assist men to make more responsible and safer choices about buying commercial sex. Van Brunschot (2003) evaluated a Prostitution Offender Program in a Canadian city and highlighted how the John School did not provide a balanced view of prostitution or give the other side of the exploitation story but retold 'worst case scenarios' that are not a representative and balanced picture. The 'sex as work' argument is not entertained on programmes and there are no accounts from women who voluntarily sell sex and those who are not damaged by sex work. Information that has been given about the context of the Change programme in the UK appears to present only the negative aspects of child sexual exploitation, drug use, health issues and how men are breaking the law. Men are not told their full legal rights regarding the freedom to purchase sex between two consenting adults and no health and safety information is provided to make them and their sexual partners more educated about safe sexual behaviour. Alternatives to the street market are not discussed on the programmes, missing the opportunity to divert men away from the street into less visible but legal sex markets such as escorting.

Programmes that do not examine sexual behaviour, sexual desires and sexual and emotional needs essentially ignore the root cause of why men visit sex workers. Given that the motivations for seeking commercial sex have been clearly documented (see Chapter 2) and that the reasons are many (for instance loneliness, marriage breakdown and other personal problems), the absence of any therapeutic understanding in such programmes is irresponsible. The Change programme is fuelled by a discourse that some men are 'socially inadequate' because they find it 'difficult to interact with women', with officers on the programme ridiculing men who fantasize about their relationships with sex workers (*The Sharp End*, 2007). Given recent information about the possible rates of sexual addiction among men who visit sex workers (Gordon-Lamoureux 2007), the content of the programmes needs to be considered with responsibility and care, taking into account the assessment of potential addiction and the provision of therapeutic need (Gold and Heffner 1998; Plant and Plant 2003).

Arguments have also been made about the unfair nature of the programmes based on legal theory. Brooks-Gordon (2005: 436) asks 'How can the programme be justified if the main activity of buying sex is not against the law?' Legal theorists have questioned the legal basis of the court diversion process because of the prerequisite of an admission of guilt. If a man is charged with a kerb-crawling offence, whether innocent or guilty, he is presented with an option of taking the re-education programme (and paying a fee) or going to court. To avoid court, the man must plead guilty to the charge, attend the programme and receive a caution as well as the humiliation of the label of 'sexual deviant'. Those who are innocent may opt for court diversion without realizing they could be acquitted in court. There is a strong likelihood that those who are innocent will still opt for the court diversion scheme rather than a court appearance in order to get the ordeal over with and prevent getting a criminal record. The 'voluntariness' of the programme is suspect as the 'choice' to attend the programme is coercive and brings into question whether 'due process' is sidestepped (Fischer *et al.* 2002).

Finally, there are several problems with the 'shaming' element of 'rehabilitation' programmes. Evidence suggests from studies on clients that shame is not a necessary consequence of buying sex, and that for many men the process of shaming would not act as a deterrent as it does not translate into behavioural change (Coy, *et al.* 2007: 25). Where shaming is a key principle of punishment, there are untold damaging effects that can upset personal lives which are disproportionate to the non-custodial offence. The 'shaming' element of the programme and the emphasis on social punishment through disgrace and humiliation (not only to the individual but their family) is a significant part of the re-education programmes. Sawyer *et al.* (1998) conclude that as a result of a psycho-education programme in Minnesota, there were unforeseen negative effects from the programme. Individuals were pathologized by being labelled as deviant, creating emotional problems made worse by stigma, shame and humiliation. With no emphasis on 'reintegration' or 'reparation', the basics of restorative justice and rehabilitation schemes in other parts of the criminal justice system, men are told how they are damaging and irresponsible, practising 'risky' and illegal behaviour, and then sent on their way. Braithwaite (1989), along with feminist criminologists, warn against using systems of shaming in crimes that are sensitive or are of a sexual nature (Adler 2003). Sending men on programmes where shaming is a key part of the rehabilitation is similar to the 'degradation ceremonies' that Lee (1995) identifies in cautioning young people in pre-courts. Fischer *et al.* (2002: 396) note that the public message from the aims of the programmes is significantly different from the reality because the programmes are based on 'morality, blaming and shaming'. The moralistic content of the programme that blames individuals for what is considered to be sexual misdemeanours by the state is a direct mechanism of labelling a group as sexually deviant.

Educational awareness

Nowhere to be found in the recent policy review and outcome is the need to educate men who engage in the sex industry about safety, sexual health, respectable behaviour and good practice. Although, like many other academics, I reject the premise and practice of rehabilitation programmes for this group of men, I recognize that there is scope for wider educational programmes for the general population of men and specifically men who buy sex. Groom and Nandwini (2006) conclude from a study in Glasgow of men who buy sex that this group needs to be targeted from a public health perspective. Specific education about health, risky sexual behaviours and how to engage in respectful commercial interactions is an urgent requirement for this group of men who often do not engage in mainstream health services. In other parts of the world, men who buy sex are targeted for their key role in the early stages of sexual infection and HIV epidemics and programmes are designed to promote condom use and educate about sexual behaviour with multiple and frequent partners (O'Farrell 2001). While the rate of sexually transmitted infections in the UK increases (for instance cases of chlamydia rose by 103 per cent from 1997 to 2002 (Ward *et al.* 2005: 467)), the infection rates among female sex workers is declining, suggesting that it is men and not women involved in commercial sex that are at risk and spread infection (*ibid.*).

Alongside key health messages there is scope to educate men about the contract that should exist between a sex worker and a customer where there are rights to regression and protection if the client breaks the contract. The German health authorities initiated an information campaign during the World Cup to inform men of how to behave when visiting a sex worker or a brothel (BBC News, 15 May 2006). All of these legitimate (and essential) educational needs can be done on a much wider scale to increase impact and coverage outside a criminalization framework.

An awareness programme specifically for men who buy sex could be an effective prevention initiative to promote the safety of women and the self-regulation of the industry. Just as there are many outreach projects for sex workers, there could also be outreach programmes that provide information to men who buy sex.[18] The following information could form the basis of an educational programme:

- ensuring men are aware of how to negotiate a service;
- what is meant by a contract with a sex worker;
- respecting the worker's rules;
- how to spot exploited women or bad management in parlours;
- how to choose a well-run parlour;
- issues of personal safety for themselves and women;
- actions to take in violent situations;
- where to report crimes;
- addictions to sex work and where to get therapeutic help;
- how to spot money scams;
- drugs and sexual health awareness;
- facts about the law.

HIV prevention and sexual health programmes ignore the patterns of human sexuality, established through research, at their peril (Kelly and Kalichman 1995). The Internet and cybercommunities have already been highlighted as an arena for sex education and a place to deliver sexual healthcare advice (Schnarch 1997). Given the prevalence of men who buy sex, a more responsible education awareness campaign via the Internet could be cost-effective and react to the questions and queries that men often ask each other on websites and message boards.

Male sexuality, 'respectability' and New Labour

The government's approach currently makes explicit assumptions that there is something inherently morally wrong in the exchange of sex for money and that the purchase and sale of commercial sex is detrimental to public order, personal morality and wider gender relationships. There is nothing inherently violent in exchanging sex for money and imposing a judgement on this is simply a moral, religious-based ideology supporting heteronormative concepts of how sexuality should be expressed. Targeting both men who buy sex from the street and female sex workers leaves a status quo of pure vulnerability: women have no choice but to work in deeply dangerous conditions as underlining causes of why women enter sex work are not addressed. In addition, social policy refuses to provide safer working conditions or tackle the negative cultural messages relating to women who sell sex.

The premise of the Strategy rests with the assumption that the sex worker is being abused by the man who is paying her for sex, even if she is consenting and voluntarily involved in sex work. This overriding assumption fails to take into account the debate about agency and choice exercised by some women who voluntarily earn money through their sexual labour (Weitzer 2005). The starting point that the Strategy takes, that commercial sex cannot be work and that there is no voluntary consent, ultimately means that men who buy sex can only be framed as abusers and 'users', rather than as legitimately seeking out sexual services for payment under the sex worker's conditions. The long-awaited promise from New Labour in 1999 that government decision-making would build on a 'better use of evidence and research in policy-making' (David Blunkett, Cabinet Office 1999) to deliver long-term goals for social policy were, in the case of managing the sex industry and many other social issues, merely empty words.

How can street prostitution be eradicated if the basic premise of selling and buying sex is still legal? The complicated aftermath that the Strategy has left means that the law remains contradictory by allowing consensual commercial sexual services yet criminalizing men who look for sex on the street. The rise of the victims' discourse complicated by a narrow view of the nature of sex work and the outright rejection of formal managed zones determines current prostitution policy and the levels of violence and safety experienced by some of the most vulnerable women in society. With a u-turn on the government's own recommendation to change the laws against women working together indoors (Sanders 2007a) and attempts to close down indoor establishments where there are no concerns about exploitation (Sanders and Campbell 2007b), no forward steps have been taken to legitimize, regulate or control the indoor sex markets.

The root causes of street prostitution go much further than men simply looking for cheap sexual thrills but are located in the social position of women who are economically disadvantaged, dislocated from main-stream society and excluded from welfare provisions thus maintaining a lifestyle of marginalization, often trapped in violent and drug-dependent relationships. Any plans to eradicate street prostitution need to look beyond the male client as the scapegoat to consider wider structural mechanisms that make prostitution the only option for some women. Considering these arguments, it is only with scepticism that policies driven by a criminalizing agenda can be a safe and feasible solution.

Caution must be observed in any attempts to introduce rehabilitation programmes as emergency correctives for men who are arrested and labelled as 'kerb-crawlers'. The criticisms and limitations of diversion as a general tactic for crime control (Sanders 1988) suggest that the voluntary nature of any diversion is misleading and usually undermines due process in law. Further, the moral disapproval through the market-ing strategy that promotes buying sex as morally indefensible and unacceptable sexual behaviour reinforces a certain sexual and social order. While fines and driving bans are distant instrumental sanctions to punish those who are 'out of control', the moral message of respectability is the powerful tool for keeping order. Ordinary men, who have a comfortable public and private life, one to which others are encouraged to aspire, are under attack for lapses of self-control, sexual non-conformity and state-defined irresponsibility. Under New Labour, 'faulty persons' will be the subject of social punishments that reach beyond a ticking off from the state.

Notes

1 Peng (2007) describes how, in Taiwan, the images of the client as either dominant or exploitative have resulted in the Swedish model being favoured and calls for the *piao-ke* (sex buyers) to be held culpable.
2 A case in point of the state acceptance of the diversity of sexuality is the 801st mayor and mayoress of Cambridge who are a transsexual couple, inaugur-ated in May 2007.
3 'Crackdown pledged on sex with trafficked women' (*Guardian*, 18 July 2007). See: http://www.guardian.co.uk/crime/article/0,,2128881,0 0.html.

4 See Pitcher *et al.* (2006: 4, Table 1.1) for an outline of the additional three main pieces of legislation that regulate prostitution in Scotland.

5 Coy *et al.* (2007) reported how research methodology based on police kerb-crawler operations failed due to very few men being arrested, resulting in a redesign of the study.

6 Campaign to deter kerb-crawling – see: http://www.homeoffice.gov.uk/documents/kerb-crawling-marketing-material/.

7 For a full review of the implications of the Strategy see: 'The prostitution strategy: implications for community safety', *The Community Safety Journal*, 6 (1).

8 The *Coordinated Prostitution Strategy* proposed a change in the soliciting laws for sex workers to introduce a 'new rehabilitative approach to loitering and soliciting – the penalty will vary according to persistence' (p. 39). This essentially will combine the 'exiting' model with the criminal justice system.

9 'Men held in street vice crackdown' (20 June 2007). See: http://news.bbc.co.Uk/l/hi/england/suffolk/6221264.stm.

10 A study in Finland by Koskela and Tani (2005) found that women who lived and worked in known street prostitution areas used a range of resistance strategies when approached by men looking to buy sex.

11 'Campaign to target kerb-crawlers' (BBC News, 13 May 2007). See: http://news.bbc.co.uk/2/hi/uk_news/6647655.stm.

12 'Get out and stay out' campaign. See: http://www.wolverhampton.gov.uk/policing_safety/crime_law/street_sex_trade/campaign/default.htm.

13 Kerb-crawling operation 'success'. See: http://news.bbc.co.uk/2/hi/uk_news/england/south_yorkshire/6460247.stm.

14 'Arrests in red light district crackdown', *Norfolk Evening News 24*, 26 July 2007.

15 Superintendent Peter Nicholson was quoted on the intentions of the crackdown in Leeds in March 2007. See: http://www.westyorkshire.police.uk/section-item.asp?sid = 12&iid = 3252 (retrieved 21 March 2007).

16 Campaign to Stop Dodgy Punters – see: http://www.crimestoppers-uk.org/solving/campaignsandinitiatives/dodgypunters/.

17 http://www.northants.police.uk/default.asp?action = article&ID = 15069

18 See UK Network of Sex Work Project: http://www.uknswp.org.uk.

Chapter 8

Moral panic: the 'punter' as danger

This chapter applies the sociological concept of the 'moral panic' to the case of men who buy sex, in particular the kerb-crawler. I apply the five criteria set out by Goode and Ben-Yehuda (2004) to establish whether a moral panic exists, charting how general anxieties regarding male violence, sexuality and dangerousness have been mapped onto the discourses that surround men who buy sex from women. The concept of the moral panic has been chosen to explain the unfolding developments over the past two decades that have reframed male purchasers of sex and produced a specific social reaction. I provide evidence to argue that media representations, institutions of decision- and policy-making and knowledge production (and here I refer also to academics) foster and perpetuate certain mythologies and exaggerated anxieties about this group of men. Recent legacies of sexual dangerousness surrounding the customers of sex workers are traced through to modern debates that have influenced regime change, legal and policy frameworks and policing practice. The UK discourses that adopt 'the problem of men' as a starting point for prostitution policy is explored alongside the perspectives of radical feminists and the case of Sweden criminalizing the buying of sex. Finally, this chapter explores the consequences of an exaggerated social reaction: the impact on sex workers, the maintenance of cultural values of disposability and a system of sexual and social control built on constructing 'risky' male sexuality.

Applying the concept of moral panic

The concept of the moral panic, originally coined by Stan Cohen (1972) and now prolific in both lay and academic language, refers to the fear or concern created about a group, category or behaviour that is out of proportion to the danger of a few or the real extent of disruption that a behaviour causes. The now famous example of the disturbances between Mods and Rockers in the seaside town of Clacton in the UK on Easter Sunday in 1964 prompted Cohen to develop the concept. This incident attracted exaggerated media attention, policing practice and state intervention around 'youth violence' which was disproportionate to the damage and harm actually caused. Since this incident was used to develop the moral panic concept, researchers have applied the theory to social reactions that have been inflated beyond appropriateness. Examples include marijuana and sexual psychopath laws in the USA (Goode and Ben-Yehuda 1994), the Internet and sexuality (Hamilton 1999) and paedophilia in the UK and USA (Bell 2002; Critcher 2002; Jenkins 1998).

What is the concept and why is it useful?

Cohen (1972: 191) described the value of the moral panic concept as a way of making sense of the social reactions to a real or supposed threat to 'positions, statuses, interests, ideologies and values'. Celebrating the relevancy of the concept in contemporary society, Goode and Ben-Yehuda (1994: 29) state that 'the concept of the moral panic expands our understanding of social structure, social process and social change'. Although commentary on the rise of the 'risk society' has argued that the concept of the moral panic is now defunct (Ungar 2001), the concept still allows the interrogation of the creation of moral and ideological boundaries alongside the construction of a 'folk devil' that becomes the focus of social anxieties. In the case of men who buy sex, it is useful to test whether the concept applies because of this basic conundrum: why have kerb-crawlers been given significant attention in politics and policy when sex workers have not been highlighted as a group of women whose safety and protection is a social issue, despite over a hundred murders in the past decade (see Kinnell 2006a)? By analysing the criteria of the moral panic, it can be established how different groups have reacted to the 'problem of prostitution' to assess whether the consequences of kerb-crawling are disproportionate and whether the sense of threat from men who buy sex has been exaggerated.

The Process: creating a moral panic

Cohen analysed the reactions of five segments of society to establish whether a moral panic occurred: the press, the public, agents of social control and law enforcers, politicians and law-makers and action groups. Implicitly the reactions of these five segments of society will be reviewed through the application of five indicators that constitute a moral panic as outlined by Goode and Ben-Yehuda (1994: 33): concern, hostility, consensus, disproportionality and volatility.

Concern

Concern about the sexual behaviour of men who buy sex as kerb-crawlers and fear from specific community groups about safety is well documented in the media, through community resident groups and some research. By mobilising financial resources, cultural capital and networks, small numbers of individuals have formed resident groups which have gained direct access to the public and political arena and received considerable attention and policing resources in order to promote anti-prostitution sentiment (Sagar 2005; Williams 2005).

One example is of a campaign against kerb-crawlers in Wolverhampton in the West Midlands of the UK in 2006, supported by health authorities, the local police, city council and the community. Reporting to act specifically in accordance with the wishes of members of the community, the Prostitution Task Group in Wolverhampton ran a poster campaign featuring a white man's face behind bars under a gutter, with the words 'Kerb-crawlers end up behind bars', 'Wolverhampton hates kerb-crawling. So get out and stay out'.[1] The head of the task group commented, 'We wanted the campaign to be direct and hard hitting. We're sure the message will remind the would-be kerb-crawler of the consequences of their actions and stop them in their tracks. The strong imagery also reminds would-be kerb-crawlers that their actions belong, literally, to the gutter.' The Director of Public Health commented in support of the enforcement focus on kerb-crawlers:

> The police and courts' commitment to bringing kerb-crawlers to justice and the local media's naming and shaming of those caught and convicted has proved to be a most effective weapon against this vile trade. But praise must also go to the residents of All Saints and Blakenhall who have backed the campaign and have been prepared to stand up and be counted in spite of concerns for their own safety.[2]

The powerful imagery and language evident in the Wolverhampton anti-kerb-crawler campaign sends out misinformation (that men arrested for kerb-crawling could face a prison sentence), but has explicit implications for the stereotypes and dangerous messages that are reinforced about the women who work in the street sex industry. Stating that men who buy street sex are dirty, disgusting and contaminated also implies that the women who they interact with are of the same status. The Association of Police Officers celebrated this poster campaign at the annual 'vice conference' in 2007; in addition, the designers won an award for the creative poster campaign. State-sanctioned images, language and messages of hatred are at the heart of the contradiction of the law, as buying and selling sex between consenting adults remains legal.

Local residents in some areas where street sex work occurs, such as those in Birmingham, Bradford and Doncaster, have become powerful change agents (see Hubbard 1998; Pitcher *et al.* 2006). Small numbers of residents who are unhappy about prostitution in their neighbourhoods have used the political and media channels to voice their concerns. The problem is framed as harassment of non-prostitute women propositioned by men in cars, decreasing house prices, public sex acts, noise and disturbance at night, drugs paraphernalia and dealing, economic damage to businesses and concerns for children witnessing prostitution in their recreation time. There is some evidence that the concern has become fear, particularly for women who are harassed by men looking for sex workers or who fear that they are at risk of harassment (Koskela and Tani 2005).

Through community involvement and activism, prostitution has been recast as 'urban disorder' in the UK, Canada (Van Brunschot 2003) and Australia (Kerkin 2003) as residents become key voices in urban planning decisions. Those who are tolerant towards prostitution or have not been affected by its presence are most likely not to engage in community politics nor advocate for alternative solutions. The community has become the 'new victim' as mobilized voices have identified themselves as victims of the harmful and negative impacts of prostitution (Fischer *et al.* 2002: 394).

Hostility

There are two clear examples of how men who buy sex from street sex workers become newsworthy, attracting condemnation and hostility. First, when men in powerful positions, either celebrities or high-profile professionals, are caught engaging in street sex or liaising with a sex worker, they are treated with disgust and contempt. For example, in June 1995, British actor Hugh Grant was arrested in Los Angeles for picking up sex worker Divine Brown and paying $60 for oral sex.[3] Both were arrested and Grant received unprecedented media coverage, resulting in a live public apology to explain his actions on the popular American *Tonight Show*, grossing the largest show audience to date. In May 2002, the host of BBC's *Have I Got News for You* Angus Deayton, was humiliated by a kiss and tell story sold to the *News of the World* which printed the front page headline: 'Deayton's sex romp with vice girl', which affected his career and reputation. These examples generally humiliate the middle-class men and show contempt for the woman as a deviant.

At a more localized level, several years of resident campaigns against the existence of street prostitution and kerb-crawlers have successfully framed men who buy sex as being a threat to the community's safety. One example of hostility against sex workers and kerb-crawlers is of the Street Watch prostitution action group which started in the Balsall Heath area of Birmingham in the early 1990s. This group then moved when street prostitution was displaced to neighbouring Edgbaston in the late 1990s (Hubbard 1998; Williams 2005). Following geographical displacement, the 'Rotton Park Action Group' was set up in 1997 and continues to work with the local policing partnerships to eradicate prostitution from the streets.

Resident groups like Rotton Park, which is still in operation at the time of writing, have a permanent history in contemporary community policing. Kantola and Squires (2004: 81) report that in the 1984 parliamentary debates, MPs celebrated the actions of local residents who were working against the problem of street prostitution to protect their neighbourhoods. These debates specifically constructed men who looked for street-based commercial sexual services as 'the problem' and the public discourse in relation to kerb-crawling grew in strength. By allowing the voices of a minority of disgruntled residents to monopolize the agenda and become the main 'claims makers', attitudes towards prostitution are overwhelmingly negative, promoting solutions based on enforcement, eradication and removal rather than coexistence. The 'Wolverhampton hates kerb-crawlers' campaign supported by the authorities identifies that resident hostility overrides any coexistence solutions in certain communities. Even when the majority of residents, sex workers and local authority officials agreed that there should be a workable, non-criminal solution through managed zones in Liverpool, the political support through the Home Office was absent, immediately discounting the views of those more tolerant to commercial sex (Bellis *et al.* 2007).

The media has been a key 'meaning-maker' in the social construction of the sex industry, and particularly women involved in selling sex, contributing to the global sustenance of social stigma of this group (Hallgrimsdottir, *et al.* 2006). Alongside community and political discourses that demonstrate hostility towards the kerb-crawler, contemporary media authors have also reported with disgust men who buy sex as a threat to the social and moral order. Cohen (1972: 30) noted three distinct processes that the media adopted to define a group or behaviour as a moral panic: 'exaggeration and distortion' by using emotive language to create mythical stories and extend the seriousness of the event; 'prediction' of recurring 'problems' that need to be addressed permanently; and 'symbolization' through specific language connected to the 'deviancy'. Such criteria are evident in an analysis of the treatment of kerb-crawlers by local media reporting. For example, long-standing enforcement strategies carried out in Teeside, North East England have been reported frequently in the headlines of the *Evening Gazette*: 'Fines of vice shame men' (29 October 2004); 'Secret cameras snare town's vice "Tourists"' (9 September 2004); 'Moment of shame' (25 June 2004). The 2007 government campaign against kerb-crawling has used the media to effectively spread the shaming message: 'Kerb crawlers were today warned they face having their personal lives destroyed when they are caught carrying out their sleazy activities in Ipswich's red-light district' (*Evening Star*, 2 June 2007). Headlines such as 'Praise for a kerb-crawler pest plan' (BBC News, 29 December 2005) and the media naming and shaming campaigns against individuals only fuel negative images of men who seek commercial sex and construct them as sex offenders. The persistent stories of 'vice' and unruly male sexual predators on the streets exaggerate the extent of the problem, creating continual alarm and fear in the public who begin to believe and internalize the fears and hatred of a minority. Weitzer (2006) argues that the strength of the religious-based moral crusade against the sex industry which represents the views of a few becomes powerful as the moral message gathers strength and success through examples such as these individual media reports, localized campaigns and support from key stakeholders at a national level.

'Symbolization' is created through the specific language used to describe kerb-crawlers as 'deviant' and uncivil and forms part of the hostility strategies (see below for a more detailed discussion of language). Specific imagery, terminology and jargon are applied, repeated and normalized to separate out different groups and define one as a threat: 'Division is made between "us" – good, decent, respectable folk – and "them" – deviants, bad guys, undesirables, outsiders, criminals, the underworld' (Goode and Ben-Yehuda 1994: 34). The Wolverhampton anti-kerb-crawler campaign that features a man in the gutter creates the image that the men who buy sex, contrary to the research evidence, are men who are unscrupulous, evil, dangerous and criminal offenders. The media becomes a chief 'claims maker' as all men who buy sex are constructed as a threat to respectable society. The media has a significant role in wider social and legal changes that stem from the strength of the moral panic. Bell (2002) describes how a British newspaper, the *News of the World*, successfully campaigned to change the law on sex offenders after the murder of 8-year-old Sarah Payne in July 2002. With the same hostility if not the same intensity, the media have constantly promoted the message that buying street sex is uncivil and an unwanted behaviour, and through 'naming and shaming' promotes the humiliation of individuals and the criminalization of kerb-crawling and street prostitution as appropriate controlling measures.

Consensus

Goode and Ben-Yehuda (1994) state that one of the central criteria for assessing whether a reaction is strong enough for a moral panic is whether there is widespread sentiment that the behaviour or group is 'wrong doing'. It is this point on consensus that is not straightforward in the evidence to establish whether a moral panic exists. Although the evidence above demonstrates the concern for the kerb-crawler and inflated threats about the behaviour, there has not been the universal condemnation against men who buy sex like there has in other moral panics, such as the case of harms against children (Bell 2002: 533). Moral entrepreneurs have been challenged by alternative voices who call for a more nuanced approach to managing sex work. Some campaign groups have spoken out against the criminalization of kerb-crawlers: in the 1990s, the English Collective of Prostitutes (1997) set up the Campaign Against Kerb Crawling Legislation. Responding to the *Paying the Price* consultation document on prostitution, the UK Network of Sex Work Projects strongly argued against demonizing men who buy sex and for supplying misinformation about the relationship between men who buy sex, violence, sexual health and sex work.

The political arena has seen a small number of moderates speaking out against the criminalization of men. Ken Livingstone, the Mayor of London, pointed out that criminal approaches to kerb-crawling would increase the victimization of men and women and that there was a concern that certain men (those who adhered to the stereotype of the punter or 'other', including ethnic minority groups of men) would be targeted as suspicious through the increased powers given to the police under the intentions of reducing kerb-crawling (cited in Brooks-Gordon and Gelsthorpe 2003: 443). In addition, the Liberal Democrats in 2006 supported plans to pilot managed zones in Liverpool and did not condemn men who buy sex but supported alternative methods of managing prostitution.[4]

Despite some level of opposition to the support for criminalizing men who buy sex from the street, concern and fear expressed by a small number of communities remains the strongest voice and therefore appears as a consensus. The hostility of a small group of residents in the All Saints and Blakenhall area of Wolverhampton is translated to the whole city, as officials praise and support the message that 'Wolverhampton hates kerb-crawlers'. The kerb-crawler is constructed as an outsider, a predatory, dirty male who sidles into known 'red light districts', sneaky and furtive, trying to barter for sexual 'goods' without detection. He is the 'other' not only because of his sexual deviance and uncivil behaviour, but perhaps because of a racialized and class-based construction of 'risky' men. Emphasizing Douglas's (1986) theory of risk and blame, Hollway and Jefferson (1997: 260) remind us that 'this blaming of the outsider builds loyalty and this assists social cohesion'. The resident groups that form around 'the problem of prostitution' construct a 'them' (on the wrong side of state and social laws) and 'us' (as law-abiding and 'normal' citizens) through the fear of crime narrative. For a moral panic to form there does not need to be a consensus from the entire population, as geographically localized 'concerned' communities gain power, status and resources through strategic engagement in the political process, campaigning and community policing (Van Brunschot 2003). Where elite views and strong community voices are synchronized this becomes a driving force in the formation of the moral panic and it appears as if a consensus against the behaviour exists. These processes are part of what Weitzer (2006) describes as a moral crusade against prostitution.

Disproportionality

Goode and Ben-Yehuda (1994: 36) describe the criteria of disproportionality, key to Cohen's original definition of the moral panic, as 'the degree of public concern over the behaviour itself, the problem it poses, or condition it creates is far greater than is true . . . public concern is in excess of what is appropriate if concern were directly proportional to objective harm.' The emergence of disproportionate and exaggerated images and conceptions about the threat and harms caused by men who buy sex can be traced across the postwar decades.

In the 1950s postwar years, the unacceptability of prostitution was solidified as 'romantic love' became the dominant ideal in postmodernity (Giddens 1992) and normative couplings became the 'proper' sexual outlet. It began to be established that it was disrespectable for men to 'consort' with 'fallen women' as less men had their first sexual experience with sex workers and sex outside marriage became normative. In the 1970s the dominant discourses of violence against women and the dangers of men influenced the construction of men who buy sex. Media anxiety around the single case of the 'Yorkshire Ripper' in the UK in the 1970s led to fear and anxiety, and public condemnation of kerb-crawling. The case of the 'Yorkshire Ripper' is worth examining in more detail because of its historical prominence in the construction of the image of who buys and who sells sex.

Reigniting historical fears about 'Jack the Ripper' killing women in the East End of London in the 1880s, the serial killer Peter Sutcliffe who became known as the 'Yorkshire Ripper' (his crimes were based largely in Bradford and Leeds during 1975–80), have a bearing on the present-day construction of men who buy commercial sex from women. In the case of Peter Sutcliffe, at all levels of reporting, recording and investigation, street prostitution featured significantly in the way in which the stories that surrounded the 13 murders were constructed and reported. During the five-year police investigations (that were a catalogue of errors, oversights, professional blunders and ineffective operations: see Cross (1981)), the construction of three of the murder victims as 'active' and 'known' prostitutes had a major bearing on how the investigation team constructed the images of different victims, and more importantly, what type of person the killer would be.[5]

When reading the details of the investigations, trial and media reports of the Yorkshire murders, it is clear that the cultural production of a certain type of male who visited 'red light districts' and bought street sex was part of the mythology that constructed the serial killer. Hollway (1981: 37) notes how Sutcliffe's visits to 'red light districts' were considered normalized sexual violence as an acceptable part of aggressive masculinity. After the two murders in October 1975 and January 1976 of women who were supposedly known as prostitutes, men who visited street sex markets were linked with sexual violence. In a press release in October 1979, a senior West Yorkshire police detective made connections between the killer's hatred for prostitutes with a general view of disgust towards such women: 'He has made it clear that he hates prostitutes. Many people do. We, as a police force, will continue to arrest prostitutes. But the Ripper is now killing innocent girls' (cited in Smith 1989: 175). Apathy towards the sex workers as murder victims was evident (Bland 1992). The acceptance of women involved in prostitution as targets for men with hatred towards them is clear as the serious plea for public assistance to find the killer was only issued after 'innocent' (ie. non-prostitute) women became targets.

Smith (1989) describes how the mythology surrounding Sutcliffe as a 'prostitute killer' that was held by the police and the media had a strong influence in the ill-fated direction of the investigation. As a result of the flawed theory, the image of the killer was constructed as an 'outsider', an 'other' who was not from the local community. Despite excellent photofits of the killer from women who had survived attacks, and nine arrests of Sutcliffe during the period, he was never a serious suspect because he did not appear to be a 'killer' of women or indeed someone who would visit 'red light districts'. What Smith (1989: 171) notes is that it is not the differentness that is glaring in the case of Sutcliffe, but his ordinariness that investigators failed to see which led to major errors and a conviction only by chance.

At the trial, the image of the prostitute 'user' was reinforced. Walkowitz (1992: 232) explains how Sutcliffe was transformed from a shy family man to a 'horror show' monster, troubled as a child and dominated by his overbearing wife. Feminists at the time, although they campaigned hard against the view that Sutcliffe was a 'perverted kind of moralist' but was in fact simply a woman killer, also made strong links between sexual violence and all male sexuality. The construction of a sexual murderer, something that continues to be a rare occurrence (Soothill 1993), as an example of the type of men who buy sex on the street invokes dangerous and unjustified connections between male sexuality and sexual danger. Walkowitz (1992: 238) traces how the radical feminists used the case of Sutcliffe to put forward their argument that normative male sexuality is pathological by relying on the train of thought that equated Sutcliffe's extreme violence as a deep-rooted form of a more general misogyny in society. Sutcliffe began to symbolize violence against all women and the view that other ordinary men, especially those visiting street sex markets, could be capable of such horrors. Walkowitz (1992: 230) notes that at the time of the Yorkshire murders, the case 'provoked and reinforced purity campaigns to clean up red light districts and to outlaw smut', reinforcing the stigma that many sex workers already experienced. Bland (1992: 240) recounts how 'displays of sexual violence' such as sex and porn shops were attacked by women after the 13th murder in December 1980. Women picketed, sprayed graffiti and set up their own self-defence classes as Sutcliffe represented the potential violence of all men against women. Walkowitz (1992) concludes that the feminists who campaigned on the back of the Sutcliffe murders in the 1980s contributed to the politicization of sexuality where stories of sexual dangerousness and who were the sexual predators were constructed. Feminists became an active part of the cultural production of sexual danger resulting in a failure to recognize where the differences in violence lie, the role of the state in creating conditions of violence and the damage of universalizing misogyny and violence.

This exaggerated public tale about men who buy sex, which is far removed from much of the reality of men and how they interact with sex workers, continues through random, isolated cases of murder against sex workers. Extreme cases of recent and past serial killers who have targeted vulnerable sex workers such as Robert Pickton in Vancouver, Canada (Jiwani and Young 2006), Gary Ridgway in Washington State, USA (Levi-Minzi and Shields 2007) and the case of the Yorkshire Ripper in the UK make generalized links between men who buy sex and inevitable violence, cruelty and murder.

Disproportionality by constructing men who buy sex as a threat to social order is also evident during the late 1980s and 1990s which saw a 'new' fear attached to men who buy sex. Although the general moral panic about HIV/AIDS (Weeks 1989) scapegoated female sex workers as one group of 'infectors' that threatened public health (Faugier 1994; Lawless et al. 1996), customers of commercial sex were also described as a risk category. Atchison et al. (1998: 177) describe how epidemiological concerns of HIV/AIDS during the 1990s included the construction of 'risky' male sexual behaviour among men who buy sex. Buyers of sex were considered to be a risk to themselves, their partners and part of a wider public health risk. Brooks-Gordon and Gelsthorpe (2003) note that the kerb-crawling legislation of England and Wales is derived from a range of other fears and concerns for the safety of the public, namely the public fear of HIV and child protection rhetoric that determine the powers given to the police and the seriousness attached to the minor, non-custodial offence of kerb-crawling.

Today, there is continuing evidence to suggest that the case of men who buy sex, particularly the kerb-crawler, fits the criterion of disproportionality, particularly in official documents. Evident in US policy and legislation of the Bush administration, Weizter (2006: 34) describes how a moral crusade led by the Christian alliance and radical feminists 'make universalistic and often unverifiable claims about the nature and extent of a particular social evil'. In the UK, official discourses have adopted a new language that has become accepted, uncontested and familiar terminology in formal documents, strategies and official communication. Words that are particularly pejorative, most notably 'the user', are now the everyday monikers applied to men who purchase sex in policy. The first government document for fifty years on prostitution, that promises a 'process of reform' from 'outdated, confusing and ineffective' laws (David Blunkett, Home Secretary, Home Office 2004: 5), adopts a moral tone from the outset, regarding men who buy sex as morally reprehensible at best and are afforded the term 'the prostitute user' (*ibid.*: 17) throughout all government documents (see Chapter 7).

The fashionable term 'the user' was accompanied by another deliberately loaded term: 'demand'. Speaking of the 'demand' side of the sex industry makes specific links to the economic markets of the sex industry and the existence of 'demand' (buyers) as the main reason why sellers (female sex workers) exist at all. 'Demand' is a curious term that refers to an unknown, arbitrary mass of men who are responsible and blamed for the increase in commercial sex in the global markets and indeed the wider commodification of the female (and child) body. The terminology of 'the user' and 'demand' is important because it immediately refers back to the victimhood narrative of female sex workers who are considered to be without choice, free will or any elements of decision-making powers or control over their bodies. The reality is that these two ideologies, of nasty wrongdoing men on the one hand and poor innocent female victims on the other, mutually reinforce a gendered ideology that commercial sex is immoral, violence against all women and consequently men who buy sex are only abusers.

Other generalized misinformation about all men who buy sex as spreaders of disease, perpetuating the drugs industry, 'white slavery' and 'trafficking' (see Chapter 7 and O'Connell Davidson 2003), adds to the disproportionate fears created around this type of sexual behaviour and group of men. These perspectives have led Brooks-Gordon and Gelsthorpe (2003: 447) to identify how these constructions influence the images we have of which men buy sex: 'We now see the punter [and the pimp] aligned as coercive and abusive characters from whom the public should be protected.' The experiences, stories and identities of men who buy sex are still shrouded in secrecy – few men speak with the media about their activities and the only real testimonies come through online sources, leaving the media free to sensationalize, generalize and construct damaging images of disproportionality.

Volatility

The final criterion to test whether a moral panic occurs is the precarious ebb and flow of the concerns and reactions to the issue. Anxieties about the kerb-crawler as a nuisance have subsided over time only to be reignited by either policy initiatives or specific incidents, like high-profile murders. As the small conviction rates for the offence of kerb-crawling show (see Chapter 7), police forces rarely give this area full attention but react to local and national politics on a sporadic and inconsistent basis. Kerb-crawler 'crackdowns' can suddenly erupt but then lie dormant for a while, although the fear never really dissipates. The re-emergence of the issue is often fuelled by complaints from residents and pressure from councils and local authorities to address a social issue which is an easy target because of the powerlessness of those involved.

Without difficulty, the case of the kerb-crawler fits the five criteria set out by Goode and Ben-Yehuda to establish whether a moral panic exists. Arguing that there is a moral panic over men who buy sex which has gathered momentum over the past fifty years does not justify harmful behaviour or violence against women. Yet simply saying there is a moral panic does not move the debate forward. Exploring the underlining motivations for misinformation and exaggeration about narratives of dangerous male sexuality are the next point of example.

Male sexuality as danger

There are several segments of society that are responsible for reinforcing the generalization that all men who buy sex are dangerous and a threat to the social order. Below I examine how feminist scholars have contributed to this debate and the influences of the Swedish law against buying sex.

Feminist panics about 'the punter'

Alongside popular culture and media representations, academic analysis has contributed to the cultural production of the image of the purchaser of sex as a dangerous and uncivil character who is an abuser of women. Radical feminists who seek to abolish prostitution construct 'the problem of prostitution' as the problem of male sexuality. O'Connell Davidson (2003: 56), citing arguments put forward by Barry (1995) and Jeffreys (1997), suggests: 'In "radical" feminist analyses of prostitution, men who buy sex often become indistinguishable from those who commit acts of rape or incest.' Jefferys (1997: 4) states that a man who buys sex can only be a 'prostitution abuser' because he reduces women to 'sexual objects' by purchasing power and control over her body. Male sexual behaviour in commercial sex is characterized by Jefferys (*ibid.*) as 'barter, promiscuity and emotional indifference'. It is very unclear which aspect of the sex worker–client transactions and markets are referred to as all men who buy sex are lumped together in an unsophisticated assessment of the power relations between men and women in the sex industry.

This essentialist reductionism which is promoted by radical feminists, described by Scoular (2004a: 345) as an 'uncompromised account of domination', refuses to connect real life micro-relationships and dynamics between sex workers and male clients to anything other than 'over-determined gendered power dynamics' (*ibid.*). The day-to-day interactions of sex workers and clients, the many different forms of commercial sex relationship, the false dichotomies between commercial and non-commercial relations and the shifting nature of sexual cultures are overlooked as the panic about the punter takes over. Reductionist arguments that simplify prostitution as the surrendering of the female body to the male 'objectifier' advocate for the punishment of men who buy sex, controlling and re-educating them through 'treatment' programmes.

Some radical feminist socio-legal arguments support and encourage the targeting of all men who buy sex as harmers of women. Madden Dempsey (2005) presents a legal argument in favour of 'prostitute-use' as the main focus of the law. The victim debate and the 'forced prostitution' extremes are applied to explain why all men who visit sex workers should be the target of criminalization alongside 'violent pimps, pimp/partners, and sex traffickers'. Madden Dempsey uses the concept of 'abstract endangerment' to refer to remote harm that is created to the sex worker by putting her at an unacceptable risk of harm. Such a simplistic view of the client–sex worker relationship misses the reality that much prostitution is not 'forced' and the large indoor sex market is organized differently with a reduced level of violence and coercion (see Sanders and Campbell 2007a). Narrow arguments that equate buying sex with sexual aggression and control have the same effect as the moral messages from the media and misinformation in policy. If the concept of 'abstract endangerment' was applied to the current conditions which the state sanctions as acceptable for sex workers to experience, then the culprits of exploitation and abuse of women lie equally with the state. The harmful products of sex work, such as violence against women, are not an intrinsic part of commercial sex but are a product of the system within which it exists. Echoing the arguments of Zatz (1997) and Scoular (2004a), the criminalization of the sex industry with the resulting stigma, marginalization and moral rhetoric that feeds into social and criminal justice policies are of themselves regimes of harm that perpetuate the cultural reproduction of hatred towards sex workers and double standards regarding female sexuality.

Arguments against the radical feminist view are both philosophical (Shrage 1989) and based on legal theory and testimonies from sex workers about their experiences and rights (Kempadoo and Doezma 1999). O'Connell Davidson (2003) draws on empirical findings from a multi-site pilot study across six countries throughout the world (Anderson and O'Connell Davidson 2003) to oppose the arguments for penalizing men who buy sex as the solution to effective action to reduce the abuse of women. First, there are significant cross-cultural differences in the social meanings of the consumption of sex. There are complex differences in the pressure to perform masculinity by either engaging in commercial sex or abstaining from it at various life-stages and ages, meaning that 'normal' masculinity is closely linked with the sex industry. Second, young men and boys are more likely to come under social pressure to engage with the sex industry, suggesting that cultural norms dictate who is buying sex. Third, how clients perceive migrant sex workers was not simply an expression of mastery over a female body but involves racial or ethnic hierarchies and 'a complex configuration of attitudes towards race, migration, sexuality and prostitution' (O'Connell Davidson 2003: 56). Finally, O'Connell Davidson documents and argues against the abolitionist call to penalize men who buy sex because clients display abhorrence towards forced prostitution and trafficking and are concerned with engaging in only 'free' prostitution. Such evidence clearly identifies the homogeneity of men who buy sex, and how a 'one-size-fits-all' approach that places men at the centre of any legislative system is a flawed, naive policy response.

The Swedish Model: a continued pathology against men

The moral panic that is influenced by feminist analysis and knowledge production draws on historical legacies of sexual dangerousness, male sexuality and violence towards women in the context of prostitution. Contemporary policy examples show how the fear of the 'user' has been constructed while at the same time the cyclical loop of distorted information has strongly influenced social and criminal justice policy in some parts of Europe. The example of Sweden is used to suggest the international and cross-cultural nature of the social reaction and the breadth of the moral panic.

The rise of the 1999 Act Prohibiting the Purchase of Sexual Services (one law in a package of measures against male violence) has a political history in Sweden which can be traced back to the early 1980s (Svanstrom 2004). From a state which had effectively absorbed the feminist movement and equality politics, the first commission on prostitution in 1981–2 framed the debate around human dignity rather than gender equality, stating that prostitution was against individual freedom. The early debates that were later vindicated in contemporary legislation were based on arguments about 'the commercialization of women's bodies', being 'counterproductive to equality' and 'contempt for women' (Svanstrom 2004: 230). The centring of blame was evident from 1981: 'Men who bought sexual services from drug-addicted women should be punished' (commission report, cited in Svanstrom 2004: 228). During the mid-1990s, there was increasing support from feminists across political parties to 'criminalize the john' (Scoular 2004b).

The 1999 law made it a crime to purchase a temporary sexual relationship and the law now criminalizes the actual transaction. Kulick (2003; 2004) identifies how the policy response encompasses a whole range of wider moral panics about the status of Sweden and its internal stability in light of its entry into the European Union. Commenting on the latest in a line of punitive laws that have abolished gay bathhouses, prohibited erotic dance and strip clubs and forcibly incarcerated people with HIV, Kulick (2005) argues that the Swedish government has acted out of concern for their 'national sexuality'. Punitive actions against other lifestyles and sexualities are a result of reinforcing 'good sexuality' as morally comprehensible, socially sanctioned and not involving money.

Other commentators have identified that despite Sweden's international reputation for liberal attitudes and socialist structures, the nation-state has promoted other moral panics around activities involving 'risk', sexuality and 'deviance'. Gould (2001) notes a weak liberal tradition and a desire for social purity as the driving force behind several moral panics in Sweden. The new laws to 'protect' sex workers by punishing men who buy sex are a replica of the laws to further criminalize drug consumption by penalizing the consumer of drugs (possession of drugs became an imprisonable offence in 1993), offering 'users' only rehabilitation through the criminal justice system (Gould 2001: 450). The same 'restrictive line' has significantly influenced prostitution policy. Although officially framed in the language of gender equality, Kulick (2003) highlights the fact that Sweden's motivation, which was in the opposite direction to the majority of European countries that have opted for more liberal methods of managing prostitution (Boutellier 1991; Pakes 2003), had other international and national concerns at its heart. Kulick (2004) describes how anxieties over foreign women 'invading' the country can be dated back to the early 1990s when Sweden held a referendum on entering the EU. Fears about foreigners and the liberal practices of other countries spiralled into a prohibition of prostitution policy supported by politicians from the social democrat party.

Supporters of the new law claim that Sweden is the first country to make a stand against the oppression of women and children through prostitution: 'This groundbreaking law is a cornerstone of Swedish efforts to create a contemporary, democratic society where women and girls can live lives free of all forms of male violence' (Ekberg 2004: 1187). Other Swedish academics are more sceptical of the objectives as the concern about men's violence against women in social policy bulldozed other considerations for the effective management of prostitution: 'Prostitution was redefined in the public discourse into a form of structural as well as individual violence against women' (Leander 2005: 118). Commentary since the Swedish law was introduced suggests that the law has merely been symbolic – an expression of what is acceptable sexual behaviour – and to deter men who may be interested in seeking commercial sex (Kaspersson 2006). The impact of the law has been minimal on behaviour: in 2006 Swedish police stated that 'prostitution on the streets is on the increase in Sweden and has returned to earlier levels'.[6]

The symbolic nature of the legislation seems apparent when the numbers of men arrested under the new law are examined. Ekberg (2004: 1195), who praises the new law for its success, reports that 734 men were arrested in five years from 1999 to 2004 resulting in 140 convictions, most of which resulted in a fine. In 2004 there were only 154 reported crimes for the purchase of sex resulting in 48 convictions (Leander 2005: 122). Given that it has been predicted that at least 13 per cent of the Swedish male population have purchased sex (Ekberg 2004: 1194), these statistics suggest the law is having minimal effect on apprehending men or slowing down commercial sexual consumption. With only one man sent to prison since the law was implemented, and the same numbers of women on the streets (after an initial reduction), prostitution has not been eradicated in the slightest. Behavioural patterns have continued as men visit neighbouring Denmark and Estonia to buy sex as well as use the Internet to arrange meetings with sex workers (Kaspersson 2006). Even with claims that the main purpose of the law is 'normative' (Ekberg 2004: 1209), Swedish men continue to buy sex in other countries or from markets other than the street, showing the law has had little effect in changing attitudes or behaviour.

The prohibition law has brought with it other negative consequences. Convictions essentially require testaments from sex workers to provide that evidence that the man was engaged in a 'temporary sexual relationship'. Most cases have been dropped because of a lack of evidence while women are harassed by the police to provide evidence. Three separate evaluation reports of the law (all from different sources) have concluded that there has been no significant decrease in sex workers since the law was introduced and that hidden prostitution had increased (Scoular 2004b: 199). As Kaspersson (2006) has argued, the symbolic and deterrent effect in the law to criminalize men who buy sex has been overestimated, yet its infectious power to spread the message that men who buy sex are criminal offenders has had more success.

The stance that prostitution is violence against all women has shaped the policy in the UK, as well as significantly influencing the law in Finland and Norway. The Scottish Executive have introduced a gender-neutral criminal offence that penalises both seller and buyer. From 2007 all behaviours that are considered nuisance or offensive from sex workers or clients have been criminalized in Scotland. New kerb-crawling laws introduced in Scotland in 2007 include a penalty of £1,000 for men caught 'kerb-crawling', further criminalizing and at the same time demonizing the client (see Self 2006). The move towards criminalization in Scotland comes after a Private Member's Bill to introduce tolerance zones was defeated in 2003 (see Scoular 2004b). Northern European states taking an abolitionist line by criminalizing the purchasing of sex symbolize a backlash against other European liberal states that have traditionally opted for a legalized or decriminalized system whereby safety, regulation and employment rights are at the heart of the law.

Men who act violently towards sex workers

While I argue that a moral panic surrounding the kerb-crawler exists because the disruption, danger and violence posed by a few men in commercial sex are extended to all clients, the rub is that sex workers do experience high levels of violence in working environments.[7] The nuances of evidence regarding sex workers' experiences of violence suggest that the street is overwhelmingly more dangerous than indoor sex markets (Hausbeck and Brents 2000; Raphael and Shapiro 2004; Sanders and Campbell 2007a). Levels of violence mean that street sex workers in the UK are twelve times more likely to die from violence at work than other women their own age (Ward, Day and Weber 1999) and 18 times more likely in the USA (Potterat *et al.* 2004). Street workers in the UK have reported multiple incidents of violence (Campbell and Kinnell 2001; Church *et al.* 2001; Day and Ward 2001; May *et al.* 1999; McKeganey and Barnard 1996; Phoenix 2000).

Understanding the complexities of violence against sex workers is an important part of the argument against generalizing that all men who visit sex workers are violent or potentially violent men. First, a self-report survey of 77 men who identified as clients in Greater Vancouver, Canada, found that past reports of physical violence in both a commercial and non-commercial setting were low, 80.3 per cent (n = 61) said they had not committed a violent act, including refusal to pay, against a sex worker (Lowman and Atchison 2006: 290). These authors conclude:

> While it is certainly true that men commit most of the violence experienced by sex workers, it appears that a relatively small proportion of sex buyers account for most of the violence; many do not assault, rob, rape or murder sex workers ... Much of the literature on the frequency and nature of sex buyer violence appears to be empirically overestimated and theoretically underspecified. (Lowman and Atchison 2006: 293)

There is evidence that repeat offenders are responsible for a disproportionate number of offences (Kinnell 2006a). Data from the Ugly Mug system of reported attacks against sex workers (see Penfold et al. 2004) in the London area demonstrate that a relatively small number of men who buy sex on the street are responsible for multiple attacks on sex workers (Kinnell 2006a: 152). Further evidence from a 1999 study of kerb-crawlers in London by Brooks-Gordon (2006: 192) highlights that only a fifth of the sample of men arrested had convictions for violent offences (21 per cent: 16/77) suggesting that the large majority of clients are not violent. Detailed analysis of the offender profiles of men arrested for kerb-crawling leads Brooks-Gordon (2006: 197) to conclude: 'Just as the violence within prostitution occurs in a minority of exchanges, there are some serious violent and sexual acts committed by kerb-crawlers that involve a very small number of repeat offenders.' In the USA, homicide data sets compared by Brewer et al. (2006) suggest that between 1982 and 2000, 35 per cent of sex worker murders were perpetrated by serial killers. Brewer et al. (2007) note that violent clients were much more likely to have a criminal history of violence, marking them out from the rest of the client population. Equally, it must be remembered that while the majority of violence against women in prostitution is committed by men who pose as clients, violence against sex workers is also committed by romantic partners, acquaintances and drug dealers, robbers and opportunistic criminals, while other women and sex workers are also perpetrators of hate crimes against vulnerable sex workers (see Kinnell 2006a: 156).

When the complexities of violence patterns and the victimization of sex workers are simplified, dangerous generalizations are made. For instance, while recognizing the demographic diversity among clients,

Coy *et al.* (2007: 3) confuse and generalize men who are violent and misogynistic with those who are not: 'What commonalities there are centre on attitudes and beliefs, suggesting that the socio-cultural context of masculinity is more significant than sex buyers' personal characteristics and circumstances.' Such generalizations ignore key research findings such as that by Monto and Hotaling (2001) that explore the extent of rape myth beliefs (attitudes that support sexual violence against women) among 1,286 men arrested for hiring a street sex worker in San Francisco, Las Vegas and Portland, Oregon. This research established that, although the overwhelming majority of clients did not hold such rape myths, a small number of respondents did express high levels of rape myth beliefs such as attraction to violent sexuality and sexual conservatism. This important study, combined with the evidence above, strongly suggests that the violence committed against sex workers is the action of a small number of men and certainly not a feature of all men who purchase sex.

There are material and cultural factors that are important when understanding violence specifically directed at women who sell sex. Localized cultures of masculinity and values of machismo mean that not 'all men' are subjected to the same misogynistic values or perform the same aggressive behaviour. There are significant social divisions among male attitudes and therefore it is not a necessary fact that all men who buy sex are part of one patriarchal system that wants to and enjoys oppressing women. A balance of information does have to be restored: most transactions go without incident; most clients are not sexual predators; most clients do not use violence, force or robbery. Crucially, many clients respect the rules of sex workers and practise safe sex. Other indoor sex work venues, where the power dynamics between sex workers and clients are more balanced because of safer environments, promote client responsibility and allow sex workers more control. Of most concern is that the moral panic around men who buy sex does not promote the safety or rights of sex workers or the responsibility of male clients as the message to eradicate prostitution blurs any real solutions.

Consequences of the social reaction

This chapter has argued and presented evidence to demonstrate that a moral panic exists around the kerb-crawler which influences how all men who buy sex are treated and the social reaction to commercial sex. A symbolic and institutional shift has occurred in recent decades from the acceptability (or mild ambivalence) of buying sex to the construction of such behaviour as anti-social (at least in the case of the street market), uncivil and a danger to women, children and the cohesion of communities. This current position leaves male sexual desire, pleasure and sexuality a target for punitive enforcement strategies, individual blame and social humiliation. The moral panic against the kerb-crawler has implications for others who are caught up in the reactions against men who buy sex and sex workers.

Criminalizing kerb-crawlers endangers sex workers

Policies and policing practices that criminalize and target men who buy sex increase the danger for sex workers, particularly those that work from the street. It has previously been established that where there have been high-profile policing crackdowns and increased surveillance in areas used by street sex workers, risks for women increase (Hart and Barnard 2003; Sanders 2004b; Surrat et al. 2004). With the emphasis on criminalizing both sex workers and men who buy sex, visible policing that aims to arrest and prosecute will have dangerous consequences for sex workers. Sex workers experience an increasingly hostile and volatile working environment, making the market more competitive and creating cause for women to reduce their screening strategies when assessing if a potential customer will be a 'good' customer (Sanders 2005a: 97–101). A reduction in customers because of police surveillance means that women need to stay out late into the night and take more risks to gain the same amount of money. Where custom reduces, this encourages women to engage in other acquisitive crimes or make money through unsafe sex practices.

The increase in policing has changed the nature of the street beat and made it increasingly unsafe. Less popular are the traditional routines of standing on a street corner or women staking out their territories, aware of who's who and where people work. The consequences of policing are that women are reducing the amount of time they advertise on the street but arrange to meet regular clients by mobile phone or at other locations. Anecdotally, other public places have been used for connecting potential clients with sex workers including betting shops, pubs, roadside and all-night cafes, car parks, truck stops, taxi ranks and bus stops. The changing location of interactions between sex workers who work from a street-based market and men seeking commercial sex make it notoriously difficult to engage women who are in most need of services such as health and drug treatments (Jeal and Salisbury 2004).

Maintaining cultural values of disposability

Any policy that states that an activity should not be tolerated is immediately condemning the actors who are involved. The government message that 'street prostitution shall not be tolerated' (Home Office 2004) maintains the image that those women involved in prostitution are worthless and worthy only of intolerance. Such a philosophy can only fuel direct action against sex workers from vigilantes and those who morally object to prostitution are vindicated in their extreme intolerant views. It has already been established that rejecting street sex workers sends a specific cultural message to society that such women are not acceptable. Lowman (2000) points to a 'discourse of disposability' surrounding media and public opinion on street sex work. The use of inappropriate and stereotypical language such as 'prostitute' and 'vice' during the vast media coverage of the Ipswich murders perpetuates the idea that sex workers are to be blamed for putting themselves in danger, and it is only to be expected that they are maimed, raped and murdered because of what they do, their loose morals and general disrespectability.

Kinnell (2006b) has illustrated the presence of the 'discourse of disposability' in media and policy debates in the UK, linking this to the high levels of violence and murder rates among street sex workers. Sanders and Campbell (2007a) argue that policy and some policing practice define street sex workers in a way that increases their status as a vulnerable sexual minority and sends out distinct cultural messages that these women are not to be tolerated. While sex workers are targeted by violent men in unprotected conditions, the government has a responsibility to denounce the negative images that permeate social attitudes and ultimately leave women even more vulnerable to hate crimes and fatal violence.

'Risky' male sexuality as a system of social control

The 'problem of men' in the prostitution conundrum can be understood through explanation of the persistent discourses of the fear of crime, concerns about violence against women and individual anxieties that are reproduced on a social level. Explaining the persistence of the discourse of the fear of crime in modernity, Hollway and Jefferson (1997: 266) centralize the role of the moral panic: 'The inability of modern governments to contain and control the manifold crises that beset them makes "crisis management" arguably the key art of government and moral panics a key discursive strategy in their management.' Hollway and Jefferson (1997: 260) note how the construction of the 'other' through a 'galaxy of folk devils' is endemic in modern society as a mechanism that perpetuates fear and anxieties: 'Folk devils tend to share certain features which make the fear of crime discourse such a powerful modernist tool in the quest for order.'

The fear of crime discourse is a useful concept through which the development of the 'problem of the kerb-crawler' can be understood. 'Fear of crime is a peculiarly apt discourse within the modernist quest for order since the risks it signifies, unlike other late modern risks, are *knowable, decisionable (actionable)*, and potentially *controllable'* (*ibid.*: 265 original italics). Like many 'others' (young 'hoodies', schizophrenics in the community, the black male, the Muslim Asian male, the promiscuous prostitute), the 'kerb-crawler' is an easy target for the fear of crime narrative and the construction of 'risk' because they conform to these three characteristics. Kerb-crawlers are 'knowable': they can be individually identified; their behavioural patterns are obvious, as are their intentions and geographical locations. Equally, their 'victims' are easily identifiable: the local community, mainly women and children, and also 'vulnerable' drug-addicted sex workers. Men apprehended for 'kerb-crawling' have little defence and are powerless to resist police intervention. This makes them actionable. It is these 'offenders' who are a sitting target for crime control strategies as they appear controllable through state and social deterrents and punishments.

Cohen's (1972) original thesis identified how the creation of a moral panic contributed to a 'system of social control' as it influenced how officials and agencies react to the behaviour through processes of 'sensitization', 'diffusion' and 'innovation'. First, male violence has become synonymous with the sex industry as the activities of commercial sex have come to symbolize only violence against women. Second, diffusion of issues from local, geographically specific communities to a national level (i.e. 'tackling demand') escalates local control to a national, persistent 'problem'. The picture of terrorized neighbourhoods, filthy streets clogged up with used condoms and needles, fearful children and petrified non-prostitute women who are harassed by armies of menaces in cars becomes the backdrop of a 'national' problem, discounting the views of other parts of the community, mediation experiences between concerned parties and less confrontational community–sex worker relationships (Pitcher *et al.* 2006). New research on the perceptions of community residents and local businesses that witness, live and work alongside street prostitution suggests that opinions about men who buy sex are more ambiguous and that there is not an overall condemnation.[8] Third, new measures in the form of 'rehabilitation' and 're-education' programmes, increased powers given to the police and courts and a public deterrence campaign provide a coordinated approach to controlling sexuality and form part of wider mechanisms of social control (see Chapter 7).

Individual anxieties, which have both a real and exaggerated basis, are channelled through powerful institutions (media, police, government) to become socially accepted anxieties. Through individual concerns, men who buy sex become legitimate targets for controlling strategies, enforcement, social punishments and criminalization. Hollway and Jefferson (1997: 262) argue that anxieties in individual psyches are reproduced in 'cultural, political and organizational spheres'. Concerns for 'stranger danger' male violence against women and children (opposed to the routine violence in the domestic sphere) are an important part of the construction of kerb-crawlers as sexual predators. Freak serial killers who target sex workers allow individuals to make psychological links between men who buy sex and sexual violence against women. Douglas (1986: 42) explains how risk is about 'trying to turn uncertainties into probabilities'. Incidents like that of the murders of five women involved in street sex work in the UK in December 2006, allow a smooth narrative between the fear of 'the street', the fear of non-normative sex and risky male sexuality. Dangerous male sexuality has become integral to characteristics expressed about street prostitution. Alongside repeated images and exaggerated attention to the street characterized only by constant drug dealing and taking, violent 'pimps', organized criminal gangs, child exploiters and nefarious untrustworthy women, the kerb-crawler has been included in those who are 'dangerous', 'risky' and hated.

The 'risk' culture is responsible for the emergence of punitive approaches and social policy adopting an anti-male stance. Hollway and Jefferson (1997) note how public fears have increased in the light of paedophilia and concerns about failing registration systems of convicted offenders. This has resulted in all men arrested for kerb-crawling having DNA samples taken and their profile maintained on a database as connections are made between this type of sexual behaviour and sinister, dangerous sexual crimes. However, criminal policy does not target all men who buy sex as the potential 'stranger danger' or even tarnish their reputations because of a loss of 'respectability'. O'Connell Davidson (2003: 61) comments:

> It is difficult to imagine any government enthusiastically applying legal penalties to middle-class men who use 'discrete' forms of prostitution such as escort agencies or high-class hostess clubs, and still harder to imagine governments intervening in the consumption of forms of commercial sex that are more closely linked to mainstream businesses in the print, film, leisure and tourism industries.

Suggesting that a moral panic surrounds the reaction to, understanding of and criminal interventions applied to men who buy sex is not to deny the realities of the sex industry, the high levels of violence and the appalling treatment of some sex workers by men who are violent. But these harms are not intrinsic to commercial sex and are not produced by men as a category but are produced by some individuals as a result of cultural values of disposability and a structural environment that increases danger for women and denies their safety.

The 'sexual revolution' did not have any lasting effects on fully expanding our understanding of diversity in sexuality, lifestyles and behaviours but referred specifically to a heteronormative form of sexual relationships and interactions. Under Wolfenden, prostitution was considered a private sexual act and an individual moral issue. Now under the New Labour government, prostitution is reframed as a social problem, an individual pathology, one which should be controlled by social and criminal policy. This policy, or at least the strength of the message, is applied explicitly to men who buy sex from the street, but all men who buy sex are implicitly damned: 'Contemporary understandings of prostitution locate it as part of a rampant, at times highly organized, occasionally global hyper-masculine criminality' (Phoenix and Oerton 2005: 77). Scoular (2004a: 204) highlights how the construction of men who kerb-crawl as dangerous is necessary in order 'to justify the extension of social control over a dangerous new deviant'. The lack of acknowledgement of diversity among men who buy sex or that some men act responsibly (by obeying sex workers' rules, for instance) and are generally non-violent produces a short sighted policy that will waste resources and have limited long-term success.

Notes

1 http://www.wolverhampton.gov.uk/policing_safety/crime_law/street_sex_trade.

2 Press release: http://www.wolverhamptonhealth.nhs.uk/comms/press/released.asp?ID=526.

3 http://www.telegraph.co.uk/news/main.jhtml?xml=/news/1995/06/28/hughgrant.xml.

4 Press release: http://www.libdems.org.uk/news/prostitution-strategy-a-missed-opportunity-oaten.9569.html.

5 If this analysis of the Yorkshire murders was concentrating on how women involved in prostitution were constructed during the investigation, following the work of Smith (1989) and Walkowitz (1992) there could be endless description of the way the female victims were categorized as 'good' and 'bad' depending on their personal sexual histories and moral lifestyles, analysis of the way in which the police and the courts expressed opinions about some of the murdered women and the media representations that perpetuated 'the whore stigma', marginalization and degradation of the murder victims, their families and all women involved in prostitution.

6 Sveriges Radio International, 28 December 2006: http://www.sr.se/cgibin/International/nyhetssidor/amnessida.asp?programID=2054&Nyheter=0&grupp=3582&artikel=1115012.

7 Global trends describe how between 50 and 100 per cent of street sex worker samples experience physical, sexual and economic violence in their job (Kurtz

Chapter 9

Shifting sexual cultures, moving masculinities

This book has presented a snapshot of the everyday realities, motivations, conduct and experiences of largely middle-class men who buy sex from women who work in brothels or as escorts. Although the focused nature of the study limits generalizability, findings about the micro-relationships between this specific group of male clients and sex workers provides evidence of how commerce, sex and intimacy interplay within a system cloaked in stigma, secrecy and criminalization. While it is not possible to make correlations between environmental factors and the behaviours of individual men, this final chapter draws attention to the structuring of the conditions in which sex is bought and sold. I discuss the implications of commercial sex as a feature of sexualized culture and the social prescription of sexual behaviour in contemporary society within the global context of shifting mores, media activity and the overall climate of contemporary sexuality and market forces. Understanding these wider economic and cultural forces highlights the futility of policies which criminalize, pathologize and persecute the buying of sex.

Davis (1937: 744) in the *American Sociological Review* poses the conundrum of prostitution: 'Why is it that a practice so thoroughly disapproved, so widely outlawed in Western civilization, can yet flourish so universally?' Picking up this question, I will expand further on the concepts I introduced in Chapter 3 as the 'push' and 'pull' factors that provide momentum to the sex industry. Contributing to understanding further the 'sexed up' (Attwood 2006; Gill 2007) society that forms a system predicated on what McNair (2002) terms ' the striptease culture' that permeates everyday modern life, this discussion will examine the relationship between work, leisure, and commerce that fuels the desire for sexual pleasure, including commercial sex.

A changing sexual morality?

Although there appears to have been shifts in the prevalence of men buying sex in both the USA and Europe in the postwar years, suggesting downward trends (see the review of surveys by Brooks-Gordon 2006: 81–6), at the beginning of the twenty-first century, it can be argued that the wider sex industries have expanded and increased (see Harcourt and Donovan 2005), to the point that many parts of the sex industry are acceptable and mainstreamed as contemporary leisure pursuits (Bernstein 2001). Even if it is difficult to find any definitive answers to the exact degree of expansion of the commercial sex industries or prevalence of men buying sex in the general population, the extent and capacity of the sex industry, in its many different forms, has become a major economy over recent decades (Collins 2004; Moffatt and Peters 2004). Just in the UK, the geographical spread of the sex industry across small towns, suburbs, entertainment districts, city centre dwellings, private houses and, to a lesser extent, the street is indicative of its current diversity and availability. Although the extent of direct sexual services for sale is impossible to accurately quantify, there are small indicators of the extensiveness of the sex industry. For example, Jones *et al.* (2003: 215) examine the retail planning of the new generation of lap dancing clubs in the UK, which had an estimated annual turnover of £300 million in 2002. Moffatt and Peters (2004), using Internet data, calculated that in 1999 the private and parlour subsectors of the UK sex industry grossed yearly earnings of approximately £534 million.

Adaptability is one of the sex industry's strongest qualities. Sexual behaviour changes with 'techniways' as human behaviour reacts to, interacts with and configures around new technologies (Quinn and Forsyth 2005). With both visibility and availability of commercial sex signalling a new era in the sex trade, more men appear to be purchasing sex than in previous times (Ward *et al.* 2005). McNair (2002: 6) claims that sex industries are indisputably 'of major economic significance in the cultural capitalism of the twenty-first century', suggesting both a permanent and irremovable economy that is an expected if not a tolerated aspect of consumer capitalism. Even if the intricate relationship between the sex trade and global capitalism are agreed upon, for social scientists it is problematic to then assume that what is structurally evident translates into attitude or behavioural change. Do these observable structural changes represent a change in sexual morality? Has the acceptability of purchasing commercial sexual services increased in society while, in many parts of the world, the state condemns and criminalizes those who buy sex?

While there are no recent survey results to draw on that could examine attitude changes regarding commercial sex, changes to sexual attitudes in general may shed some light on shifts in sexual cultures. Scott (1998), while remaining sceptical that the so called 'sexual revolution' of the 1960s led to major changes in sexual attitudes, compares statistics in both the UK and USA to show that attitudes towards pre-marital sex and homosexuality have become less conservative, while extra-marital affairs generally remain condemned. While these trends suggest a move towards liberal sexual attitudes regarding some areas of sexuality, attitudinal measurement does not necessarily indicate behaviour. Other signs suggest that behavioural practices are not necessarily predicated by measurements of attitudes. The reasons for having sex vary widely: Meston and Buss (2007) conducted a factor analysis on two quantitative survey data sets to establish 237 reasons for having sex. The researchers suggest a hierarchical taxonomy of why humans have sex consisting of four main factors (physical, goal attainment, emotional, insecurity) which are further characterized by 13 sub-factors. Differences in sexual strategies and mating strategies are gendered and may contribute to why predominantly men buy sex and women do not. The vast range of reasons for having sex must be considered in the broader picture of why more men are purchasing sexual services according to recent comparative studies (Groom and Nandwani 2006; Ward, et al. 2005).[1]

Cross-referencing survey evidence suggests that the demographics of men who buy sex are ever varied. Current trends indicate there has been an increase in the purchase of sex across the age range and life-course (Ward, et al. 2005). Middle-aged and older men are frequent and regular customers of sex workers, despite Western cultural traditions prescribing sexual socialization for younger males through 'coming of age' rituals in the sex industry. Survey findings have usually pointed to older, widowed, divorced or separated men as the largest group of clients (Pitts, et al. 2004; Wellings et al. 1994: 138). As the therapeutic nature of sexual services is recognized for older people (Duke 2006) and people living with disabilities (Sanders 2007c), and the invention of Viagra provides more sexual ability and confidence (Loe 2004), the functions of sexual services go far beyond sexual release. In addition, there may be changes in the numbers of young men who pay for sex (see Spurrell 2006), although young people's understanding of engaging in sexual rituals for celebrations and holidays may not be interpreted as paying for sex.

There are key social facts that suggest sexual morality is moving away from traditional values as other major structural changes in socialization, belief systems and macro influences shape new generations. For instance, there is a significant relationship between the decline in religious authority and the rejection of traditional sexual values and mores (Scott 1998). As organized religion loses power, religion becomes a weaker regulator of sexuality. Cameron and Collins (2003) found that churchgoing was negatively associated with a lifetime of prostitution usage.

Religious affiliation and levels of belief are declining with each generation in the UK (Voas and Crockett 2005), loosening constraints and possibly contributing to an increase in the acceptability of and engagement in less accepted sexual practices.

Changes in sexual morality and sexual lifestyles and practices are also affected by the changes in demographics. How men live, where they live and the types of relationships they move in and out of has a significant bearing on their place in the sexual marketplace. One of the most significant social trends reported in this respect is the number of single male households:

> In 2005 there were 7 million people living alone in Great Britain compared to 3 million in 1971 ... the largest increase over the past 20 years has been among those aged 25–44 years. The proportion of men in this group who lived alone more than doubled between 1986/7 and 2005 from 7 per cent to 15 per cent. (National Statistics 2007: 16–17)

More men living on their own suggest more people are single without a (at least regular) sexual partner. Other notable recent changes in household composition have a bearing on male lifestyles. In 2006, 58 per cent of men aged 20–24 and 22 per cent aged 25–29 still lived with their parents (National Statistics 2007: 18) which could also hinder the formation of conventional relationships. With divorce averaging at 155,000 per annum and remarriage stable at 113,000 in 2005 (National Statistics 2007: 19), changing relationship formation patterns continue in the twenty-first century, suggesting that men (and women) spend considerable time alone, or move in and out of conventional relationships with periods without permanent sexual partners.

Sexual behaviour is also likely to adapt with the physical changes in men's lifestyles. As more men travel for work, work away from the home and are increasingly mobile in their everyday routines, spending time alone or without their partner is a familiar part of male economic labour patterns. Cameron and Collins (2003: 287) analysed datasets from the National Survey of Sexual Attitudes and Lifestyles in the UK and found that working away from home significantly increases the likelihood of a lifetime usage of sex workers and that such opportunity variables suggest a 'potential substantial increase in the volume of trade'. These changing demographics for the male population may contribute to the rise in the use of commercial sex to fulfil sexual and other needs.

Whether there have been significant shifts in the dominant sexual morality and how such shifts relate to actual behaviour is a sociological conundrum that will be the subject of many more articles, journals, conferences and books in the future. What is important to understand as a result of the empirical findings presented in this book is that there are strong reasons to suggest that sexual behaviour has changed even if explicit sexual attitudes and values remain somewhat conservative regarding sexual relations outside of traditional marriage, as measured by Scott. These changes in sexual behaviour are strictly gendered, as men engage in direct commercial sex while the sex industries accessed by women remain at the level of the 'feminization of sex toys' (Malina and Schmidt 1997), soft pornography (Juffer 1998), Ann Summers parties (Storr 2003) and watching male strippers (Montemurro, *et al.* 2003). Men appear to be engaging in the sex industry as a result of two powerful dynamics: the allure of the sex industry and the dissatisfaction with everyday life that makes commercial sex an attractive option for sexual and emotional gratification.

The push factors

Observations suggest that there are strong push factors that encourage men to seek out commercial sex. As discussed in Chapter 3, motivations stem from an absence of a sexual relationship, the particular sex acts that are desired, the availability of certain types of women and social barriers that contribute to constraints on finding conventional sexual partners and forming relationships. In addition to what men describe as their 'sexual needs', existing normative relationships can prove unfulfilling or are not incompatible with commercial sex, particularly long-term relationships. Changes in individual circumstance, life-choices and styles contribute to factors that open up the possibilities for commercial sex. Beyond these obvious factors that encourage men to seek out alternative sexual arrangements, there are other features of contemporary social life that need considering. This section will discuss how the pressures of everyday living and working and the relationship between marriage, the sex industry and gender roles act as push factors that encourage the abundance of and attraction to the sex industries.

Everyday pressures and the search for 'time out'

The sex industry is bound to interrelated systems of other institutions, specifically the interplay between the labour market and the leisure economy. The common condition for men and women alike in the fast intensity of modern capitalist consumerism is the need for leisure and relaxation time. The growth of health spa travel markets and mini-breaks are a testament to the need to relax, get away and recharge from the intensity and mundane routines of everyday modern living. This relaxation and leisure time is now a multi-billion pound business that can be found on the doorstep of country houses and retreats, as well as all-inclusive health tourism destinations across the world. The sex industry has become a part of leisure time, mainly for men, but to a lesser extent for women, couples and groups, as it merges with the promise of gratification, pleasure and relaxation, whether at home or abroad. Marketing and advertising appeals to the vulnerabilities and weaknesses of men, encouraging them to visit sex tourism destinations. Bender and Furman (2004: 182) analysed the contents of 20 sex tour websites and found that a recurring theme to attract male sex tourists was that of men as 'overworked' and 'unappreciated' where women are 'rewards' or 'trophies' for their hard work. In addition, such sex tour websites promote the idea that finding a foreign woman for companionship or 'just' sex will be the answer to much wider personality problems, flaws in character or poor sexual partners and that the men will find acceptance and be the centre of attention.

While the relaxation and destressing strategies of doubly-burdened women are not the issue here, men I spoke with use their visits to sex workers as 'me time': as a reward, a treat, an experience or relationship that adds to their quality of life. This did not necessarily arise out of a discourse of 'entitlement' or a belief in a male biological right to have access to sex as suggested in other studies (see Coy *et al.* 2007). Men's ability to buy sex was, of course, related to their disposable income and economic position, but this was not necessarily a translation into the desire to exercise power or domination over individual women. Stein (1979: 312/16) reported that buying sex and intimacy represented time out from 'performance pressures' and passive sexual roles were often sought. Buying time with sex workers translated into something to show for their hard slog at the office, something tangible that can transport them into a warm, doughy place where they are the focus of lavish attention for their body, mind and sometimes soul.

Visiting sex workers, spending time in a parlour, or splashing out on an overnight extended session where the rituals of normalcy can be acted out (even breakfast together over the papers has been offered as part of the service by some sex workers), presents the purchaser with the ideal 'time out' from the humdrum of everyday stress, other responsibilities, keeping up appearances and, in their view, being an ordinary 'burdened' man. Returning to the empirical study, male clients articulated the need not to be the responsible husband or father as a significant push factor for seeking out uncomplicated sex (not necessarily unemotional or detached) in the commercial environment:

> Simply the benefit for me is, I don't think it is really an affection element, it's, I have a managerial position at work, I have a lot of capital 'R' responsibility at home, more so than an average parent

with a young child does, and it gives me a little bubble of space where I can shrug some of that responsibility off and be completely relaxed and do something entirely for myself. (Patrick, 39, long-term partner, social care)

Time with sex workers was described as a suspension of reality for male clients. Whether they are consciously or unconsciously acting out the 'client role' this experience provided men with temporary alleviation from the mundane:

What I found in punting is something to look forward to, an escape from the day-to-day pressures of working 18 hours a day, 7 days a week. However, once the punt is over I step outside on a dark and cold winter afternoon, reality soon hits home. The phone starts ringing, people asking where I am, why I've been uncontactable, the mountain of work I've got to catch up on. (Steve, 47, divorced, IT)

Creating this special 'me time' does not always occur in the 'night-time' spaces that are traditionally reserved for leisure. Just like the boozy long lunch at the expense of the company, individuals often blur the traditional divides between economic production time and personal pleasures. Men who arrange to visit a sex worker during their working hours are appealing to the blurred temporal spaces of pleasure and work. Creating special time becomes even more special if it is pushing other boundaries of time, space, secrecy and privacy. Other men prefer to uphold conventional times and spaces leaving their pleasure time to the Friday night or weekend event, or timed for when their partner is away or they are on a business trip in another town or country. Working away from home, staying in hotels, blurs the boundaries of work and leisure providing opportunities for men to fill their spare time with paid-for company.

Those who challenge the existence of the sex industry will suggest that explaining the psychology behind buying sex, acts as an apology for men exploiting women in the sex industry. The social and economic capitalist system is unlikely to exist without an economic framework where market forces are not applied to sex, sexuality and the sexualization of male, female, heterosexual and gay bodies. Pressures to perform in relationships and marriage have made conventional relationships more complex which has resulted in new types of relationships, interactions and sexual practices that act as receptacles for expressions of intimacy and sexuality. At an individual level, motivations to engage in the sex industry usually do not stem from one reason and commercial sex is not mutually exclusive of conventional relationships or other forms of temporary sexual interactions.

Marriage, gender performance and capitalism

The changing status and lifestyles of men as they live on their own and without a sexual partner for longer periods cannot totally account for the rise of the sex industry, as many customers of sex workers are married or are long-term cohabiters. Men who integrate the sex industry into their moral economy and their everyday lives, often over a considerable number of years, are married and usually have little intention of ending this long-term commitment. Stein (1979) explains the existence of the 'call girl' market during the 1970s in New York City as a market for the middle classes who were committed to marriage but not sexually or emotionally fulfilled by the relationship. Still today, marriage, for some clients, is not really the institution of romantic love, fidelity and 'pure' commitment but bears more resemblance to the economic foundation of marriage in feudal times where women swapped sexual services for security and sustenance.

The relationship between marriage and prostitution has remained fundamental in the explanations of why prostitution exists. Davis (1937: 747) explains how marriage constitutes a respectable sexual institution, with all other erotic expressions 'diminishing in respectability as they stand further away from wedlock'. Prostitution appears to threaten the reproductive institution of marriage which encourages state sanctions against it. Yet the unfulfilling nature of marriage for some men means that commercial sex is a viable solution, often instead of extra-marital affairs, for gratification while also maintaining institutional commitments. McLeod (1982) attributes the reasons for men seeking commercial sex to the failure of the institution of marriage to cater for male sexual and emotional needs, rendering alternative forms of pleasure-seeking inevitable in contemporary society. Marriage is not really threatened by commercial sex, as rarely do men leave committed relationships because of paid sex. Instead, men often stay and fulfil their marriage commitments because commercial sex provides solutions to sexual and emotional needs.

Exposing the dynamics between work, marriage and commercial sex highlights the contradictions of modern-day living. Illouz (1997) explores the contradictions between consumption, culture and production that influence love and relationships in late capitalism. Drawing on Bell (1976), she highlights the contradictions of the culture of capitalism as it demands that the individual works hard, what Bunting (2004) aptly refers to as 'willing slaves' in our 'overwork' culture, while throwing ourselves to the hedonism of the night in the 'pleasure saturated cultural atmosphere' of late capitalism (Illouz 1997: 42). Illouz's thesis argues that the 'romantic ideal' constructed at the beginning of the twentieth century helps maintain the democratic ideals of consumer capitalism. The possibilities of buying temporary sexual and emotionally fulfilling interactions with sex workers can both provide temporary relief and uphold, and even perhaps increase, production and consumption. The men I spoke with were very aware that their commercial relationships, no matter how regular or irregular, were temporary, outside their conventional lives and did not immediately threaten their everyday relationships or routines like an affair perhaps would. In fact, their engagement with the sex industry made their everyday stressful lives palatable and allowed them to act out the traditional roles of husband, father, high-achieving employee and responsible citizen. The burden and intensity of modern living, entwined with personal absences or unfulfilled desires, provide the push factors to seek out temporary commercial relations.

Push factors that encourage men to engage in the sex industry stem from the construction of heterosexual masculinity, expectations to be the active sexual male and the formulaic expectations of male performance in forming and conducting sexual relationships. Socialization into the male gender role dictates that men should seek out sexual fulfilment as part of proving masculinity. Contemporary culture, displayed through many media formats, promotes the 'rights' of men to sexual pleasure through men's lifestyle magazines (Attwood 2005), and the core content of primetime television promotes the normalcy of heterosexual males actively and aggressively pursuing sex (see Kim *et al.* 2007). Butler (1990) demonstrates how gender is performed and socially regulated. Although at times buying sex can conflict with positive performances of masculinity as men internalize failure for seeking out paid sex and display the fragile nature of their male identity, masculinity is also performed as an affirmation of the sexual self through intimate and sexual relationships with sex workers.

The pull factors

This section will discuss how intense consumerism and the commodification of sex, along with strong cultural messages about the normalcy of commercial sex, are partial explanations for the popularity of commercial sex.

Commodification, culture and commerce

Illouz (1997) explains the process of the sexualization of the night-time economy as sex becomes a commodity and product of consumption, bodies are used as sales pitches, bodies are on show and a dominant feature of the mass market of leisure that is driven by alcohol and 'binge' drinking as the use of recreational drugs declines (Hadfield 2007; Measham 2004). The mass market of cultural consumption is now predicated on a 'right' to luxury goods: to have fun at the weekends, to treat oneself to quality-of-life enhancing products and experiences, and fulfil the expectations that the seductive night-time economy promises. Sex is an intrinsic part of capitalism and culture, supported by the principles of hedonism, pleasure and fulfilment. Hawkes (1996: 120), when discussing the 'liberalization of heterosexuality', notes that the market of sex is offered through 'lifestyle sex' and 'sex as leisure'. Individuals are encouraged to construct their self-identity through sexual choice and 'a form of erotic window shopping' (Hawkes 1996: 115). These cultural messages do not only shape heterosexual relationships, but the sexualization of the public sphere has extended to the 'mainstreaming of gayness' (McNair 2002: 129), where male and female bodies are commodified in popular culture.

The mass economy of the night-time entertainment industry is fuelled by an overriding theme or guiding lifestyle principle of contemporary modernity: that of self fulfilment and the dominance of an egocentric way of life, placing the individual at the centre of the social world and social interactions (Beck 1992). Illouz (1997: 32) argues that the power of consumerism in modern capitalism is built on the principle of the right to individual pleasure and for one's 'needs' to be fulfilled through consumption and money while values of constraint, sacrifice and selflessness have decreased. Whether individual pleasure is met on a regular basis in the dark spaces and places of the leisure and entertainment economy, or whether pleasure is obtained as 'treats', 'celebrations' or 'one-off's', different forms of temporary sex are part of the pleasure culture. Sex is part of leisure: whether this is extra-marital sexual liaisons, one-night flings found through alcohol-induced interactions, men engaging in group leisure activities in legal sex markets such as lap dancing clubs or individuals buying direct sexual services. Hawkes (1996) describes how the phenomenon of commodification has altered over time: in modernity, material goods were commodified and in late modernity it is self-identity that is produced and marketed. This self-identity is specifically a sexual self that comes in a pre-packaged form, to be taken off the shelf (almost literally) and pursued through conventional or less conventional forms. Choice about the construction of one's own identity no longer remains static or predictable over the life-course, but choice in sexual identity and practice is available for reconstruction as the male body is no longer constrained by socially constructed age-sets and categories (Hockey and James 2003).

The pull factors of the sex industry obviously revolve around the constructions of female sexuality that permeate everyday life. Through the powerful cogs of consumerism, a certain female form is elevated to the status of ultimate desire and commodified as obtainable for any man, however ugly or old, as long as they are willing to pay and play by the rules. The supply of these fantasies by women who work in the sex industries are not a passive dynamic in the supply-demand nexus. Lowman and Atchison (2006: 288) criticize the abolitionist argument for its narrow understanding of market forces: 'Like most other goods and services bought and sold in a consumer society, demand and supply interact: for a certain segment of the sex buyer population, their initial demand was, at least partly, supply driven.' Survey evidence from these researchers describes how 41 per cent (of 76 clients) 'said that it was the availability and/or visibility of sex workers' that first prompted their visit to a sex seller (*ibid.*). The realization of sexual desires is not the only reason for the sex industry. Being a regular client to the same sex worker is a thin disguise for conventionality, where romance, courtship rituals, 'commitment' and fidelity can be acted out in the safe confines of the commercial contract (Sanders, 2008). The dominance of the sex industry perhaps signifies a continuation, rather than a transformation, of middle-class cultural definitions of where a sexual relationship can legitimately come from, how it can be provided and the persistent merging of intimacy and commerce.

The powerful multi-billion dollar sex industry has largely been based on what Hausbeck and Brents (2002) describe as the McDonaldization of the sex industry: a standardization of the sexual services that promises to provide beautiful fantasy women for erotic, sensual and even intimate liaisons. These fantasies are promoted through corporate strategies that produce 'highly predictable production/consumption rituals to increase efficiency and profit and standardize emotional services' (Brents and Hausbeck 2007). The cogs of global capitalism have shown signs that the McDonaldization strategy is shifting to make way for new forms of marketing and organization of the sex industries. Brents and Hausbeck (2007) argue that this shift illuminates the 'touristic' strategy applied to the Nevada brothel industry that offers everyone an 'individualized, interactive, touristic' experiential sexual service not unlike buying a good quality, memorable experience in other aspects of the leisure and entertainment industry. Appealing to the tourist gaze reduces the 'deviant' status of engaging in commercial sex, as it merges with the blurriness of the entertainment economy.

Cultural messages have probably been the strongest pull factor behind the growth of the sex industry. Hawkes (1996: 9) argues that 'the power of sexual imagery' has been grasped and exploited in all aspects of cultural production. The consumption of the erotic image in public, whether to sell motorcars, mobile phones, washing powder or bingo halls, suggests there are shifts in the boundaries of acceptability in late modernity. The power and saturation of the sexual image has led Egan *et al.* (2006: xxvii) to conclude that 'our cultural imagination is thus simultaneously hypersexual (wanting sex, selling sex and making sex a spectacle)'. Bernstein (2001) has argued that the prolific and unabridged use of sex, in particular the female body form, in advertising and other mechanisms of cultural production have produced a greater acceptability of the erotic, a normalization of the desire for the erotic and increasing acceptance for men to pursue these desires. The sex industry, as the ultimate mode of consumption where money, power and erotic sexuality convene, take on new levels of acceptability in both the public and private imagination as these cultural messages become embedded and enduring. The strength of these messages is increasingly powerful and copious because of the new media technologies that did not support the sex industries in previous times.

Weber described the functions of love and the erotic as private respite from the public processes of rationalization (see Whimster 1995). The erotic was the safety valve for modern humanity, a place exempt from the excesses of rationalization, where nurturing and personal gratification could be gained without tampering with the public sphere. Illouz (1997: 195) argues against Weber, or at least for a change in the function and place of the erotic in society, by claiming that love and sex have become rationalized as a product of mass culture. Now, relationships and sex are calculated, hedonism is planned and the institutions that will provide these functions are prolific. We are told what forms of relationships and sex to want and how to conduct our needs and emotions: 'Sex – like love – is a commodity determined by the market transactions and bargaining' (Illouz 1997: 195). The demand and supply dynamics are a peculiar interplay of men wanting to realize their sexual and intimacy desires and achieve temporal isolation from their everyday roles, while some women fully realize that sexual attractiveness and intimacy is somewhat of a luxury commodity that men want to buy wrapped up in erotic, sensual sexuality (see Sanders, 2008). Yet the rational approach to consumption brings with it problems. Any basic Marxist analysis of consumption suggests that the sex industry will appear to satisfy need, but consumption can never be fulfilled. Need can never be satisfied by capitalism because what we are told is necessary for a fulfilling (sex) life is constantly altered, creating compulsive and unsatisfying consumption at the extreme end and sporadic, diverse consumption at the other.

The romantic love ideal remains a strong socializing force that is not necessarily at odds with the foundations for a thriving sex industry. Illouz argues that 'the ethic of consumerism' has been built on an 'anti-domesticity' discourse which does not promote sexual fidelity, trust in relationships and marriage as an ideal relationship or sexual restraint.

In contemporary cultural discourses marriage is not a marketing gem but is often portrayed in popular media as an asexual institution. Broadsheets are intent on telling the middle classes why 'Sex and marriage don't mix'.[2] A headline in one of the weekend papers reads depressingly 'No sex please, we're married' (Johnson 2007).[3] Revealing the extent of lacklustre marriages in the broadsheets sits idly alongside the excess of women's magazines which, on a weekly basis, promise wives thirty ways to spice up their flagging sex life with their husband. We are warned that sex has a shelf life within a marriage and as soon as children come along this heralds a sexual desert as physical intimacy becomes reserved for holidays and celebrations. Yet messages that we should all still be having sex are prolific. The profits to be made from sexual consumerism have not escaped the pharmaceutical giants. Loe (2004) notes how the cheap and easy availability of Viagra on the global drugs market has had a significant impact, particularly in the USA, on tapping into emasculated identities offering the promise of a new sexual lease of life after taking 'the little blue pill'. While messages about whether people should or should not be engaging in sexual activity and with whom are contradictory, no one, whether married, single, celibate or gay, can escape the ethic of consumption that promotes thrill-seeking behaviour, excitement, romance, adventure, intensity and sexual freedom outside conventional relationships.

The middle classes, sex and money

The organization and characteristics of the sex industry as it adapts and changes to social factors, has a significant bearing on who is involved in selling and buying sex. In some towns, which have historically seen busy street sex markets in the UK, there appears to be a reduced number of street sex workers and therefore possibly a reduced customer base in this market. Observations from grassroots involvement in the Leeds-based sex markets suggest that another tier of indoor sex markets are developing as drug using sex workers create new markets for selling sex away from direct surveillance. Outside the sauna markets, women swap sex informally for cash and goods in markets that are characterized by the dangers of traditional street sex work and are based on women's immediate networks and domestic environments. While the once relatively 'drug-free' indoor sex markets (May et al. 1999) may well be changing, at the same time other parts of the industry are attracting a larger customer base. Chic entertainment environments that are often legal offer sexual services to specifically appeal to middle-class men. These expansions exist alongside more traditional, fluid and informal sex markets where, for instance, working-class sex workers, operating from their homes, arrange to sell sex to a small number of clients over long-term periods.

It could be argued that the middle classes are monopolizing the customer base of the sex industry as business entrepreneurs, property owners, conglomerates and legitimate multinationals such as Spearmint Rhino form a lasting landmark on the high street to specifically target men with disposable income. Middle-class venues squelch in fake elegance and expectations to attract regular high-paying customers who will treat saunas, brothels and lap dancing clubs in the same way as they would their favourite restaurant or local pub. In addition, the Internet has created an expanding audience of middle-class professionals who have easy, private and permanent access to online information, who can negotiate the web and have the disposable independent income (that they can hide from their wives) to match the prices of escorts. Illouz (1997: 59) notes that traditionally the working class had more sexual freedom whereas the middle classes flocked to public spaces where flirtation, romance and permissiveness were available unlike the religiously constrained conservatism of their homes. Expansion in the sex industries may well be among the middle classes as consumption, sexualization and new media technologies shape modern life in a way that is unprecedented.

While middle-class men are targeted as the spending leisured classes, the backgrounds of women who work in the sex industry are also changing as the root causes of involvement continue to be economic profit margins contrasted to actual time spent working. Cross-cultural and historical attractions of sex work persist as women continue to receive high pay for low skilled labour (Edlund and Korn 2002). While the British sex industry has been historically characterized by wealthier middle-class males buying sex from poorer working-class women (Finnegan 1979), contemporary shifts in who works in the sex industry have seen middle class, educated women setting themselves up as entrepreneurial sex workers or paying to work in other people's lap dancing bars or brothels to benefit from the shadow economy. Such an example can be found in the best-selling memoirs of Belle de Jour (2005), *The Intimate Adventures of a London Call Girl*, whose acclaimed true story is of a Jewish university-educated 20-something woman who turned to escorting after miserable and failed day jobs.

These women are made up from groups such as those who leave mainstream jobs because the conformity and relatively low pay constrain their lifestyle, free-time and work–life balance. Although women have always used the sex industry to support their education endeavours, increasingly female students, faced with mounting debts and university fees, are opting to work in the sex markets.[4] Roberts et al. (2007) suggest there has been a 50 per cent rise in the number of London-based female students entering the sex industry as a means of earning money over the past six years, in line with the financial burdens of the higher education system. Perhaps suggesting a global trend in the rise of the student sex worker, Duval Smith (2006) reports that the numbers of young women in France who are turning to the sex industry as a lucrative enterprise to fund their college fees is significant. A study by a SUDEtudiant union conducted a survey that suggests some 40,000 female students (2 per cent) fund their studies through the sex industry. An increase in women whose backgrounds are not unstable or marginalized must be understood as part of wider processes of 'upscaling' in the sex industries in Western countries.[7]

Take what's on offer, but be damned if you do

Today, unlike fifty years ago, men who buy sex from women are at the heart of a social contradiction. They represent the tensions between mass consumerism, the sexualization of culture and the constraints of neo-liberal sexual conservatism. The cultural phenomenon of the Western sex industries takes its shape and form from other powerful overarching infrastructures and mechanisms that shape the economy and social structure of late modern capitalism. Consumer capitalism encourages, cajoles and enflames male desire by actively constructing sexual fantasies, commodifying women's bodies and normalizing commercial sex. McLeod (1982: 90) concluded that men are also victims of the social structure and the construction of male sexuality because of the pressure of the conventional male heterosexual role which emphasizes masculine prowess, dominance and sexual performance. Young boys are taught the centrality of acting out their heterosexual masculinity (Holland, *et al.* 1998), and engaging in paid-for sex is often part of the transition or 'rite of passage' from boyhood to manhood. Commercial sex also thrives on a backlash to the heavy burdens placed on men to engage in dating and courting rituals that are tinged with unsatisfactory liaisons. Sexual mismatches and the pressure to consume alcohol in order to socialize while at the same time present as an eligible, worthy and respectable potential partner is a daunting and pressurized expectation of night-time rituals. While relationship formations and intimacy are ever-changing, the normalization of the sex industry as a place for men to find what is missing in their lives is increasingly promoted in the sex industries.

Commercial sex prospers on the principles that underline contemporary consumerism. Bauman (2007) argues that in liquid modernity, the society of producers is transformed into a society of consumers where individuals become the promoter of commodities and at the same time the commodities that they promote. Mass consumer society promotes the right to personal satisfaction and encourages a self-obsession with individualism. The desire for intimacy and sex meets the cultural and economic sphere of consumption affecting value choices, partnership formation and behavioural patterns (Bauman 2007). While existing throughout pre-capitalist systems, commercial sex has been made possible today by the sexualization of the night-time economy, the commodification of sex and sexuality and the continued class structuring of sexuality. Commercial sex is allowed to thrive through direct appeals to middle-class men who have disposable income and seek solutions to the burdens of performing at work, home and in the bedroom.

The sex industry is pervasive, accessible, affordable and convenient. Culture, cultural messages, production and experience promote the acceptance of buying sex. Occupational cultures across the spectrum of manual to professional jobs operate on values of sexual prowess and sexual 'point scoring' and require displays of virility whether through humour, sport or other leisure pursuits. Corporate business often includes commercial sex as part of the company socializing etiquette where customers are courted amid the dizzy and seductive heights of the cityscape. Campbell (1998: 170) concludes that motivations to purchase sex need to be understood as an extension of, or expression of, male sexuality. A combination of push and pull factors make the sex industry a haven of temporary relief from the male sex role and the strict obligations to 'do masculinity'. Motivations for buying sex are not 'deviant' but part of the wider construction of male and female sexuality and the outcome of many different decisions and thought processes for clients, most of which are heavily influenced by cultural messages that encourage men to buy sex.

At the same time as this overwhelming sexualization of culture entices men to consume sex, punitive laws and policing and formal policy reinforce disgust and hostility towards men who buy sex from the street market (see the discussion of the Wolverhampton City Council campaign in Chapters 7 and 8). The past century has seen a shift away from traditional attitudes that medicalized and pathologized women in prostitution as deviant, who simply tempted or corrupted innocent men. Now, the idea that clients who are kerb-crawlers are deviant, abusive and dangerous to women and therefore require punishment and rehabilitation is the overarching formal attitude of officials and policy. What appeared to happen in the 2004–6 Home Office review of the prostitution laws is that violent men who target and attack sex workers in their working environment came to represent *all* men who visit commercial sex sites. Phoenix and Oerton (2005: 96) recognize that 'the relationships between adults in prostitution and their partners have been re-configured in the service of a construction of these relationships as pathological, problematic, exploitative and criminal.' Individuals apprehended for kerb-crawling are treated as if they were sex offenders. They are constructed as culprits who perpetuate abuse, who are as dirty as the gutter, a threat to the social fabric and therefore a legitimate target for criminal sanctions and social shaming.

The immediate contradiction is that there has been a policy silence on men who buy sex from indoor markets as the attitudes and discourse towards kerb-crawlers have not been applied to men who buy sex from indoor markets with the same intensity. This can be explained in several ways. First, the moral argument that it is wrong for men who buy sex from vulnerable female 'victims' is less feasible in markets where women are less vulnerable, are more likely to be drug-free and consensually working. The 'punter' as 'exploiter' discourse cannot easily be applied to the indoor markets where sauna workers and escorts are often making clear choices under few constraints about selling sex. Second, the customer base of the indoor markets is largely middle-class men, and this category has been traditionally protected from the reprimands and sanctions applied to markets that are considered 'dirty' and 'unrespectable' such as the street.

Third, there is a reluctance to demonize or legislate against men who buy sex indoors because they constitute a major part of the economy. Making buying sex from indoor markets illegal would be very hard to police and such a strategy would present major regulation problems. While critics will say that these men are unlikely to become victims of harsh policing policies, within a framework of condemning and criminalizing the purchase of sex and the strength of citizen complaints, all men who buy sex are at risk of these contradictions. For instance, the trafficking discourse is one example of how there have been calls to bring charges of rape against men who buy sex from women who are trafficked,[6] indicating that men who buy sex indoors are not safe from the moral panics against 'risky' male sexuality.

Pursuing eradication: futile, simplistic and failing

The concept of eradicating demand for commercial sex is the underlining principle of the UK government's prostitution strategy (along with other countries such as Sweden, Scotland and Norway). Such an aim is futile and contradictory at many levels. First, the state explicitly supports the sex industry by allowing extensive sexual consumerism, commodification of bodies and the economic forces (such as female poverty) underpinning the sex industry to flourish. Many parts of the sex industry are sanctioned by the state through licensing, sporadic and inconsistent policing, informal agreements between owners and regulators, as well as explicit tolerance for legal markets. Lowman and Atchison (2006: 288) argue that because of the supply/demand market forces that make commercial sex available and partly sanctioned by the state, '... the proposal to criminalize the purchase of sexual services and decriminalize their sale – the law adopted in Sweden – becomes a form of institutionalized entrapment.' These contradictions and complexities mean that the state cannot be a straightforward ally in any attempts to reduce sexual exploitation and the harm of women. O'Connell Davidson (2003: 60) makes the position of the state clear: 'The state plays an important role in shaping the consumption of commercial sex, not simply by permitting or tolerating certain types of consumption, but also by endorsing, perpetuating or promoting the social divisions and status hierarchies that are so central to clients' choices as consumers.' The call from governments for men to individually resist temptation, find sexual expression only in those institutions where sex is considered 'respectable', or alternatively accept sexual dissatisfaction, celibacy or masturbation, or resist cultural pressures that dictate the male role is at odds with other fundamental cultural messages. Bernstein (2001: 411) pointed out several years ago that the mass expansion and diversification of the sex industry leading to 'cultural normalization', is in direct opposition to the social and criminal justice policies that seek to criminalize buying sex. Bernstein calls this contradiction the simultaneous normalization and problematization of commercial sex (Bernstein 2001: 409).

Prohibitionists who advocate that 'demand' can be removed through educational awareness (Coy et al. 2007), are challenging the fundamental institutions of capitalism and implicitly suggest that the sex industry can be managed by taking on the forces of capitalism, media and new technology formats that make sexualization and commodification so prolific. The eradication agenda is opposing durable cultural messages about sex that are not necessarily new but centuries old: the embedded commodification of sex and of bodies (homosexual or heterosexual, male or female), the overpowering 'ethic of consumption' and the emphasis on performing masculinity through sex.

Can educational programmes really challenge these forces? O'Connell Davidson (2003: 62) optimistically suggests: 'If policy-makers around the world are concerned to reduce overall levels of demand for prostitution, there is a need for extensive and long-term education work to bring about a fundamental re-visioning of sexuality, age, gender relations and prostitution.' If indeed it were possible to overstep complex structural factors of capitalism, sexual relations between men and women, biological differences and deep-rooted gender constructions, then 'demand' could potentially be diminished given a profound change in social values and cultural practices (Stein 1979). Yet philosophically envisaging a society without commercial sex seems utopian. Davis (1937: 753) argues that a society where prostitution was absent could only be one where there was ultimate sexual freedom, without marriage, sexual constraint or values such as monogamy and sexual jealousy, and no institutional controls over sexual expression: 'Free intercourse for pleasure and friendship is the greatest enemy of prostitution.' Policies to eradicate parts of the sex industry, with a heavy influence on 'tackling demand' through poster campaigns and beer mat gimmicks, are a gross underestimation of the nature, extent and causation of the sex industries and the relationship between the state and the maintenance of commercial sex.

Second, eradication policies that are motivated by a fundamental belief that certain forms of sexual practices between adults are wrong are at odds with the basis of democratic law. This argument can be explained by understanding why the government upholds the legality of selling and buying sex between consenting adults, while at the same time promoting the message that prostitution is wrong. The first point to make in explaining this contradiction is that it is still a basic premise of democracy that morality cannot be the basis of the law and cannot inform the definition of when a crime is committed because moral values, and particularly those relating to sexuality, are not universally shared (Soble 2002). If morality were the basis of the law then many sexual practices which offend one powerful group (such as homosexuality, anal or oral intercourse, masturbation, adultery, fornication, nudity, public kissing or group sex) would be outlawed. However, the state does come into play, through laws and social control agencies, when the matter considered is one of public order and maintenance. Where there is a need to protect vulnerable individuals, prevent unambiguous cases of exploitation and coercion, and reduce public nuisance, as in any other commercial sectors, the state has a role.

Third, policies and systems that have the objective of eradicating demand ignore the class structuring of the sex industries and the historical legacies that purchasing sex are built on. Adults exchanging sex for money cannot be outlawed because the fundamental transactional and economic premise of exchanging sex and/or intimacy for money is the basis of many relationships. The trade-offs between intimacy and sex with commerce are deep rooted in systems of payment and the meaning of money as compensation, where there is 'an equal exchange of values and a certain distance, contingency, bargaining and accountability among parties' (Zelizer 1996: 482). Rendering the economic exchange of sex for money against the law would be nonsensical as it would undermine relationships that are considered conventional and customary. It is within these wider frameworks of the relationship between commerce, sex and intimacy that the realities of prostitution and the sex industry must be understood in order for justice to override hypocrisy and contradiction.

Given the unbridled 'ethic of sexual consumption' that would take immense social and cultural changes to reverse, the aim of protecting sex workers and reducing harm and exploitation should be the priority of policy and policing. There are direct and straightforward methods to subvert negative attitudes and practices against sex workers. One option is for a decriminalized minimally regulated indoor market that would enable women to work safely and collectively, brothel owners to work within occupational health and safety guidelines and licensing laws, and resources to target obvious cases of exploitation. A cultural change, brought about by regulatory laws and state messages, could begin to remove the ambiguous social status of those working in sex industries and instead replace the stigma with the status of sexual labourer and professional. As Shrage (1989: 359) states, reforming the practice and profession of commercial sex transactions would replace those aspects of prostitution that are considered repugnant in certain sectors with a different form of institution that legitimates sex workers' skills and abilities and reduces harm, violence and cultural negativity.

Returning finally to the empirical study that forms the basis of this book, it is important to remember when discussing 'men who buy sex' that they are human beings. I witnessed humanity and humility expressed by a group of men who are generally regarded as misfits. The men I spoke with, listened to and discussed sexuality and lifestyles with during this research had little intention of seeking to control or dominate the women they paid for services. Harming, humiliating or harassing women was not part of the men's morality and was far removed from the principles which informed their engagement with sex workers. I was struck by the depth of men's relationships with and their considered feelings for sex workers, the processes of understanding their own sexual selves and sometimes the struggles to reconcile their personal lives with public expectations. Many relationships clients had with sex workers were similar to non-commercial relationships and built on integrity and honesty. Although this research is based on only a micro-snapshot of a large and diverse population of men, and without wishing to draw attention away from the victimization of sex workers by some men, demonizing a group of men who could be at the forefront of responsible commercial sex sat uncomfortably with my personal interactions with the research respondents.

One of the youngest interviewees, Jeremy, a 24-year-old student, volunteered because he hoped the research would somehow feed into a more realistic awareness of the whole sex industry:

> I would like to contribute something that would maybe cast the industry in a better light and make people think that working girls aren't just drug addicts who are forced by pimps and clients aren't just sleazy men in raincoats and don't wear condoms. I think it would be good if people sort of realized that there is a lot of nice people involved and it's not always a bad thing.

For some time voices and attitudes like Jeremy's have been missing from the debate on the place of commercial sex in society. I hope this book, that reveals partial truths, goes some way to identifying another side of the complex story of the sale of what can be pleasurable and intimate sexual services.

Notes

1 Historical trend data is missing from sources available to researchers. This makes measuring patterns of prevalence of buying sex over a longer period of time difficult to assess.
2 'Why we stopped having sex', *Observer*, 8 October 2006. See: http://www.observer.guardian.co.uk/woman/story/0,,1887440,00.html.
3 'No sex please, we're married', *Guardian*, 6 January 2007. See: http://www.guardian.co.uk/family/story/0,,1982971,00.html.
4 'Female students turn to prostitution to pay fees', *Times*, 8 October 2006. See Times Online: http://www.timesonline.co.uk/tol/life_and_style/education/student/news/article665019.ece.
5 The attractions of male escort work (flexible working hours, part-time working and multiple job opportunities) may account for suggested rises in this sex market (Cameron *et al.* 1999).
6 'Crackdown pledged on sex with trafficked women', *Guardian*, 18 July 2007. See: http://www.guardian.co.uk/gender/story/0,,2128883,00.html.

Appendix

List of interviewees

Pseudonym	Age	Occupation	Marital status	Monthly expenditure on sexual services	Number of years buying sex
Matthew	39	Teacher	Married	£150	5
Benny	70	Retired trucker	Widowed	£80	3
Sol	58	Self-employed	Widowed	£45	8
Brian	37	Manual worker	Married	£50	20
Alastair	30	IT	Long-term partner	£200	6
Anthony	31	Customer services	Long-term partner	£200	14
Kelvin	36	Charity worker	Single	£50	1
Tom	60	Social care	Widowed	£200	1
Stuart	38	Media	Single	£250	10
Jeff	57	Senior management	Married	£100	10
Minty	27	IT	Single	£300	1
Farzel	28	Sales	Single	£200	3
John	58	Sales	Divorced/ separated	£100	30
Steve	47	IT	Divorced/ separated	£250	3
Dean	34	Sales	Single	£200	4
Jeremy	24	Student	Single	£100	3
Paulo	54	Property developer	Married	£300	30
Richard	56	Media	Divorced/ separated	£200	1
Paul	56	Retired bank manager	Married	£150	25
Billy	43	Manufacturing	Married	£100	5
Vernon	50	Teacher	Divorced/ separated	£100	3

Darren	36	Customer services	Long-term partner	£80	5
Tony	55	Pilot	Married	£150	30
Fazel	22	Student	Single	£60	3
Mitchell	49	Managing director	Married	£150	6
Ross	54	Engineering	Single	£100	3
Terry	68	Lawyer	Married	£500	20
Andy	31	Sales	Long-term partner	£100	3
Howard	49	Academic	Married	£150	10
Alan	59	Retired	Divorced/separated	£100	4
Ron	51	Teacher	Divorced/separated	£100	8
George	58	IT	Married	£400	3
Liam	70	Retired academic	Widowed	£200	6
Patrick	39	Social care	Long-term partner	£300	3
Noah	30	Manufacturing	Single	£150	1
Norman	50	Engineering	Married	£400	25
Ali	27	Manufacturing	Long-term partner	£50	3
Arthur	50	Army	Married	£200	33
Edward	38	Engineering	Long-term partner	£150	10
Jonny	51	IT	Married	£400	23
Graham	52	Public sector	Divorced/separated	£300	3
Michael	45	Public sector	Divorced/separated	£100	10
David	45	Social care	Divorced/separated	£80	5
Boris	56	Retired accountant	Married	£300	16
Mikey	38	IT	Married	£100	5
Trey	24	Student	Single	£50	3
Craig	38	Sales	Single	£150	10
Daniel	41	Teacher	Single	£150	3
Adam	32	Media	Long-term partner	£100	6
Morris	55	Academic	Married	£100	10

Bibliography

Adler, C. (2003) 'Young women offenders and the challenge of restorative justice', in E. McLaughlin, R. Fergusson, G. Hughes and L. Westmarland (eds), *Restorative Justice. Critical Issues*. Buckingham: Open University Press, pp. 117–26.

Agustin, L. M. (2005) 'New research directions: the cultural studies of commercial sex', *Sexualities*, 8 (5): 618–31.

Anderson, B. (1983) *Imagined Communities: Reflections on the Origin and Spread of Nationalism*. New York: Verso.

Anderson, B. and O'Connell Davidson, J. (2003) *Is Trafficking in Human Beings Demand Driven? A Multi-Country Pilot Study*. Geneva: International Organization for Migration.

Annandale, D. (2005) *Call Me Elizabeth*. London: Little Brown Book Group.

Ashbee, E. (2007) *The Bush Administration, Sex and the Moral Agenda*. Manchester: Manchester University Press.

Association of Chief Police Officers (2004) *Policing Prostitution: ACPO's Policing Strategy and Operational Guidelines for Dealing with Experience and Abuse Through Prostitution*. London: Home Office.

Atchison, C., Fraser, L. and Lowman, J. (1998) 'Men who buy sex: preliminary findings of an exploratory study', in J. Elias, V. Bullough, V. Elias and J. Elders (eds), *Prostitution: On Whores, Hustlers and Johns*. New York: Prometheus Books, pp. 172–203.

Attwood, F. (2005) ' "Tits and ass and porn and fighting". Male heterosexuality in magazines for men', *International Journal of Cultural Studies*, 8 (1): 83–100.

Attwood, F. (2006) 'Sexed up: theorizing the sexualization of culture', *Sexualities*, 9 (1): 7–94.

Barnard, M. (1993) 'Violence and vulnerability: conditions of work for street working prostitutes', *Sociology of Health and Illness*, 15 (1): 5–14.

Barnard, M., McKeganey, N. and Leyland, A. (1993) 'Risk behaviours among male clients of female prostitutes', *British Medical Journal*, 307 (6900): 361–2.

Barry, K. (1995) *Prostitution and Sexuality*. New York: New York University Press.

Bauman, Z. (2005) *Liquid Life*. Cambridge: Polity Press.

Bauman, Z. (2007) *Consuming Life*. Cambridge: Polity Press.

Beck, U. (1992) *Risk Society: Towards a New Modernity*. London: Sage.

Becker, H. (1963) *Outsiders: Studies in the Sociology of Deviance*. London: Free Press of Glencoe.

Bell, D. (1976) *The Cultural Contradictions of Capitalism*. London: Harper Collins.

Bell, V. (2002) 'The vigilant(e) parent and the paedophile. The *News of the World* campaign 2000 and the contemporary governmentality of child sexual abuse', *Feminist Theory*, 3 (1): 83–102.

Belle de Jour (2005) *The Intimate Adventures of a London Call Girl*. London: Phoenix.

Bellis, M. A., Watson, F. L. D., Hughes, S., Cook, P. A., Downing, J., Clark, P. and Thomson, R. (2007) 'Comparative views of the public, sex workers, businesses and residents on establishing managed zones for prostitution: analysis of a consultation in Liverpool', *Health and Place*, 13 (3): 603–16.

Bender, K. and Furman, R. (2004) 'The implications of sex tourism on men's social, psychological, and physical health', *Qualitative Report*, 9 (2): 176–91.

Berger, P. and Luckmann, T. (1976) *The Social Construction of Reality*. New York: Doubleday.

Bernstein, E. (2001) 'The meaning of the purchase: desire, demand and the commerce of sex', *Ethnography*, 2 (3): 389–420.

Birch, M. and Miller, T. (2000) 'Inviting intimacy. The interview as therapeutic opportunity', *International Journal of Social Research Methodology*, 3 (3): 189–202.

Bland, L. (1992) 'The case of the Yorkshire Ripper: mad, bad beast or male?', in J. Radford and D. Russell (eds), *Femicide: The Politics of Woman Killing*. Buckingham: Open University Press, pp. 233–52.

Boutellier, J. (1991) 'Prostitution, criminal law and morality in the Netherlands', *Crime, Law and Social Change*, 15 (2): 201–11.

Boynton, P. and Cusick, L. (2006) 'Sex workers to pay the price', *British Medical Journal*, 332 (28 January): 190–1.

Braithwaite, J. (1989) *Crime, Shame and Reintegration*. Cambridge: Cambridge University Press.

Brents, B. and Hausbeck, K. (2007) 'Marketing sex: US legal brothels and late capitalist consumption', *Sexualities*, 10 (4): 425–39.

Brewer, D. (2000) 'Prostitution and the sex discrepancy in reported number of sexual partners', *Proceedings of the National Academy of Science*, 97 (22): 12385–8.

Brewer, D., Dudek, J., Potterat, J., Muth, S., Roberts, J. and Woodhouse, D. (2006) 'Extent, trends and perpetrators of prostitution-related homicide in the United States', *Journal of Forensic Science*, 51 (5): 1101–8.

Brewer, D., Potterat, J., Muth, S., Roberts, J. M., Dudek, J. and Woodhouse, D. (2007) *Clients of Prostitute Women: Deterrence, Prevalence, Characteristics and Violence*. Washington, DC: US Department of Justice.

Brewis, J. and Linstead, S. (2000a) *Sex, Work and Sex Work*. London: Routledge.

Brewis, J. and Linstead, S. (2000b) ' "The worst thing is the screwing" (1): consumption and the management of identity in sex work', *Gender, Work and Organization*, 7 (2): 84–97.

Brooks-Gordon, B. (2005) 'Clients and commercial sex: reflections on *Paying the Price*: a consultation paper on prostitution', *Criminal Law Review*, 425–43.

Brooks-Gordon, B. (2006) *The Price of Sex: Prostitution, Policy and Society*. Cullompton: Willan.

Brooks-Gordon, B. and Gelsthorpe, L. (2003) 'Prostitutes' clients, Ken Livingstone and a new Trojan Horse', *Howard Journal*, 42 (5): 437–51.

Browne, J. and Minichiello, V. (1995) 'The social meanings behind male sex work: implications for sexual interactions', *British Journal of Sociology*, 46 (4): 598–622.

Bryant, C. (1982) *Sexual Deviancy and Social Proscription*. New York: Human Sciences Press.

Bunting, M. (2004) *Willing Slaves. How the Overwork Culture is Ruling Our Lives*. London: Harper Perennial.

Busza, J. (2006) 'Having the rug pulled from under your feet: one project's experience of the US policy reversal on sex work', *Health Policy and Planning*, 21 (4): 329–32.

Butler, J. (1990) *Gender Trouble: Feminism and the Subversion of Identity*. London: Routledge.

Cabezas, A. (2004) 'Between love and money: sex, tourism and citizenship in Cuba and the Dominican Republic', *Signs: Journal of Women in Culture and Society*, 29 (6): 987–1015.

Cameron, S. and Collins, A. (2003) 'Estimates of a model of male participants in the market for female heterosexual prostitution services', *European Journal of Law and Economics*, 16 (1): 271–88.

Cameron, S., Collins, A. and Thew, N. (1999) 'Prostitution services: an exploratory empirical analysis', *Applied Economics*, 31 (12): 1523–9.

Campbell, R. (1998) 'Invisible men: making visible male clients of female prostitutes in Merseyside', in J. Elias, V. Bullough, V. Elias and G. Brewer (eds), *Prostitution: On Whores, Hustlers and Johns*. New York: Prometheus Books, pp. 155–71.

Campbell, R. and Kinnell, H. (2001) ' "We shouldn't have to put up with this": street sex work and violence', *Criminal Justice Matters*, 42 (Winter): 12.

Campbell, R. and Storr, M. (2001) 'Challenging the kerb crawler rehabilitation programme', *Feminist Review*, 67 (Spring): 94–108.

Carabine, J. (ed.) (2004) *Sexualities. Personal Lives and Social Policy*. Bristol: Policy Press.

Carnes, P. (2001) *Out of the Shadows. Understanding Sexual Addiction*, 3rd edn. Minnesota, MN: Hazelden.

Castells, M. (1996) *The Rise of the Network Society*. Oxford: Blackwells.

Chambers, W. (2007) 'Oral sex: varied behaviours and perceptions in a college population', *Journal of Sex Research*, 44 (1): 28–42.

Chetwynd, J. and Plumridge, E. (1994) 'Knowledge, attitudes and activities of male clients of female sex workers: risk factors for HIV', *New Zealand Medical Journal*, 107 (3): 351–3.

Church, S., Henderson, M., Barnard, M. and Hart, G. (2001) 'Violence by clients towards female prostitutes in different work settings: questionnaire survey', *British Medical Journal*, 322 (3 March): 524–5.

Cohen, S. (1972) *Folk Devils and Moral Panics*. London: MacGibbon & Kee.

Collins, A. (2004) 'Sexuality and sexual services in the urban economy and socialscape: an overview', *Urban Studies*, 41 (9): 1631–42.

Connell, R. W. (1995) *Masculinities*. Cambridge: Polity Press.

Cooper, A., McLoughlin, I. and Campbell, K. (2000) 'Sexuality in cyberspace: update for the 21st century', *CyberPsychology and Behavior*, 3 (4): 521–36.

Cotterill, P. (1992) 'Interviewing women: issues of friendship, vulnerability and power', *Women's Studies International Forum*, 15 (5): 593–606.

Coy, M., Horvath, M. and Kelly, L. (2007) *'It's Just Like Going to the Supermarket': Men Buying Sex in East London*. London: Child & Woman Abuse Studies Unit, London Metropolitan University.

Critcher, C. (2002) 'Media, government and moral panic: the politics of paedophilia in Britain 2000–1', *Journalism Studies*, 3 (4): 521–35.

Cronin, B. and Davenport, E. (2001) 'E-rogenous zones: positioning pornography in the digital economy', *Information Society*, 17 (1): 33–48.

Cross, R. (1981) *The Yorkshire Ripper: The In-depth Study of a Mass Killer and His Methods*. London: HarperCollins.

Cusick, L. and Berney, L. (2005) 'Prioritizing punitive responses over public health: commentary on the Home Office consultation document *Paying the Price*', *Critical Social Policy*, 25 (4): 596–606.

Daniels, C. (2006) *Priceless: My Journey Through a Life of Vice*. London: Hodder & Stoughton.

Davis, K. (1937) 'The sociology of prostitution', *American Sociological Review*, 2 (5): 744–55.

Day, S. and Ward, H. (2001) 'Violence towards female prostitutes', *British Medical Journal*, 323 (28 July): 230.

Delacoste, F. and Alexander, P. (1988) *Sex Work: Writings by Women in the Sex Industry*. London: Virago.

Douglas, M. (1986) *Risk Acceptability According to the Social Sciences*. London: Routledge & Kegan Paul.

Dressel, P. and Petersen, D. (1982) 'Becoming a male stripper: recruitment, socialization, and ideological development', *Work and Occupations*, 9 (4): 387–406.

Duke, K. (2006) 'Project retains prostitutes as care workers for elderly people', *British Medical Journal*, 332: 685.

Duncombe, J. and Marsden, D. (1996) 'Whose orgasm is this anyway? "Sex work" in long-term heterosexual relationships', in J. Weeks and J. Holland (eds), *Sexual Cultures, Communities, Values and Intimacy*. London: Macmillan, pp. 220–58.

Duncombe, J. and Jessop, J. (2002) ' "Doing rapport" and the ethics of "faking friendship"', in M. Mauthner, M. Birch, M. Jessop and T. Miller (eds), *Ethics in Qualitative Research*. London: Sage, pp. 107–22

Durkin, K. (1997) 'Misuse of the Internet by pedophiles: implications for law enforcement and probation practice', *Federal Probation*, 61 (3): 14–18.

Durkin, K. and Bryant, C. (1995) ' "Log on to sex": some notes on the carnal computer and erotic cyberspace as an emerging research frontier', *Deviant Behaviour*, 16 (2): 179–200.

Duval Smith, A. (2006) '40,000 French students join sex trade to fund degrees', *Independent* (London), 31 October.

Earle, S. and Sharp, K. (2007) *Sex and Cyberspace: Men who Pay for Sex*. Aldershot: Ashgate.

Ebo, B. (ed.) (1998) *Cyberghetto or Cybertopia: Race, Class and Gender on the Internet*. New York: Praeger.

Edwards, T. (2006) *Cultures of Masculinity*. London: Routledge.

Edlund, L. and Korn, E. (2002) 'A theory of prostitution', *Journal of Political Economy*, 110 (1): 181–214.

Efthimiou-Mordant, A. (2002) 'Sex working drug users: out of the shadows at last', *Feminist Review*, 72 (1): 82–3.

Egan, D. (2003) 'I'll be your fantasy girl, if you'll be my money man: mapping desire, fantasy and power in two exotic dance clubs', *Journal for the Psychoanalysis of Culture and Society*, 8 (1): 277–96.

Egan, D. (2005) 'Emotional consumption: mapping love and masochism in an exotic dance club', *Body and Society*, 11 (4): 87–108.

Egan, D. (2006) *Dancing for Dollars and Paying for Love*. New York: Palgrave Macmillan.

Egan, D., Frank, K. and Johnson, M. (eds) (2006) *Flesh for Fantasy. Producing and Consuming Exotic Dance*. New York: Thunder's Mouth Press.

Ekberg, G. (2004) 'The Swedish law that prohibits the purchase of sexual services: best practices for prevention of prostitution and trafficking in human beings', *Violence Against Women*, 10 (10): 1187–18.

Ellis, A. (1959) 'Why married men visit prostitutes', *Sexology*, 25 (3): 344–60.

English Collective of Prostitutes (1997) 'Campaigning for legal change', in G. Scambler and A. Scambler (eds), *Rethinking Prostitution*. London: Routledge, pp. 83–104.

Faugier, J. (1994) 'Bad women and good customers: scapegoating, female prostitution and HIV', in C. Webb (ed.), *Living Sexuality Issues for Nursing and Health*. London: Scutar Press, pp. 50–64.

Faugier, J. and Cranfield, S. (1995) 'Reaching male clients of female prostitutes: the challenge for HIV prevention', *AIDS Care*, 7 (Supplement 1): S21–S32.

Finnegan, F. (1979) *Poverty and Prostitution: A Study of Victorian Prostitutes in York*. Cambridge: Cambridge University Press.

Fischer, B., Wortley, S., Webster, C. and Kirst, M. (2002) 'The socio-legal dynamics and implications of "diversion": the case study of the Toronto "John School" diversion programme for prostitution offenders', *Criminal Justice*, 2 (4): 385–410.

Fox, N. and Roberts, C. (1999) 'GPs in cyberspace: the sociology of a "virtual community"', *Sociological Review*, 47 (4): 643–71.

Frank, K. (1998) 'The production of identity and the negotiation of intimacy in a "gentleman's club"', *Sexualities*, 1 (2): 175–201.

Frank, K. (2002) *G-Strings and Sympathy*. Durham, NC: Duke University Press.

Frank, K. (2006) 'Observing the observers: reflections on my regulars', in D. Egan, K. Frank and M. Johnson (eds), *Flesh for Fantasy*. New York: Thunder's Mouth Press, pp. 111–38

Freund, M., Lee, N. and Leonard, T. (1991) 'Sexual behaviour of clients with street prostitutes in Camden, New Jersey', *Journal of Sex Research*, 28 (4): 579–91.

Freund, M., Leonard, T. and Lee, N. (1989) 'Sexual behaviour of resident street prostitutes with their clients in Camden, New Jersey', *Journal of Sex Research*, 26 (4): 460–78.

Gaffney, J. (2007) 'A co-ordinated prostitution strategy and response to paying the price – but what about the men?', *Community Safety Journal*, 6 (1): 27–33.

Gaffney, J. and Beverley, K. (2001) 'Contextualising the construction and social organisation of the commercial male sex industry in London at the beginning of the twenty-first century', *Feminist Review*, 67 (Spring): 133–41.

Gagnon, J. H. and Simon, W. (1973) *Sexual Conduct. The Social Sources of Human Sexuality*. Chicago, IL: Aldine.

Gagnon, J. H. and Simon, W. (1987) 'The sexual scripting of oral genital contacts', *Archives of Sexual Behavior*, 16 (1): 1–25.

Gall, G. (2006) *Sex Worker Union Organising: An International Study*. London: Palgrave Macmillan.

Gibbens, T. and Silberman, M. (1960) 'The clients of prostitutes', *British Journal of Venereal Diseases*, 36 (1): 113–17.

Giddens, A. (1992) *The Transformation of Intimacy: Sexuality, Love and Eroticism in Modern Societies*. Stanford, CA: Stanford University Press.

Gill, R. (2007) 'Postfeminist media culture', *European Journal of Cultural Studies*, 10 (2): 147–66.

Glover, E. (1969) *The Psychopathology of Prostitution*. London: Institute for the Study and Treatment of Delinquency.

Goffman, E. (1959) *The Presentation of Self in Everyday Life*. Edinburgh: University of Edinburgh Press.

Goffman, E. (1963) *Stigma: Notes on the Management of Spoiled Identity*. Englewood Cliffs, NJ: Prentice Hall.

Goffman, E. (1983) 'The interaction order', *American Sociological Review*, 48 (1): 1–17.

Gold, S. N. and Heffner, C. L. (1998) 'Sexual addiction: many conceptions, minimal data', *Clinical Psychology Review*, 18 (3): 367–81.

Gomes do Espirito Santo, M. E. and Etheredge, G. D. (2002) 'How to reach clients of female sex workers: a survey "by surprise" in brothels in Dakar, Senegal', *Bulletin of the World Health Organization*, 80 (9): 709–13.

Goodall, R. (1995) *The Comfort of Sin. Prostitutes and Prostitution in the 1990s*. Folkestone: Renaissance Books.

Goode, E. and Ben-Yehuda, N. (1994) *Moral Panics: The Social Construction of Deviance*. Oxford: Blackwell.

Goodyear, M. G. and Cusick, L. (2007) 'Protection for sex workers', *British Medical Journal*, 334 (7584): 52–3.

Gordon-Lamoureux, R. J. (2007) 'Exploring the possibility of sexual addiction in men arrested for seeking out prostitutes: a preliminary study', *Journal of Addictions Nursing*, 18 (1): 21–9.

Gould, A. (2001) 'The criminalisation of buying sex: the politics of prostitution in Sweden', *Journal of Social Policy*, 30 (3): 437–56.

Grentz, S. (2005) 'Intersections of sex and power in research on prostitution: a female researcher interviewing male heterosexual clients', *Signs: Journal of Women in Culture and Society*, 30 (4): 2091–113.

Griffiths, M. (2000) 'Excessive Internet use: implications for sexual behaviour', *CyberPsychology and Behavior*, 3 (4): 537–52.

Groneberg, D. A., Molline, M. and Kusma, B. (2006) 'Sex work during the World Cup in Germany', *Lancet*, 368 (9538): 840–1.

Groom, T. and Nandwini, R (2006) 'Characteristics of men who pay for sex: a UK sexual health clinic survey', *Sexually Transmitted Infections*, 82 (5): 364–7.

Hadfield, P. (2007) 'Young people, alcohol and nightlife in British cities', in A. Recasens (ed.), *Violence between Young People in Leisure Zones: Findings from the EC Daphne 2 Programme*. Brussels: Vubpress, pp. 173–90.

Hakim, S. and Rengert, G. (eds) (1981) *Crime Spillover*. Beverly Hills, CA: Sage.

Hallgrimsdottir, H., Phillips, R. and Benoit, C. (2006) 'Fallen women and rescued girls: social stigma and media narratives of the sex industry in Victoria, BC from 1980 to 2005', *Canadian Review of Sociology and Anthropology*, 43 (3): 265–82.

Hamilton, A. (1999) 'The net out of control – a new moral panic: censorship and sexuality', in Liberty (ed.), *Liberating Cyberspace*. London: Pluto Press, pp. 169–88

Harcourt, C. and Donovan, B. (2005) 'The many faces of sex work', *Sexually Transmitted Infections*, 81 (3): 201–6.

Hardey, M. (2002) 'Life beyond the screen: embodiment and identity through the Internet', *Sociological Review*, 50 (4): 570–85.

Hart, A. (1998) *Buying and Selling Power: Anthropological Reflections on Prostitution in Spain*. Oxford: Westview Press.

Hart, G. and Barnard, M. (2003) '"Jump on top, get the job done": strategies employed by female prostitutes to reduce the risk of client violence', in E. A. Stanko (ed.), *The Meanings of Violence*. London: Routledge, pp. 32–48.

Haste, C. (1992) *Rules of Desire: Sex in Britain. World War I to the Present*. London: Chatto & Windus.

Hausbeck, K. and Brents, B. (2000) 'Inside Nevada's brothel industry', in R. Weitzer (ed.), *Sex for Sale*. London: Routledge, pp. 217–43.

Hausbeck, K. and Brents, B. (2002) 'McDonaldization of the sex industries? The business of sex', in G. Ritzer (ed.), *McDonaldization: The Reader*. Thousand Oaks, CA: Pine Forge Press, pp. 91–106

Hawkes, G. (1996) *Sex and Pleasure in Western Culture*. Cambridge: Polity Press.

Hearn, J. and Morgan, D. (eds) (1990) *Men, Masculinities and Social Theory*. London: Unwin Hyman.

Hester, M. and Westmarland, N. (2004) *Tackling Street Prostitution: Towards A Holistic Approach*. London: Home Office.

Hockey, J. and James, A. (2003) *Social Identities Across the Life Course*. Basingstoke: Palgrave Macmillan.

Hoff, G. (2006) 'Power and love: sadomasochistic practices in long term committed relationships', *Electronic Journal of Human Sexuality*, 9.

Hoffman, E. (2007) 'Open-ended interviews, power and emotional labour', *Journal of Contemporary Ethnography*, 36 (3): 318–46.

Hoigard, C. and Finstad, L. (1992) *Backstreets: Prostitution, Money and Love*. Cambridge: Polity Press.

Holland, J., Ramazanoglu, C., Sharpe, S. and Thomson, R. (1998) *Male in the Head: Young People, Heterosexuality and Power*. London: Tufnell Press.

Hollway, W. (1981) '"I just wanted to kill a woman." Why? The Ripper and male sexuality', *Feminist Review*, 9 (October): 33–40.

Hollway, W. and Jefferson, T. (1997) 'The risk society in an age of anxiety: situating the fear of crime', *British Journal of Sociology*, 48 (2): 255–66.

Holzman, H. and Pines, S. (1982) 'Buying sex: the phenomenology of being a john', *Deviant Behaviour*, 4 (1): 89–116.

Home Office (2004) *Paying the Price: A Consultation Paper on Prostitution*. London: HMSO.

Home Office (2005) *Consultation: On the Possession of Extreme Pornographic Material*. London: HMSO.

Home Office (2006) *Coordinated Prostitution Strategy*. London: HMSO.

Hubbard, P. (1997) 'Red-light districts and toleration zones: geographies of female street prostitution in England and Wales', *Area*, 29 (2): 129–40.

Hubbard, P. (1998) 'Community action and the displacement of street prostitution: evidence from British cities', *Geoforum*, 29 (3): 269–86.

Hubbard, P. (2002) 'Sexing the self: geographies of engagement and encounter', *Social and Cultural Geography*, 3 (4): 365–81.

Hubbard, P. (2004) 'Cleansing the metropolis: sex work and the politics of zero tolerance', *Urban Studies*, 41 (9): 1687–702.

Hubbard, P. and Sanders, T. (2003) 'Making space for sex work: female street prostitution and the production of urban space', *International Journal of Urban and Regional Research*, 27 (1): 73–87.

Hughes, D. (2001) 'Prostitution Online'. See: www.uri.edu/artsci/wms/Hughes/demads.htm.

Hughes, D. (2004) 'The use of new communication technologies for sexual exploitation of women and children', in R. Whisnant and C. Stark (eds), *Not for Sale: Feminists Resisting Prostitution and Pornography*. Toronto: Spinifex Press, pp. 38–55.

Illouz, E. (1997) *Consuming the Romantic Utopia*. Berkeley, CA: University of California Press.

Jaget, C. (1980) *Prostitutes: Our Life*. London: Falling Wall Press.

Jamieson, L. (1998) *Intimacy: Personal Relationships in Modern Societies*. Cambridge: Polity Press.

Jamieson, L. (1999) 'Intimacy transformed? A critical look at the "pure relationship"', *Sociology*, 33 (3): 477–94.

Jeal, N. and Sailsbury, C. (2004) 'Self-reported experiences of health services among female street-based prostitutes: a cross-sectional survey', *British Journal of General Practice*, 54 (504): 515–19.

Jeffreys, E. (2006) 'Governing buyers of sex in People's Republic of China', *Economy and Society*, 35 (4): 571–93.

Jeffreys, S. (1997) *The Idea of Prostitution*. Melbourne: Spinifex Press.

Jenkins, P. (1998) *Moral Panic: Changing Concepts of the Child Molester in Modern America*. New Haven, CT: Yale University Press.

Jiwani, Y. and Young, M. L. (2006) 'Missing and murdered women: reproducing marginality in news discourse', *Canadian Journal of Communication*, 31 (4): 895–917.

Johnson, A. (2007) 'No sex please, we're married', *Guardian* (London), 6 January.

Johnson, A. and Mercer, C. (2001) 'Sexual behaviour in Britain: partnerships, practices and HIV risk behaviours', *Lancet*, 358: 1835–42.

Jones, H. and Sager, T. (2001) 'Crime and Disorder Act 1998: prostitution and the Anti-Social Behaviour Order', *Criminal Law Review*, November: 873–85.

Jones, P., Shears, P. and Hillier, D. (2003) 'Retailing and the regulatory state: a case study of lap dancing clubs in the UK', *International Journal of Retail and Distribution Management*, 31 (4/5): 214–19.

Jones, S. (ed.) (1995) *CyberSociety. Computer-mediated Communication and Society*. Thousand Oaks, CA: Sage.

Jordan, J. (1997) 'User pays: why men buy sex', *Australian and New Zealand Journal of Criminology*, 30 (1): 55–71.

Juffer, J. (1998) *At Home with Pornography: Women, Sexuality, and Everyday Life*. New York: New York University Press.

Kantola, J. and Squires, J. (2004) 'Discourses surrounding prostitution policies in the UK', *European Journal of Women's Studies*, 11 (1): 77–101.

Kaspersson, M. (2006) 'The problem with symbolic legislation and deterrence: the case of the Swedish prostitution law', *British Society of Criminology* (Glasgow), 6 July.

Kates, S. and Belk, R. (2001) 'The meanings of Lesbian and Gay Pride Day', *Journal of Contemporary Ethnography*, 30 (4): 392–429.

Kelly, J. A. and Kalichman, S. C. (1995) 'Increased attention to human sexuality can improve HIV/AIDS prevention efforts: key research issues and directions', *Journal of Consulting and Clinical Psychology*, 63 (6): 907–18.

Kempadoo, K. and Doezema, J. (1999) *Global Sex Workers*. London: Routledge.

Kennedy, M. A., Klein, C., Gorzalka, B. B. and Yuille, J. C. (2004) 'Attitude change following a diversion program for men who solicit sex', *Journal of Offender Rehabilitation*, 40 (1/2): 41–60.

Kerkin, K. (2003) 'Re-placing difference: planning and street sex work in a gentrifying area', *Urban Policy and Research*, 21 (2): 137–49.

Kibby, M. and Costello, B. (1999) 'Displaying the phallus: masculinity and the performance of sexuality on the Internet', *Men and Masculinities*, 1 (4): 352–64.

Kilvington, J., Day, S. and Ward, H. (2001) 'Prostitution policy in Europe: a time for change?', *Feminist Review*, 67 (Spring): 78–93.

Kim, J. (2007) 'From sex to sexuality: exposing the heterosexual script on primetime network', *Journal of Sex Research*, 44 (2): 145–57.

Kinnell, H. (1990) 'Prostitutes and their clients in Birmingham: action research to measure and reduce risks of HIV', *The AIDS Letter*, no. 19, June/July, Royal Society of Medicine.

Kinnell, H. (2006a) 'Murder made easy: the final solution to prostitution?', in R. Campbell and M. O'Neill (eds), *Sex Work Now*. Cullompton: Willan, pp. 141–68.

Kinnell, H. (2006b) 'Clients of female sex workers: men or monsters?', in R. Campbell and M. O'Neill (eds), *Sex Work Now*. Cullompton: Willan, pp. 212–62

Kinsey, A., Pomeroy, W. and Martin, C. (1948) *Sexual Behaviour in the Human Male*. Philadelphia, PA: W. B. Saunders.

Korn, J. (1998) 'My sexual encounters with sex workers: the effects on a consumer', in J. Elias, V. Bullough, V. Elias and G. Brewer (eds), *Prostitution: On Whores, Hustlers and Johns*. New York: Prometheus Books, pp. 204–7.

Koskela, H. and Tani, S. (2005) ' "Sold out!" Women's practices of resistance against prostitution related sexual harassment', *Women's Studies International Forum*, 28 (5): 418–29.

Kulick, D. (2003) 'Sex in the New Europe', *Anthropological Theory*, 3 (2): 199–218.

Kulick, D. (2004) 'Sex in the New Europe: the criminalization of clients and Swedish fear of prostitution', in S. Day and H. Ward (eds), *Sex Work, Mobility and Health in Europe*. London: Kegan Paul, pp. 215–40.

Kulick, D. (2005) 'Four hundred thousand Swedish perverts', *GLQ: A Journal of Lesbian and Gay Studies*, 11 (2): 205–35.

Kurtz, S., Surratt, H., Inciardi, J. and Kiley, M. (2004) 'Sex work and "date" violence', *Violence Against Women*, 10 (4): 357–85.

Lash, S. (1990) *The Sociology of Postmodernism*. London: Routledge.

Laskowski, S. (2002) 'The new German Prostitution Act – an important step to a more rational view of prostitution as an ordinary profession in accordance with European Community law', *International Journal of Comparative Labour Law and Industrial Relations*, 18 (4): 479–91.

Lawless, S., Kippax, S. and Crawford, J. (1996) 'Dirty, diseased and undeserving: the positioning of HIV positive women', *Social Science and Medicine*, 43 (9): 1371–7.

Leander, K. (2005) 'Reflections on Sweden's measures against men's violence against women', *Social Policy and Society*, 5 (1): 115–25.

Lee, D. (1997) 'Interviewing men: vulnerabilities and dilemmas', *Women's Studies International Forum*, 20 (4): 553–64.

Lee, M. (1995) 'Pre-court diversion and youth justice', in L. Noaks (ed.), *Contemporary Issues in Criminology*. Cardiff: University of Wales Press.

Leonard, T. (1990) 'Male clients of female street prostitutes: unseen partners in sexual disease transmission', *Medical Anthropology Quarterly*, 4 (1): 41–5.

Lever, J. and Dolnick, D. (2000) 'Clients and call girls: seeking sex and intimacy', in R. Weitzer (ed.), *Sex for Sale*. London: Routledge, pp. 85–100.

Levi-Minzi, M. and Shields, M. (2007) 'Serial sexual murderers and prostitutes as their victims: difficulty profiling perpetrators and victim vulnerability as illustrated by the Green River case', *Brief Treatment and Crisis Intervention*, 7 (1): 77–89.

Levine, J. and Madden, L. (1988) *Lyn. A Story of Prostitution*. London: Women's Press.

Link, B. G. and Phelan, J. C. (2001) 'Conceptualizing stigma', *Annual Review of Sociology*, 27 (3): 363–85.

Litzinger, S. and Gordon, K. C. (2005) 'Exploring relationships among communication, sexual satisfaction, and marital satisfaction', *Journal of Sex and Marital Therapy*, 31 (5): 409–24.

Loe, M. (2004) *The Rise of Viagra: How the Little Blue Pill Changed Sex in America*. New York: New York University Press.

Loebner, H. (1998) 'Being a john', in J. Elias, V. Bullough, V. Elias and G. Brewer (eds), *Prostitution: On Whores, Hustlers and Johns*. New York: Prometheus Books, pp. 221–5

Lowman, J. (2000) 'Violence and the outlaw status of (street) prostitution in Canada', *Violence Against Women*, 6 (9): 987–1011.

Lowman, J. and Atchison, C. (2006) 'Men who buy sex: a survey in the Greater Vancouver Regional District', *Canadian Journal of Sociology and Anthropology*, 43 (3): 281–96.

McKeganey, N. (1994) 'Why do men buy sex and what are their assessments of the HIV-related risks when they do?', *AIDS Care*, 6 (3): 289–301.

McKeganey, N. and Barnard, M. (1996) *Sex Work on the Streets*. Buckingham: Open University Press.

McLeod, E. (1982) *Working Women: Prostitution Now*. London: Croom Helm.

McNair, B. (2002) *Striptease Culture: Sex, Media and the Democratization of Desire*. London: Routledge.

Madden Dempsey, M. (2005) 'Rethinking Wolfenden: prostitute-use, criminal law, and remote harm', *Criminal Law Review*, 444–55.

Maher, L. (2000) *Sexed Work: Gender, Race and Resistance in a Brooklyn Drug Market*. Oxford: Oxford University Press.

Malina, D. and Schmidt, R. A. (1997) 'It's a business doing pleasure with you: sh! A women's sex shop case', *Marketing Intelligence and Planning*, 15 (7): 352.

Mansson, S. A. (2006) 'Men's demand for prostitutes', *Sexologies*, 15 (2): 87–92.

Matthews, R. (1984) 'Streetwise? A critical review of the Criminal Law Revision Committee's Report on "Prostitution in the Street"', *Critical Social Policy*, 4 (1): 103–11.

Matthews, R. (1986) 'Beyond Wolfenden? Prostitution, politics and the law', in R. Matthews and J. Young (eds), *Confronting Crime*. London: Sage, pp. 188–210.

Matthews, R. (2005) 'Policing prostitution: ten years on', *British Journal of Criminology*, 45 (6): 877–95.

May, T., Edmunds, M. and Hough, M. (1999) *Street Business: The Links Between Sex and Drug Markets*, Police Research Series Paper 118. London: Home Office Policing and Reducing Crime Unit.

May, T., Harocopos, A. and Hough, M. (2000) *For Love or Money: Pimps and the Management of Sex Work*, Police Research Series Paper 134. London: Home Office Policing and Reducing Crime Unit.

Measham, F. (2004) 'The decline of ecstasy, the rise of "binge" drinking and the persistence of pleasure', *Probation Journal*, 51 (4): 309–26.

Melrose, M. (2002) 'Labour pains: some considerations on the difficulties of researching juvenile prostitution', *International Journal of Social Research Methodology*, 5 (4): 333–51.

Meston, C. M. and Buss, D. M. (2007) 'Why humans have sex', *Archives of Sexual Behavior*, 36 (3): 477–507.

Miers, D. (2004) *Regulating Commercial Gambling. Past, Present and Future*. Oxford: Oxford University Press.

Miller, W. I. (1999) *Anatomy of Disgust*. Cambridge, MA: Harvard University Press.

Moffatt, P. G. and Peters, S. A. (2004) 'Pricing personal services: an empirical study of earnings in the UK prostitution industry', *Scottish Journal of Political Economy*, 51 (5): 675–90.

Montemurro, B., Bloom, C. and Madell, K. (2003) 'Ladies' night out: a typology of women patrons of a male strip club', *Deviant Behaviour*, 24 (4): 333–52.

Monto, M. A. (1999) *Clients of Street Prostitutes in Portland, Oregon, San Francisco and Santa Clara, California, and Las Vegas, Nevada 1996–1999*. Portland, OR: University of Portland.

Monto, M. A. (2000) 'Why men seek out prostitutes', in R. Weitzer (ed.), *Sex for Sale*. London: Routledge, pp. 67–83.

Monto, M. A. (2001) 'Prostitution and fellatio', *Journal of Sex Research*, 38 (1): 140–5.

Monto, M. A. and Garcia, S. (2001) 'Recidivism among the customers of female street prostitutes: do intervention programs help?', *Western Criminology Review*, 3 (2).

Monto, M. A. and Hotaling, N. (2001) 'Predictors of rape myth acceptance among male clients of female street prostitutes', *Violence Against Women*, 7 (3): 275–93.

Monto, M. A. and McRee, N. (2005) 'A comparison of the male customers of female street prostitutes with national samples of men', *International Journal of Offender Therapy and Comparative Criminology*, 49 (5): 505–29.

Morgan Thomas, R. (1990) 'AIDS risks, alcohol, drugs and the sex industry: a Scottish study', in M. Plant (ed.), *AIDS, Drugs and Prostitution*. London: Routledge.

Morse, E., Simon, P., Balson, P. and Osofsky, H. (1992) 'Sexual behavior patterns of customers of male street prostitutes', *Archives of Sexual Behavior*, 21 (4): 347–57.

Mower, M. (2006) 'The Way Out Project: the Hull Kerb-Crawler Re-Education Programme', *Sex as Crime*, British Society of Criminology and British Sociological Association Joint Workshop, The Conservatoire, University of Central England.

Muncer, S., Burrows, R., Pleace, N., Loader, B. and Nettleton, S. (2000) 'Births, deaths, sex and marriage . . . but very few presents? A case study of social support in cyberspace', *Critical Public Health*, 10 (1): 1–18.

National Statistics (2007) *Social Trends 37*, London: Palgrave.

Nip, J. (2004) 'The relationship between online and offline communities: the case of the queer sisters', *Media, Culture and Society*, 26 (3): 409–28.

Nixon, K., Tutty, L., Downe, P., Gorkoff, K. and Ursel, J. (2002) 'The everyday occurrence: violence in the lives of girls exploited through prostitution', *Violence Against Women*, 8 (9): 1016–43.

O'Connel, R. (2003) *A Typology of Child Cybersexploitation and Online Grooming Practices*. Preston: Cyberspace Research Unit, University of Central Lancaster.

O'Connell Davidson, J. (1995) 'British sex tourists in Thailand', in M. Maynard and J. Purvis (eds), *Heterosexual Politics*. London: Routledge, pp. 44–68.

O'Connell Davidson, J. (1998) *Prostitution, Power and Freedom*. Cambridge: Polity Press.

O'Connell Davidson, J. (2003) ' "Sleeping with the enemy"? Some problems with feminist abolitionist calls to penalise those who buy commercial sex', *Social Policy and Society*, 2 (1): 55–64.

O'Connell Davidson, J. and Layder, D. (1994) *Methods, Sex and Madness*. London: Routledge.

O'Farrell, N. (2001) 'Enhanced efficiency of female-to-male HIV transmission in core groups in developing countries: the need to target men', *Journal of Sexually Transmitted Diseases*, 28 (2): 84–91.

O'Neill, M. (1996) 'Researching prostitution and violence: towards a feminist praxis', in M. Hester, L. Kelly and J. Radford (eds), *Women, Violence and Male Power*. Buckingham: Open University Press, pp. 130–47.

O'Neill, M. and Campbell, R. (2006) 'Street sex work and local communities: creating discursive spaces for genuine consultation and inclusion', in R. Campbell and M. O'Neill (eds), *Sex Work Now*. Cullompton: Willan, pp. 33–41.

Pakes, F. (2003) 'Tolerance and pragmatism in the Netherlands: euthanasia, coffee shops and prostitution in the "purple years" 1994–2002', *International Journal of Police Science and Management*, 5 (4): 217–28.

Pauw, I. and Brener, L. (2003) '"You are just whores – you can't be raped": barriers to safer sex practices among women street sex workers in Cape Town', *Culture, Health and Sexuality*, 5 (6): 465–81.

Penfold, C., Hunter, G., Campbell, R. and Barham, L. (2004) 'Tackling client violence in female street prostitution: inter-agency working between outreach agencies and the police', *Policing and Society*, 14 (4): 365–79.

Peng, Y. W. (2007) 'Buying sex. Domination and difference in the discourses of Taiwanese piao-ke', *Men and Masculinities*, 9 (3): 315–36.

Pheterson, G. (1993) 'The whore stigma', *Social Text*, 37 (1): 37–64.

Phoenix, J. (2000) 'Prostitute identities: men, money and violence', *British Journal of Criminology*, 40 (1): 37–55.

Phoenix, J. and Oerton, S. (2005) *Illicit and Illegal. Sex, Regulation and Social Control*, Cullompton: Willan.

Pickering, H., Todd, J., Dunn, D., Pepin, J. and Wilkins, A. (1992) 'Prostitutes and their clients: a Gambian survey', *Social Sciences and Medicine*, 34 (1): 75–88.

Pitcher, J., Campbell, R., Hubbard, P., O'Neill, M. and Scoular, J. (2006) *Living and Working in Areas of Street Sex Work: From Conflict to Coexistence*. Bristol: Policy Press.

Pitts, M. K., Smith, A., Grierson, J., O'Brien, M. and Misson, S. (2004) 'Who Pays for sex and why? An analysis of social and motivational factors associated with male clients of sex workers', *Archives of Sexual Behaviour*, 33 (4): 353–8.

Plant, M.A. and Plant, M.L. (2003) 'Sex addiction: a comparison with dependence on psychoactive drugs', *Journal of Substance Use*, 8 (4): 260–6.

Pleace, N., Burrows, R., Loader, B., Muncer, S. and Nettleton, S. (2000) 'On-line with the friends of Bill W: social support and the Net', *Sociological Research Online*, 5 (2).

Plummer, K. (1995) *Telling Sexual Stories. Power, Change and Social Worlds*. London: Routledge.

Plumridge, E., Chetwynd, S., Reed, A. and Gifford, S. (1996) 'Patrons of the sex industry: perceptions of risk', *AIDS Care*, 8 (4): 405–16.

Plumridge, E., Chetwynd, S. J., Reed, A. and Gifford, S. (1997) 'Discourses of emotionality in commercial sex: the missing client voice', *Feminism and Psychology*, 7 (2): 165–81.

Potterat, P., Brewer, D., Muth, S., Rothenberg, R., Woodhouse, D., Muth, J., Stites, H. and Brody, S. (2004) 'Mortality in a long-term open cohort of prostitute women', *American Journal of Epidemiology*, 159 (8): 778–85.

Prasad, M. (1999) 'The morality of market exchange: love, money and contractual justice', *Sociological Perspectives*, 42 (2): 181–215.

Pryce, A. (2004) '"Only odd people wore suede shoes": careers and sexual identities of men attending a sexual health clinic', *Nursing Inquiry*, 11 (4): 258–70.

Pyett, P. and Warr, D. (1997) 'Vulnerability on the streets: female sex workers and HIV risk', *AIDS Care*, 9 (5): 539–47.

Quinn, J. F. and Forsyth, C. J. (1995) 'Describing sexual behavior in the era of the Internet: a typology for empirical research', *Deviant Behavior*, 26 (2): 191–207.

Raphael, J. and Shapiro, D. (2004) 'Violence in indoor and outdoor prostitution venues', *Violence Against Women*, 10 (2): 126–39.

Reid, E. (1999) 'Hierarchy and power: social control in cyberspace', in M. Smith and P. L. Kollock (eds), *Communities in Cyberspace*. London: Routledge, pp. 107–33.

Rheingold, H. (2000) *The Virtual Community*. Cambridge, MA: MIT Press.

Riberio, M. and Sacramento, O. (2005) 'Violence against prostitutes. Findings of research in the Spanish-Portuguese frontier region', *European Journal of Women's Studies*, 12 (1): 61–81.

Roberts, N. (1994) 'The whore, her stigma, the punter and his wife', *New Internationalist*, 252 (February).

Roberts, R., Bergström, S. and La Rooy, D. (2007) 'Commentary: UK students and sex work: current knowledge and research issues', *Journal of Community and Applied Social Psychology*, 17 (1): 141–6.

Rogers, A. (2005) 'Chaos to control. Men's magazines and the mastering of intimacy', *Men and Masculinities*, 8 (2): 175–94.

Roseneil, S. (2007) *Sociability, Sexuality and the Self*. London: Routledge.

Sagar, T. (2005) 'Street Watch: concept and practice', *British Journal of Criminology*, 45 (1): 98–112.

Sagar, T. (2007) 'Tackling on-street sex work: Anti-Social Behaviour Orders, sex workers and inclusive inter-agency initiatives', *Criminology and Criminal Justice*, 7 (2): 153–68.

Sanchez Taylor, J. (2001) 'Dollars are a girl's best friend? Female tourists' sexual behaviour in the Caribbean', *Sociology*, 35 (3): 749–64.

Sanders, A. (1988) 'The limits of diversion from prosecution', *British Journal of Criminology*, 28 (4): 513–32.

Sanders, T. (2002) 'The condom as psychological barrier: female sex workers and emotional management', *Feminism and Psychology*, 12 (4): 561–6.

Sanders, T. (2004a) 'A continuum of risk? The management of health, physical and emotional risks by female sex workers', *Sociology of Health and Illness*, 26 (5): 1–18.

Sanders, T. (2004b) 'The risks of street prostitution: punters, police and protesters', *Urban Studies*, 41 (8): 1703–17.

Sanders, T. (2005a) *Sex Work: A Risky Business*. Cullompton: Willan.

Sanders, T. (2005b) 'It's just acting: sex workers' strategies for capitalising on sexuality', *Gender, Work and Organization*, 12 (4): 319–42.

Sanders, T. (2005c) 'Blinded by morality? Prostitution policy in the UK', *Capital and Class*, 86 (Summer): 9–16.

Sanders, T. (2005d) 'Researching sex work: dynamics, difficulties and decisions', in D. Hobbs and R. Wright (eds), *A Handbook of Fieldwork*. London: Sage, pp. 201–22

Sanders, T. (2005e) 'Researching the online sex work community', in C. Hine (ed.), *Virtual Methods in Social Research on the Internet*. Oxford: Berg, pp. 67–80.

Sanders, T. (2006a) 'Behind the personal ads: the indoor sex markets in Britain', in R. Campbell and M. O'Neill (eds), *Sex Work Now*. Cullompton: Willan, pp. 95–115.

Sanders, T. (2006b) 'Sexing up the subject: methodological nuances in researching the female sex industry', *Sexualities*, 9 (4): 449–68.

Sanders, T. (2007a) 'No room for a regulated market? The implications of the Co-ordinated Prostitution Strategy for indoor sex industries', *Community Safety Journal*, 6 (1): 34–44.

Sanders, T. (2007b) 'Becoming an ex-sex worker: making transitions out of a deviant career', *Feminist Criminology*, 2 (1): 1–22.

Sanders, T. (2007c) 'The politics of sexual citizenship: commercial sex and disability', *Disability and Society*, 22 (5): 439–55.

Sanders, T. (2008) 'Male sexual scripts: intimacy, sexuality and pleasure in the purchase of commercial sex', *Sociology*, 52

Sanders, T. and Campbell, R. (2007a) 'Designing out violence, building in respect: violence, safety and sex work policy', *British Journal of Sociology*, 58 (1): 1–18.

Sanders, T. and Campbell, R. (2007b) 'What's criminal about indoor sex work?', in K. Williams, P. Birch, G. Letherby and M. Cain (eds), *Sex as Crime*. Cullompton: Willan.

Santos-Ortiz, M., Lao-Melendez, J. and Torres-Sanchez, A. (1998) 'Sex workers and elderly male clients', in J. Elias, V. Bullough, V. Elias and G. Brewer (eds), *Prostitution: On Whores, Hustlers and Johns*. New York: Prometheus Books, pp. 208–20.

Sawyer, S., Metz, M., Hinds, J. and Brucker, R. (2001) 'Attitudes towards prostitution amongst males: "a consumers' report"', *Current Psychology* 20 (3): 363–76.

Sawyer, S., Rosser, B. R. S. and Schroeder, A. (1998) 'A brief psychoeducational program for men who patronize prostitutes', *Journal of Offender Rehabilitation*, 26 (34): 111–25.

Schnarch, D. (1997) 'Sex, intimacy and the Internet', *Journal of Sex Education and Therapy*, 22 (1): 15–20.

Schutz, A. (1967) *The Phenomenology of the Social World*. Chicago, IL: Northwestern University Press.

Schwalbe, M. and Wolkomir, M. (2001) 'The masculine self as problem and resource in interview studies of men', *Men and Masculinities*, 4 (1): 90–103.

Scott, J. (1998) 'Changing attitudes to sexual morality: a cross-national comparison', *Sociology*, 32 (4): 815–45.

Scoular, J. (2004a) 'Criminalising "punters": evaluating the Swedish position on prostitution', *Journal of Social Welfare and Family Law*, 26 (2): 195–210.

Scoular, J. (2004b) 'The "subject" of prostitution: interpreting the discursive, symbolic and material postition of sex/work in feminist theory', *Feminist Theory*, 5 (3): 343–55.

Scoular, J., Pitcher, J., Campbell, R., Hubbard, P. and O'Neill, M. (2007) 'What's anti-social about sex work? The changing representation of prostitution's incivility', *Community Safety Journal*, 6 (1): 11–17.

Scully, D. (1990) *Understanding Sexual Violence: A Study of Convicted Rapists*. Boston, MA: Unwin Hayes.

Seidler, V. (ed.) (1992) *Men, Sex and Relationships*, London: Routledge.

Self, H. (2003) *Prostitution, Women and Misuse of the Law: The Fallen Daughters of Eve*. London: Frank Cass.

Self, H. (2006) 'Regulating prostitution', in B. B. Gordon and M. Freeman (eds), *Law and Psychology Current Legal Issues*. Oxford: Oxford University Press, pp. 472–84.

Shaffir, W. and Stebbins, R. (eds) (1991) *Experiencing Fieldwork. An Inside View of Qualitative Research*. London: Sage.

Sharp, K. and Earle, S. (2003) 'Cyberpunters and cyberwhores: prostitution on the Internet', in Y. Jewkes (ed.), *Dot Cons. Crime, Deviance and Identity on the Internet*. Cullompton: Willan, pp. 36–52.

Sharpe, K. (1998) *Red Light, Blue Light: Prostitutes, Punters and the Police*. Aldershot: Ashgate.

Sharpe, K. (2000) 'Sad, bad and (sometimes) dangerous to know: street corner research with prostitutes, punters and the police', in R. King and E. Wincup (eds), *Doing Research on Crime and Justice*. Oxford: Oxford University Press, pp. 362–72.

Shaver, F. (2005) 'Sex work research: methodological and ethical challenges', *Journal of Interpersonal Violence* 20 (3): 296–319.

Shaw, D. (1998) 'Gay men and computer communication: a discourse of sex and identity in cyberspace', in S. Jones (ed.), *Virtual Culture. Identity and Communication in Cybersociety*. London: Sage, pp. 133–45.

Shostak, A. (1981) 'Oral sex: new standards of intimacy and an old index of troubled sexuality', *Deviant Behaviour*, 2 (1): 127–44.

Shrage, L. (1989) 'Should feminists oppose prostitution?', *Ethics*, 99 (2): 347–61.

Shrage, L. (1994) *Moral Dilemmas of Feminism*. London: Routledge.

Skeggs, B. (1997) *Formations of Class and Gender*. London: Sage.

Slamah, K. (1999) 'Transgenders and sex work in Malaysia', in K. Kempadoo and J. Doezema (eds), *Global Sex Workers*. London: Routledge, pp. 210–14.

Smith, J. (1989) *Misogynies*. London: Faber & Faber.

Soble, A. (ed.) (2002) *The Philosophy of Sex*, 4th edn. Lanham, MD: Rowman & Littlefield.

Soothill, K. (1993) 'The serial killer industry', *Journal of Forensic Psychiatry*, 4 (2): 341–54.

Soothill, K. (2004a) 'Sex talk', *Police Review*: 20–1.

Soothill, K. (2004b) 'Parlour games: the value of an Internet site providing punters' views of massage parlours', *Police Journal*, 77 (1): 43–53.

Soothill, K. and Sanders, T. (2004) 'Calling the tune? Some observations on *Paying the Price: A Consultation Paper on Prostitution*', *Journal of Forensic Psychiatry and Psychology*, 15 (4): 642–59.

Soothill, K. and Sanders, T. (2005) 'The geographical mobility, preferences and pleasures of prolific punters: a demonstration study of the activities of prostitutes' clients', *Sociological Research Online*, 10 (1).

Spurrell, C. (2006) 'Who pays for sex? You'd be surprised', *Times*, 7 November.

Stanko, E. (1996) 'Warnings to women: police advice and women's safety in Britain', *Violence Against Women*, 2 (1): 5–24.

Stein, M. (1974) *Lovers, Friends, Slaves. Nine Male Sexual Types: Their Psychosexual Transactions with Call Girls*. New York: Berkeley Publishing and Puttnam & Sons.

Stoller, R. (1976) *Perversions: The Erotic Form of Hatred*. New York: Harvester Press.

Storr, M. (2003) *Latex and Lingerie: The Sexual Dynamics of Ann Summers Parties*. Oxford: Berg.

Sullivan, E. and Simon, W. (1998) 'The client: a social, psychological and behavioural look at the unseen patron of prostitution', in J. E. Elias, V. L. Bullough, V. Elias and G. Brewer (eds), *Prostitution: On Whores, Hustlers and Johns*. New York: Prometheus Books, pp. 134–54.

Surrat, H., Inciardi, J., Kurtz, S. and Kiley, M. (2004) 'Sex work and drug use in a subculture of violence', *Crime & Delinquency*, 50 (1): 43–59.

Svanstrom, Y. (2004) 'Criminalising the john – a Swedish gender model?', in J. Outshoorn (ed.), *The Politics of Prostitution*. Cambridge: Cambridge University Press, pp. 225–44.

Thatcher, A. (2001) 'Sex education: after modernity', *International Journal of Children's Spirituality*, 6 (2): 243–1.

The Sharp End (2007) *'Changing Course': How Hampshire Constabulary is using Classroom Sessions to Successfully Rehabilitate Kerb Crawlers*. Published for the Home Office by Square One Publishing.

Thomsen, S., Stalker, M. and Toroitich-Ruto, C. (2004) 'Fifty ways to leave your rubber: how men in Mombasa rationalise unsafe sex', *Sexually Transmitted Infections*, 80 (5): 430–4.

Tremlett, G. (2006) 'Europe's brothel – in a corner of Spain', *Guardian* (London), 24 June.

Ungar, S. (2001) 'Moral panic versus risk society: the implications of the changing sites of social anxiety', *British Journal of Sociology*, 52 (2): 271–91.

Van Brunschot, E. G. (2003) 'Community policing and "John Schools"', *Canadian Review of Sociology and Anthropology*, 40 (2): 215–32.

Van Doorninck, M. and Campbell, R. (2006) ' "Zoning" street sex work: the way forward?', *Sex Work Now*. Cullompton: Willan, pp. 62–92.

Vanwesenbeeck, I. (2001) 'Another decade of social scientific work on sex work: a review of research 1990–2000', *Annual Review of Sex Research*, 12 (2): 242–89.

Vanwesenbeeck, I., de Graff, R., Van Zessen, G. and Straver, C. (1993) 'Protection styles of prostitutes' clients: intentions, behaviour and considerations in relation to AIDS', *Journal of Sex Education Theory*, 19 (1): 79–92.

Veena, N. (2007) 'Revisiting the prostitution debate in the technology age: women who use the Internet for sex work in Bangkok', *Gender, Technology and Development*, 11 (1): 97–107.

Voas, D. and Crockett, A. (2005) 'Religion in Britain: neither believing nor belonging', *Sociology*, 39 (1): 11–28.

Walkowitz, J. (1980) *Prostitution and Victorian Society: Women, Class, and the State*. Cambridge: Cambridge University Press.

Walkowitz, J. (1992) *City of Dreadful Delight. Narratives of Sexual Danger in Late-Victorian London*. London: Virago.

Wang, Y. and Fensenmaier, D. (2004) 'Assessing motivation of contribution in online communities: an empirical investigation of an online travel community', *Electronic Markets*, 13 (1): 33–45.

Ward, H., Day, S. and Weber, J. (1999) 'Risky business: health and safety in the sex industry over a 9-year period', *Sexually Transmitted Infections*, 75 (5): 340–3.

Ward, H., Mercer, C. H., Wellings, K., Fenton, K., Erens, B., Copas, A. and Johnson, A. M. (2005) 'Who pays for sex? An analysis of the increasing prevalence of female commercial sex contacts among men in Britain', *Journal of Sexually Transmitted Infections*, 81 (6): 467–71.

Waskul, D. (ed.) (2004) *net.seXXX: Readings on Sex, Pornography and the Internet.* New York: Peter Lang.

Weeks, J. (1989) *Sex, Politics and Society: The Regulation of Sexuality Since 1800.* London: Longman.

Weinberg, M. S., Shaver, F. M. and Williams, C. J. (1999) 'Gendered sex work in the San Francisco Tenderloin', *Archives of Sexual Behavior*, 28 (3): 503–21.

Weitzer, R. (2000) 'Why we need more research on sex work', in R. Weitzer (ed.), *Sex for Sale*. London: Routledge, pp. 1–16

Weitzer, R. (2005) 'Flawed theory and method in studies of prostitution', *Violence Against Women*, 11 (7): 934–49.

Weitzer, R. (2006) 'Moral crusade against prostitution', *Society*, 43 (March–April): 33–8.

Wellings, K., Field, J., Johnson, A. and Wadsworth, J. (1994) *Sexual Behaviour in Britain: The National Survey of Sexual Attitudes and Lifestyles*. London: Penguin.

West, D. J. and Villiers, B. D. (1992) *Male Prostitution*. London: Duckworth.

Whimster, S. (1995) 'Max Weber on the erotic and some comparisons with the work of Foucault', *International Sociology*, 10 (4): 447–62.

Whittaker, D. and Hart, G. (1996) 'Research Note: managing risks: the social organisation of indoor sex work', *Sociology of Health and Illness*, 18 (3): 399–413.

Williams, K. (2005) ' "Caught between a rock and hard place": police experiences with legitimacy of Street Watch partnerships', *Howard Journal*, 44 (5): 527–37.

Winick, C. (1962) 'Prostitutes' clients' perceptions of the prostitute and themselves', *International Journal of Social Psychiatry*, 8 (3): 289–97.

Winick, C. and Kinsie, P. M. (1971) *The Lively Commerce*. Chicago, IL: Quadrangle.

Wolfenden Report (1957) *Commission on Homosexual Offences and Prostitution.* London: HMSO.

Wood, E. (2000) 'Working in the fantasy factory: the attention hypothesis and the enacting of masculine power in strip clubs', *Journal of Contemporary Ethnography*, 29 (1): 5–31.

Wortley, S., Fischer, B. and Webster, C. (2002) 'Vice lessons: a survey of prostitution offenders enrolled in the Toronto John School Diversion Program', *Canadian Journal of Criminology*, 44 (4): 369–402.

Wyatt Seal, D. and Ehrhardt, A. (2003) 'Masculinity and urban men: perceived scripts for courtship, romantic and sexual interaction with women', *Culture, Health and Sexuality*, 5 (4): 295–319.

Xantidis, L. and McCabe, M. P. (2000) 'Personality characteristics of male clients of female commercial sex workers in Australia', *Archives of Sexual Behaviour*, 29 (2): 165–76.

Yang, C. (2000) 'The use of the Internet among academic gay communities in Taiwan: an exploratory study', *Information, Communication and Society*, 3 (2): 153–72.

Zatz, N. (1997) 'Sex work/sex act: law, labour and desire in constructions of prostitution', *Signs*, 22 (2): 277–308.

Zelizer, V. (1996) 'Payments and social ties', *Sociological Forum*, 11 (3): 481–95.

Zelizer, V. (2005) *The Purchase of Intimacy*. Princeton, NJ: Princeton University Press and Oxford University Press.

Index

Added to a page number 't' denotes a table and 'n' denotes notes.

recruitment
   procedure 17–21
   framing the official context 21–3
   trust and power dynamics 23–7
   research questions 16–17
employment, research respondents
   34t, 35
emptiness 104
encouragement, online message
   boards 74–5
English Collective of Prostitutes 138,
   168
entertainment, sex as 43
entrepreneurial sex workers 63, 71,
   102
environmental issues 149
eradication of prostitution 7, 203–7
erotic 198
erotopian landscape 3
escort market 2, 63, 207n
essentialist reductionism, radical
   feminism 174
ethnicity 34t, 35, 39
everyday pressures, motivation to buy
   sex 191–3
exaggeration, media reporting 167
expenditure, sexual services 34t, 35–6
exploitation
   client assessment of 53–6
   of male clients 106–7
explorers 48t

falling in love 104–6
fantasy fulfilment 46
fathers, research respondents 34t
fear of crime 182–3
fellatio 3, 12n, 37n
felt identity 121–3, 129
female sex workers
   assessing exploitation of 53–6
   as business women/service
      providers 101
   as 'carriers of disease' 8
   commodification and objectification
      of 86
   criminalization 145, 153
   demand as reason for existence of
      172

emotional labour performed by 90
endangerment through
   criminalization 181
entrepreneurial 63, 71, 102
freelance, Thailand 63
inclusion on Punternet 64
management of personal websites
   64
participation in online sex work 64
praise of field reports 65–6
protection of 205–6
risk and safety applied to 50–1
sexual difficulties and importance
   of pleasing 100
sexually transmitted infection 158
skill of creating and preserving
   illusions 102
US homicide data 179
violence against 178–80, 186n
who sell sex to women 4
see also client–sex worker
   relationships; street sex
   workers; student sex workers
female sexuality 8
feminism see radical feminism
field reports
   multiple authors and audiences
      68–70
   revelations of sexual identities 67–8
   role in sex industry 64, 65–7, 86
folk devils 182
force 137
forced prostitution 174
France, student sex workers 201
free intercourse 204–5
freelance sex workers, Thailand 63
friends, coming out to 128–9
friendship
   regular client–sex relationships 96–8
   through virtual communities 79–82

gay sexuality, acceptance of 130, 136
gender dynamics, researcher–
   respondent relationships 26–7
gender performance, motivation to
   buy sex 195
generalizations 179–80
genuine friendship 96–7